ASPEN PUBLISHERS

Friedman's
Practice Series

Edited by

Professor Joel Wm. Friedman

Tulane University Law School
Jack M. Gordon Professor of Procedural Law & Jurisdiction

Law & Business

AUSTIN   BOSTON   CHICAGO   NEW YORK   THE NETHERLANDS

© 2007 Aspen Publishers (reprint of 2005 edition by Precedent Press).
All Rights Reserved.
http://lawschool.aspenpublishers.com

No part of this publication may be reproduced or transmitted in any form
or by any means, electronic or mechanical, including photocopy, recording,
or any information storage and retrieval system, without permission
in writing from the publisher. Requests for permission to make copies
of any part of this publication should be mailed to:

>Aspen Publishers
>Attn: Permissions Department
>76 Ninth Avenue, 7th Floor
>New York, NY 10011-5201

To contact Customer Care, e-mail customer.care@aspenpublishers.com,
call 1-800-234-1660, fax 1-800-901-9075, or mail correspondence to:

>Aspen Publishers
>Attn: Order Department
>PO Box 990
>Frederick, MD 21705

Printed in the United States of America.

1 2 3 4 5 6 7 8 9 0

ISBN 978-0-7355-7349-9

About Wolters Kluwer Law & Business

Wolters Kluwer Law & Business is a leading provider of research information and workflow solutions in key specialty areas. The strengths of the individual brands of Aspen Publishers, CCH, Kluwer Law International and Loislaw are aligned within Wolters Kluwer Law & Business to provide comprehensive, in-depth solutions and expert-authored content for the legal, professional and education markets.

CCH was founded in 1913 and has served more than four generations of business professionals and their clients. The CCH products in the Wolters Kluwer Law & Business group are highly regarded electronic and print resources for legal, securities, antitrust and trade regulation, government contracting, banking, pension, payroll, employment and labor, and healthcare reimbursement and compliance professionals.

Aspen Publishers is a leading information provider for attorneys, business professionals and law students. Written by preeminent authorities, Aspen products offer analytical and practical information in a range of specialty practice areas from securities law and intellectual property to mergers and acquisitions and pension/benefits. Aspen's trusted legal education resources provide professors and students with high-quality, up-to-date and effective resources for successful instruction and study in all areas of the law.

Kluwer Law International supplies the global business community with comprehensive English-language international legal information. Legal practitioners, corporate counsel and business executives around the world rely on the Kluwer Law International journals, loose-leafs, books and electronic products for authoritative information in many areas of international legal practice.

Loislaw is a premier provider of digitized legal content to small law firm practitioners of various specializations. Loislaw provides attorneys with the ability to quickly and efficiently find the necessary legal information they need, when and where they need it, by facilitating access to primary law as well as state-specific law, records, forms and treatises.

Wolters Kluwer Law & Business, a unit of Wolters Kluwer, is headquartered in New York and Riverwoods, Illinois. Wolters Kluwer is a leading multinational publisher and information services company.

CHECK OUT THESE OTHER GREAT TITLES:

Friedman's Practice Series
Outlining Is Important But PRACTICE MAKES PERFECT!

All Content Written By *Top Professors* • 100 Multiple Choice Questions • Comprehensive *Professor* Answers and Analysis for Multiple Choice Questions • *Real Law School* Essay Exams • Comprehensive *Professor* Answers for Essay Exams • Free Digital Version

Available titles in this series include:

Friedman's Civil Procedure

Friedman's Constitutional Law

Friedman's Contracts

Friedman's Criminal Law

Friedman's Criminal Procedure

Friedman's Property

Friedman's Torts

ASK FOR THEM AT YOUR LOCAL BOOKSTORE
IF UNAVAILABLE, PURCHASE ONLINE AT
HTTP://LAWSCHOOL.ASPENPUBLISHERS.COM

ABOUT THE EDITOR

Joel Wm. Friedman
Tulane Law School

Jack M. Gordon Professor of Procedural Law & Jurisdiction, Director of Technology

BS, 1972, Cornell University; JD, 1975, Yale University

Professor Joel Wm. Friedman, the Jack M. Gordon Professor of Procedural Law & Jurisdiction at Tulane Law School, is the lead author of two highly regarded casebooks -- "The Law of Civil Procedure: Cases and Materials" (published by Thomson/West) and "The Law of Employment Discrimination" (published by Foundation Press). His many law review articles have been published in, among others, the Cornell, Texas, Iowa, Tulane, Vanderbilt, and Washington & Lee Law Reviews.

Professor Friedman is an expert in computer assisted legal instruction who has lectured throughout the country on how law schools can integrate developing technologies into legal education. He is a past recipient of the Felix Frankfurter Teaching Award and the Sumpter Marks Award for Scholarly Achievement.

Table of Contents

ESSAY EXAMINATION QUESTIONS

CRIMINAL LAW ESSAY EXAM #1	1
CRIMINAL LAW ESSAY EXAM #2	7
CRIMINAL LAW ESSAY EXAM #3	15
CRIMINAL LAW ESSAY EXAM #4	23
CRIMINAL LAW ESSAY EXAM #5	31

ESSAY EXAMINATION ANSWERS

CRIMINAL LAW ESSAY EXAM #1	39
CRIMINAL LAW ESSAY EXAM #2	55
CRIMINAL LAW ESSAY EXAM #3	71
CRIMINAL LAW ESSAY EXAM #4	89
CRIMINAL LAW ESSAY EXAM #5	105

MULTIPLE CHOICE

100 CRIMINAL LAW QUESTIONS	129
100 CRIMINAL LAW ANSWERS AND ANALYSIS	269

CRIMINAL LAW
ESSAY EXAMS

QUESTIONS

CRIMINAL LAW ESSAY EXAM #1

For **QUESTIONS ONE, TWO** and **THREE**, you need only refer to the following list of state statutes for all substantive crimes. For criminal law defenses, however, refer to your own knowledge under both the common law and the Model Penal Code.

FIRST-DEGREE MURDER:

(A) A homicide perpetrated by any kind of willful, deliberate and premeditated killing; or

(B) a killing proximately caused in the perpetration of, or attempt to perpetrate, a felony.

SECOND-DEGREE MURDER:

Any murder which is committed recklessly under circumstances manifesting extreme indifference to the value of human life.

VOLUNTARY MANSLAUGHTER:

(A) A homicide that would otherwise be murder is committed in a sudden passion or heat of blood caused by provocation sufficient to deprive an average person of his self-control and cool reflection; or

(B) a homicide committed recklessly.

INVOLUNTARY MANSLAUGHTER:

A homicide committed negligently.

ROBBERY:

The taking of anything of value belonging to another from the person of another, or that is in the immediate control of another, by use of force or intimidation, when the offender leads the victim to reasonably believe he is armed with a dangerous weapon. Robbery is a felony carrying a sentence of no less than 3 and no more than 40 years in prison.

RAPE:

Sexual intercourse with another person by force or threat of force against the will of the other person. Rape is a felony carrying a sentence of up to 20 years in prison.

ATTEMPT

An attempt to commit any other crime is a felony carrying a sentence of up to five years in prison.

Question #1

Frank and his wife Martha had been married just under four years. Martha told Frank that she was dissatisfied with the relationship and wanted some time apart. Frank voluntarily took an apartment a couple of miles away. Frank also persuaded Martha to go to marital counseling with him on several occasions during the period of their separation.

One night, Frank took Martha to dinner and she told him she thought the marriage was over and that she wanted to date someone that she had met. Frank returned her to their house and went back to his apartment. He drank a six-pack of beer. He called a close friend to discuss what Martha had said. The friend told him that Martha must not be taking his efforts at reconciliation seriously. Now drunk, Frank decided to drive over to the house to try once more to convince Martha that he was sincere.

When he arrived at the home, he saw an automobile parked in the driveway. He did not recognize the car as one belonging to any of his wife's friends. He parked his car around the corner and walked back to the house. Observing from the rear of the house, he saw his wife and a man eating dinner and drinking wine. He then saw them kiss. The man he saw was a coworker of his wife's named Kevin, whom Frank had never seen before.

Frank decided to go home and get a camera but before doing so he let the air out of one of the tires on Kevin's car. Frank went to his apartment, drank another beer down and retrieved a camera as well as an old pistol that had belonged to his father. He tucked the pistol down in his waistband and covered it with his shirt. He then drove back to the house.

Frank spent more than an hour in the backyard of his home observing his wife and Kevin in the den and the kitchen. They then left the den area but Frank remained behind the house, thinking that Kevin was about to leave. He waited for a little bit and finally walked around to the front of the house. The car was still in the driveway and the drapes to the front guest bedroom had been closed. He listened near the window of the bedroom and heard the sounds of two people having sex.

Frank then burst through the front door of the house and into the bedroom where he found his wife and Kevin nude and he pulled out the camera and attempted to take pictures. Kevin, a former high school basketball and football player, stood at 6'3" tall and weighed about 210 pounds. Frank was slightly built, standing at about 5'8" and weighing only about 130 pounds. Kevin lunged toward Frank and Frank pulled out his gun and shot, hitting Kevin in the hip, just once. Frank immediately called the police and stayed until assistance arrived. Kevin died on the way to the hospital. Frank admitted to the police that he was pretty drunk, and he told them that he believed Kevin was going to attack him.

Part A: Discuss the possible charge or charges the prosecutor could file against Frank. What are all the arguments the defense attorney might make against those charges? What arguments, if any, are the prosecutor likely to make in response? In essence, discuss both sides of all of the issues in this case.

Part B: Now, consider the same factual scenario, but Frank suffers from a minimal brain dysfunction with an associated explosive personality disorder with paranoid features. Minimal brain dysfunction is a biochemical imbalance in the brain that prevents Frank from maintaining control over his emotional impulses, especially in stressful situations. How, if at all, do these facts affect Frank's criminal liability?

Question #2

Marty and Sally met at a bar and talked for a few hours. At about midnight, Marty invited Sally to come back to his apartment for a nightcap and Sally agreed to come. Sally drove her own car and followed Marty to his apartment.

They went up to his apartment and Marty poured each of them a scotch. They sat on the couch and began kissing. Marty and Sally talked some more and Marty told Sally that he is divorced and that he hates his ex-wife. He told Sally that "the b---h" got him put in jail for nothing, explaining that she claimed he hit her. Marty got visibly angry explaining this story to Sally. "Besides," Marty said to Sally, "as I told the police, I should have cracked her one -- she needed it. She never listened to me and NEVER," Marty said, looking at Sally, "gave me what I needed." Sally remained quiet during this time; she did not tell Marty that she had been in a physically abusive relationship before.

Feeling uncomfortable, Sally got up to leave. Marty said, "Aw, come on, you're not scared of me, are you?" Sally responded nervously, "No, I'm not scared. I should just get home, that's all." Marty was standing up near the doorway at this time. Sally moved toward the door. Marty did not move out of her way. He said, "Prove you are not scared of me, then." Marty began to kiss her again. Sally pulled away and said, "I really should be going." Marty responded, "Oh, come on," and he picked her up and carried her to the bedroom, placing her down on the bed. Sally said nothing more. Marty pulled off his clothes and then took hers off. He kissed her and she did not return the kisses. Sally was stiff and unresponsive. Marty got on top of Sally and engaged in sexual intercourse.

Sally left the house and went home. The next day, she decided to report this incident to the police. She told the police that she simply froze with fear as she was afraid he might hurt her if she did not cooperate.

You are the prosecutor in this case. What arguments will you make to support a charge of rape? What arguments will the defense attorney make against the charge?

Question #3

Feona is desperate for money. She decides she is going to rob a bank even though she has never committed a crime in her life. She figures that she should have something to scare people with but does not want to carry an operating gun because she is afraid of guns. Therefore, Feona goes to a pawn shop and buys a gun that the shopkeeper tells her is no longer operational.

Feona goes out the next day to scope out the best bank to rob. She walks around downtown for awhile and settles on First Union Bank. She goes inside and makes mental notes about the layout of the bank. When she gets outside, she scribbles a map on a piece of paper and puts it in her pocket. Feona decided to come back just before the bank closes at 3:00 p.m., at about 2:55 p.m. Feona times herself by her watch, which she has forgotten to "Spring Forward" by one hour. She was unaware that Daylight Savings Time had ended the day before.

Feona then decides to go buy a wig in the meantime. After much indecision, she gets herself a long, curly blond wig and some dark glasses. She then goes home, watches T.V. for awhile, and practices telling people to "cooperate and no one gets hurt." At 2:30 p.m. by her watch, she puts on the wig and the glasses, grabs the gun and the map and drives to the bank. Feona parks her car around the corner from the bank.

It is about 2:50 p.m. by Feona's watch, so she decides to stand around the corner from the bank for five minutes. As she stands there, she gets more nervous about the whole thing. In the meantime, a homeless man comes up to her and asks her if she has the time. She tells him to "Piss off!" The man gets angry and says, "You have got some nerve, lady, you need a personality adjustment, you know?" and continues to talk louder and insult her. To scare him off, Feona pulls out her gun and waves it at him. She is so nervous she squeezes the gun. To her shock, the gun goes off. She narrowly misses the man but, instead, hits a child who is walking with his mother in the vicinity. The child dies instantly. Feona runs to her car, deciding never to return, and gets half way home when she is arrested.

You are the prosecutor assigned to the case against Feona. Discuss all of the charges you would contemplate bringing against Feona, including the defense attorney's likely arguments against those charges. Supply the prosecutor's responses to the defense arguments, to the extent there are any.

CRIMINAL LAW ESSAY EXAM #2

For **QUESTION ONE and THREE ONLY**, refer to the following list of state statutes for all substantive crimes. For criminal law defenses, however, refer to your own knowledge under both the common law and the Model Penal Code.

FIRST-DEGREE MURDER:

(A) A homicide perpetrated by any kind of willful, deliberate and premeditated killing; or

(B) a killing proximately caused in the perpetration of, or attempt to perpetrate, a felony.

SECOND-DEGREE MURDER:

Any murder which is committed recklessly under circumstances manifesting extreme indifference to the value of human life.

VOLUNTARY MANSLAUGHTER:

(A) A homicide that would otherwise be murder is committed in a sudden passion or heat of blood caused by provocation sufficient to deprive an average person of his self-control and cool reflection; or

(B) a homicide committed recklessly.

INVOLUNTARY MANSLAUGHTER:

A homicide committed negligently.

SIMPLE BURGLARY:

The unauthorized entering of any dwelling, vehicle, watercraft, or other structure, movable or unmovable, with the intent to commit a felony or any theft therein.

Whoever commits the crime of simple burglary is guilty of a felony.

THEFT:

The taking of anything of value which belongs to another, without the consent of the other to the taking, with the intent to deprive the other permanently of the subject of the taking. Whoever commits the crime of theft is guilty of a felony.

ATTEMPT:

Whoever attempts to commit any other felony is guilty of a felony and subject to half of the penalties of the underlying felony.

Question #1

Ross, Monica, Chandler, Joey, Phoebe and Rachel are sitting around Monica's apartment. Rachel is complaining that waitressing at the Central Perk Coffee House is a living hell. Her main complaint is that the espresso machine spews foam at her on a daily basis, and that Gunther, the shop's manager, has refused to fix it. Joey suggests that they should steal the espresso machine that night after Central Perk closes and leave a ransom note for Gunther – "Promise to fix the machine or you will never see it again." Ross says, "No way. That is the stupidest idea I have ever heard. But if you do get the machine, bring me a double latte, no foam." Rachel is afraid of the idea because she figures she will be the first one suspected, but she does not say anything to the others. The other four – Monica, Chandler, Joey and Phoebe – all say that they like the idea.

Chandler asks Rachel if she has her key to the coffee house and she says yes. Everyone but Ross drives together to the coffee house after closing. When they arrive, Rachel looks for her key in her purse but realizes that she left it at home. She is secretly relieved because she does not want the coffee shop burglarized. Phoebe says, "Oh well, so much for that" and begins to turn around and go back to the car when Joey picks up a brick and heaves it through the front window of the coffee shop. An alarm goes off and Monica runs away, yelling, "Forget it! Forget it!"

Joey and Chandler climb through the front window. Phoebe and Rachel are still standing outside the coffee house. As they are standing there, an elderly woman, aged 72, walks by the coffee house, hears the alarm, sees the broken window and the two men inside rummaging around the shop, and faints from fear. When she falls to the sidewalk, her head hits the pavement so hard that she dies instantly.

While this is happening, Joey and Chandler are inside the store. They look and look for the espresso machine, and then realize that it is not there. It turns out the espresso machine had been taken out for repairs earlier that day.

What charge or charges will the prosecution consider bringing against each of the six individuals? How might the defense respond to each of those charges?

Question #2

Ally McNally is a lawyer in a small, quirky law firm, known for taking cases that no other law firm will touch. Ally, likewise, is a small, quirky woman who spends the bulk of her time unsuccessfully trying to have a love life. She has recently become smitten with a new lawyer named Luke Walker. It has not escaped Luke's notice that for the past week, Ally has always managed to be right where he is -- in the co-ed bathroom when he emerges from the stall, getting water from the water cooler, in a particular section of the library. Ally always says, "Oh, uh, well, uh, fancy meeting you here" and then she moves on. One day Ally gets up the nerve to ask Luke out on a date. Luke says "no thanks." Ally goes home and looks in the mirror and tells herself she is "okay" and resolves to try again. The next day, Ally sends Luke a dozen roses with a note saying, "I'm a really good kisser. Ally." Luke does not thank her for the flowers. Later that same day, Ally sees Luke talking to a secretary named Elaine. Ally realizes they are flirting and she becomes very upset. She e-mails Luke a message that simply says, "You are making a big mistake."

That evening, Ally sees Luke leave the office and take the same elevator down as Elaine. Ally runs to catch the next elevator. As she gets off the elevator, she runs outside the building to see them walking away together. Ally follows them for about a block and a half, when Luke turns around and sees her. "Oh for God's sake," he moans. He then taps a police officer standing nearby on the shoulder and points at Ally, saying "That woman is following and harassing me." Next thing she knows, she is in handcuffs and is arrested.

Ally is charged with stalking, which is defined as follows:

> Stalking is an intentional and repeated following or harassing of another person, when such following or harassing seriously alarms, annoys or harasses the person, and which serves no legitimate purpose.

A look into the legislative history of this "stalking statute" shows that it came about as a result of a concern over a couple of well-publicized cases. In one, a former husband repeatedly followed his former wife in a car, called her on the phone and threatened to do things to her, her current boyfriend, or her dog, slashed her tires twice, and hid outside her apartment. The police said there was little they could do when she called them. The former husband ultimately killed her. In another, a spurned co-worker followed the woman who rejected him every time she left the office until she got onto the subway, left her nasty notes at work, and finally was arrested for carrying an unlicensed weapon after she called the police, who found him waiting for her outside her house with a gun. The debate in the legislature showed that the legislative intent in passing the new statute was to get at the kind of behavior exhibited in these examples.

Webster's New World Dictionary defines "alarm" as "to strike with fear: fill with anxiety," and "annoy" as "to irritate with a nettling or exasperating effect."

You represent Ally McNally. What possible defense or defenses might you have to the charge of stalking?

Question #3

Mad Cap and June Bug are members of different rival gangs and both sell drugs. They hate each other and have gotten into fights before over being on the other's home turf. Mad Cap has sworn to his gang members that the next time he sees June Bug on his turf, he is going to "put a cap in his ass" (shoot him dead).

One day, Mad Cap encounters June Bug in Mad Cap's neighborhood. Both, as usual, are packing guns. Mad Cap goes to pass June Bug without saying anything, but intentionally bumps him on his way past him. June Bug turns around and says, "What's up?", known in gang lingo to signify, "Do you want to fight?" Mad Cap says, "You are what's up" and pulls his gun out of his pocket. June Bug laughs and says, "You expect that to scare me? You can't even keep your own mama off drugs." Mad Cap's mother is a heroin addict and everyone in the neighborhood knows it. Mad Cap is terribly ashamed of this fact and very sensitive to people's comments about it. He flies into a rage and shoots June Bug, hitting him in the abdomen. Mad Cap runs and leaves June Bug lying in the street. Unattended, a wound of that type would cause June Bug's death within twenty-four hours.

An ambulance takes June Bug to the hospital emergency room, where Dr. Green is assigned to take care of him. (Dr. Green hates gang bangers and is constantly doing unethical things in the E.R. to show he is a righteous member of society.) Dr. Green makes all conventional efforts to save June Bug but June Bug is not responding to treatment. Dr. Green is aware of a new procedure that is expensive, time-consuming and still in the experimental stages. It has a 65% chance of working on June Bug. Nonetheless, Dr. Green decides not to do the procedure. June Bug dies on the operating table.

What charge charges will the prosecutor consider bringing against Mad Cap and Dr. Green? As far as Mad Cap, consider **only two charges** which seem to you to most likely fit his deed. For both Mad Cap and Dr. Green, analyze the charges from both a prosecutorial and defense perspective.

Question #4

Winston and Charlene have been married for less than a year. Winston is about 5'9" tall and 155 pounds and Charlene is 5'10" tall and 145 pounds. Winston often (several times a week) starts fights with Charlene, getting angry at her and then slapping or hitting her. Although he has caused some black eyes and red marks, Winston has never caused serious bodily injury to Charlene. The fights often occur after Charlene has returned from being out somewhere, because Winston becomes convinced she has been cheating on him every time she goes out.

Winston has been to therapy in the past about his anger and was diagnosed with Borderline Personality Disorder, which is described in DSM IV as follows:

> A pervasive pattern of instability in interpersonal

relationships, self-image, and affects, and marked impulsivity beginning by early adulthood and present in a variety of contexts, as indicated by five (or more) of the following:

(1) frantic efforts to avoid real or imagined abandonment

(2) a pattern of unstable and intense interpersonal relationships characterized by alternating between extremes of idealization and devaluation

(3) markedly or persistently unstable self-image or sense of self

(4) chronic feelings of emptiness

(5) inappropriate, intense anger or difficulty controlling anger

(6) impulsivity in at least two areas that are potentially self-damaging (e.g., spending, sex, substance abuse, reckless driving, binge eating)

(7) transient, stress-related paranoia

(8) instability due to a marked reactivity of mood (intense depression, irritability, or anxiety usually lasting a few hours and only rarely more than a few days).

One day, Charlene returns home from shopping and Winston is fuming. He accuses her of having been out with a man. She tries to ignore him and walks into the bedroom. Winston follows her into the bedroom, screaming at her. He comes after her with his fists clenched and his face red. He slaps her hard and she falls against the wall of the bedroom. Charlene grabs for a gun that Winston keeps on the nightstand, points the gun at him and fires a shot which misses him by an inch. They struggle over the gun. Winston grabs her hand that has the gun with one of his hands and at the same time, with his other hand, grabs one of his fifteen-pound bar bells off of the floor and hits her over the head with it. Charlene dies an hour later at the hospital from the hemorrhaging of the head injury.

Assume the prosecutor charges Winston with heat of passion voluntary manslaughter, and **only that**. You are the defense attorney. Assume you think the prosecutor can meet all of the elements of heat of passion manslaughter, what other defense or defenses does Winston have? What will be the prosecution's response?

CRIMINAL LAW ESSAY EXAM #3

For **QUESTION ONE and THREE ONLY**, refer to the following list of state statutes for all substantive crimes. For criminal law defenses, however, refer to your own knowledge under both the common law and the Model Penal Code.

FIRST-DEGREE MURDER:

(A) A homicide which is intentionally perpetrated by any kind of premeditated and deliberated killing; or

(B) a killing which occurs in the perpetration of, or attempt to perpetrate, a felony.

SECOND-DEGREE MURDER:

Any murder which is committed recklessly under circumstances manifesting extreme indifference to the value of human life.

VOLUNTARY MANSLAUGHTER:

(A) A homicide committed under the influence of extreme mental or emotional disturbance for which there is reasonable explanation or excuse. The reasonableness of such explanation or excuse shall be determined from the viewpoint of a person in the actor's situation under the circumstances as he believes them to be; or

(B) a homicide committed recklessly.

INVOLUNTARY MANSLAUGHTER:

A homicide committed negligently.

RECKLESSLY ENDANGERING ANOTHER HUMAN BEING:

A person is guilty of a felony if he recklessly engages in conduct which places or may place another person in danger of death or serious bodily injury.

CHILD ABUSE:

Any person who, under circumstances or conditions likely to produce great bodily harm or death, willfully causes or permits any child to suffer, or inflicts thereon unjustifiable physical pain or mental suffering, is guilty of a felony. A child is one who is less than 17 years of age.

Question #1

Billy, Emma and Benny are best friends. They are each 15 years old and, like most kids their age, are rebellious and think their parents are really stupid. One of their favorite topics of conversation when they sit in Billy's tree house after school is the bizarre and tortured ways in which they would kill their parents.

Billy and Emma find it all a big joke, but, unbeknownst to them, Benny is dead serious. Benny often shows up to meet them with bruises or a broken bone or two. He claims he is just clumsy or got beat up at school. In reality, his father, Leonard, gets drunk and beats him on a daily basis. Benny knows his life would be easier if it were just he and his Mom.

One day after school, the three kids meet and Benny is particularly beat up. He tells the others that he was beat up at school. In reality, Leonard had beaten him with his fists and then kicked him repeatedly as he lay on the ground. Leonard then told Benny that if he ever saw him again, he would kill him. Benny's father has said this before and has obviously not carried through on his threat, but, nonetheless, Benny was scared to go home.

Benny begins to talk to Emma and Billy about killing his father. Emma and Billy laugh, and Emma says, "Oh sure, Benny, how do you want to do it – beat him with wet noodles?" Benny ignores the joke and asks the two of them to meet him outside his house at midnight. He asks Billy to bring Billy's father's gun. Emma and Billy agree, thinking this is a joke.

That evening, Benny does not go home, but hides outside in his backyard, waiting for midnight to come. Emma and Billy talk on the phone that evening and decide they will sneak out to meet Benny since they figure they will just goof around with him when they get there. Billy decides to tuck his father's handgun in his pants, anyway, since he could have a little fun scaring them with it.

Emma and Billy sneak out of their houses and meet Benny in front of his house. Benny asks if Billy brought the gun. Billy pulls the gun and yells, "Gotcha! Come near me or I'll shoot!" Benny gets furious at Billy's antics and begins to cry. Benny says, "Don't you know my father is going to kill me if I don't kill him first?" He tells them it is his father who beats them. Now, Billy and Emma see that he is serious. Billy says, "That no-good bastard," while Emma, seeing them both getting worked up, tries to talk them out of doing anything. Billy hands Benny the gun. Billy says to Emma, "Well, we are going in there with or without you. Are you coming?" Emma decides she does not want to be left outside alone so she follows them to the door. Benny opens the door, and all three go inside. Leonard was not asleep, but was waiting up for Benny in the living room, and he was drunk as a skunk. Benny's mother, Ruth, sat in the living room as well, crying softly to herself. As soon as Leonard saw Benny, he started toward Benny. Benny pulled the gun out of his pocket and shot at him. The bullet missed his father, and, tragically, hit his mother by mistake, killing her instantly.

Leonard then lunged toward Benny and grabbed the gun out of Benny's hands. Leonard took the gun and beat Benny over the head with it. Benny subsequently died as a result of severe head injuries.

The police arrest Leonard, Emma and Billy.

NOW you are the prosecutor. What are all of the possible charges you can bring against each of them. Assume Emma and Billy can be prosecuted as adults. What will be the defense attorney's responses to the charges? Argue both sides.

Question #2

Ron Miller, a United States Postal inspector, was working with a task force targeting the exploitation of children on the Internet. Miller would typically enter an Internet chat room while assuming the identity of a child. On August 3, 2002, he entered a Microsoft chat room that was not limited to adults. Using the name "Jaime14," Miller participated in the chat session and soon received a "whisper" (private communication from another chat room participant) from a "Pablito," who was actually 42-year-old Paul Conrad.

"Pablito" inquired, "Just 14 and fun?" Conrad e-mailed a photograph of himself, and Miller responded with a photograph of a female undercover officer taken when she was approximately 14 years old. "Pablito" raised the possibility of "Jaime14" visiting him at a place where they could "talk easier." "Pablito" provided an address and a telephone number. "Pablito" and "Jaime14" arranged a meeting for August 9th.

On August 9th, police posted an undercover officer at the arranged meeting site, but Conrad did not appear. Conrad e-mailed "Jaime14" that he did not show because he became nervous about meeting with her, that he was afraid someone might find out.

After Conrad did not show, the police went to his apartment and arrested him for attempted sex with a minor. The statute at issue prohibits "sexual intercourse with a child," where "child" is defined as "a person aged 15 or younger."

NOW discuss Conrad's liability.

Question #3

Donald and Kit are a husband and wife out hunting deer in a forest. It is wintertime, there are no leaves on the trees, and the temperature with the wind chill factor is about 10 degrees Fahrenheit. Donald suffers from a severe color-blindness – he only sees shades of gray. As a consequence, he relies on Kit to confirm for him whether what he has spotted is a deer.

George is hiking in the same forest. He realizes it is hunting season, so he wears a bright orange vest and stays on well-marked trails.

From his post, Donald spots an object moving about 30 yards away. He sees a gray form moving. Kit is nearby and has her own deer in sight. Donald whispers urgently, "Kit! Kit! I think I see one." Kit is afraid to take her eyes off of her own prey. In the ten years she and Donald have been hunting together, he has only been wrong once about having spotted a deer – in that one case, it was a turkey. Without taking her eyes off of her deer, Kit whispers back to Donald, "Go for it, Donny." Donald fires his rifle toward the object. George is hit in the leg by the bullet.

Part A: Assume George does not die. Assess the potential liability of Donald and Kit.

Part B: Assume instead that George does not die right away. Afraid he will get shot again, George crawls to a hidden spot behind a rock. Donald and Kit go to look for Donald's kill but do not find anything and assume he missed. It so cold out that, lying there so still, George falls asleep. Within several hours, he freezes to death in his sleep. Assess the potential liability of Donald and Kit.

Question #4

Josephine is a pharmacist. When she moved residences within the state of Utah, she forgot to notify the licensing board of her change of address. Josephine therefore never received a notice about the pending suspension of her license, and her license lapsed for failure to pay the licensing fee. Josephine took a position as head pharmacist at the local Walgreen's in the town of her new residence. One day, after she filled a prescription for sleeping pills for one of her customers, a girl who looked to Josephine to be in high school came to the counter to claim the prescription. The girl stated that she was picking up the prescription for her mother. Josephine asked for the girl's identification and saw that the girl had the same last name and address as the person on the prescription and so she released the pills to the girl. A little later, the customer showed up to claim her prescription and Josephine told her that her daughter had already picked up the prescription. The woman shouted, "My daughter! How could you? My daughter is an addict!" and stormed off to get the police. Josephine was arrested and charged with violating the following statutes:

1. It is unlawful to distribute medication without a license. Anyone who violates this section faces a period of incarceration of up to 90 days in jail, a fine of $1000 or both.

2. It is unlawful to knowingly distribute

controlled substances to a minor. Anyone who violates this section faces a period of incarceration of up to five years in jail, a fine of $5000 or both.

It turns out the girl was 15 years old. Josephine claims that she had no idea the girl was under 18 years old, and that when she looked at the identification, she did not look at the girl's birth date, but only her name and photograph. Josephine further claims that she had no idea her license was suspended. Assume that the sleeping pills were both "medication" and a "controlled substance" within the meaning of the statutes.

You are Josephine's lawyer. What arguments will you make that she is not guilty of either offense? What arguments do you expect the prosecutor to make in response? What arguments, if any, will you make in reply?

CRIMINAL LAW ESSAY EXAM #4

Question #1

89-year-old Mildred Rogers was at home when her 87-year-old neighbor and friend Martin Sellers came over for his morning visit. Martin has been experiencing bouts of senility now and then. On this day, Mildred and Martin got into an argument when Martin accused Mildred of sharing secrets with his wife. Martin's wife has been dead for ten years and Mildred tried to convince Martin of this. Martin insisted that she is alive and that Mildred was a "damned liar." Martin got madder and madder until, thoroughly distraught, he took hold of Mildred's wheelchair, to which she was confined, pushed her to the front door, and then gave her a big push out the door. He yelled after her, "I hope you die, too, then!" and slammed the front door.

The driveway sloped down toward the street, which is a quiet side street. As Mildred gathered speed and headed straight for the street, she knew she would be able to steer the wheelchair into the grass and therefore only suffer a few bruises or broken bones. Instead, she thought to herself, "Well, I have had a good run. I have to go sometime, so now is as good a time as any." She did not do anything to steer away from the street.

As her wheelchair entered the street, she was hit by a car. The driver of the car was 30-year-old Walter Knowles, who had just reached down to grab a CD off of the floor of his car when he looked up to see Mildred in the street. It was too late to stop. After Walter hit Mildred and saw how severely injured she was, he panicked and left her there as he drove off.

Mildred did not die immediately. If help had gotten to her within 10 minutes of Walter hitting her, she could have been saved. Instead, no one came along as she lay there and 15 minutes after she was hit, she died of her injuries.

The state has the following statutes:

1. When a homicide is committed by any kind of deliberate and premeditated killing, a person is guilty of murder in the first degree.

2. When a homicide is committed recklessly under circumstances manifesting extreme indifference to the value of human life, a person is guilty of murder in the second degree.

3. When a homicide is committed in a sudden passion or heat of blood caused by provocation sufficient to deprive an average person of his self-control and cool reflection, a person is guilty of voluntary manslaughter.

4. When a homicide is committed with recklessly, a person is guilty of reckless homicide.

5. When a homicide is committed negligently, a person is guilty of negligent homicide.

The police arrest Martin and Walter and charge them in the death of Mildred.

You are the prosecutor in the case. What charge or charges could you possibly bring against Martin and Walter (i.e., discuss all plausible charges)? What are likely to be the defense attorney's arguments against these charges?

Question #2

Mary Beth and Kenneth Joyner have been married for five years. They have a four-year-old girl named Annie. Two years ago, Kenneth lost his job and has been unemployed ever since. Mary Beth has been the sole breadwinner, trying to make ends meet by cleaning other peoples' homes three to four days a week. When Kenneth lost his job, he began to drink and became a very angry man. He also became violent when he was angry. Several times, he hit Mary Beth so hard, she blacked out. Kenneth would always apologize afterward and cry in Mary Beth's arms. In the last two years, he has hit her about a dozen times.

Within the last year, Kenneth has begun taking his anger out on Annie as well, getting furious when she has cried or made too much noise. The very first time he smacked Annie, Mary Beth screamed at him and hit him in the chest. Kenneth grabbed Mary Beth's hands and threw her to the ground, saying, "Don't you ever, ever interfere with my discipline or you will be very sorry." After that, Mary Beth was too afraid to intervene. Mary Beth became increasingly agitated at her daughter's behavior, afraid it would incur her husband's wrath. Mary Beth would frequently lose patience with Annie, so that neighbors and friends would hear her tell Annie she was a "very bad girl" or a "stupid girl" for any small, childish infraction.

One day Kenneth was in an especially bad mood. Mary Beth was in the kitchen trying to make Annie eat some vegetables. Annie began to scream and cry. Mary Beth told her to "shut up." Kenneth came into the kitchen and pushed Mary Beth to the floor and knocked over the chair Annie was sitting in, sending Annie falling to the floor. As Annie screamed, Kenneth kicked her repeatedly. Mary Beth whimpered and cried in a corner, afraid to move.

A neighbor heard the screams and commotion and called the police. When the police arrived, Child Welfare Services was called and Annie was taken from Mary Beth and Kenneth, who were then charged with child abuse and child neglect.

In the state in which Kenneth and Mary Beth live, "child abuse" is defined as:

> (1) Knowing or purposeful infliction of physical or mental injury upon a child;
>
> (2) A knowing or purposeful act that could reasonably be expected to result in physical or mental injury to a child; or
>
> (3) Active encouragement of any person to commit an act that results or could reasonably be expected to result in physical or mental injury to a child.

"Child neglect" is defined as:

> (1) A care giver's willful or negligent failure or omission to provide a child with the care, supervision, and services necessary to maintain the child's physical and mental health; or
>
> (2) A care giver's willful or negligent failure to make a reasonable effort to protect a child from abuse, neglect, or exploitation by another person.

The prosecution plans to include in its indictment against Mary Beth as "mental injury" the instances where Mary Beth told her child she was "bad" and "stupid" or to "shut up," and as "physical injury," the instances where Kenneth hit and kicked Annie.

As prosecutor, analyze how you would make your case against Mary Beth under the statutes. As Mary Beth's defense attorney, describe all of the arguments you might make in response to the charges, including any objections you may have about any part of the statute itself, constitutional or otherwise.

Question #3

Francine Patrick is a 48-year-old history professor at a liberal arts college. Each year, the freshman class hears the rumors about Professor Patrick from last year's class. Those rumors are: she is harsh and demanding, often getting angry with her students in class and insulting the intelligence of one student in front of others; she only takes male research assistants; and she has affairs with her male students.

Eighteen-year-old Samuel Collins is a freshman and is enrolled in Professor Patrick's history class. He has already heard all of the rumors. He is fresh off a Kansas farm and fairly naive and unworldly. On the very first day of class, Professor Patrick calls on Samuel, who has not done the reading. She asks him a question and he tells her he does not know the answer. She then proceeds to call him "an ignorant hayseed" and tells him to see her after class.

Samuel reports to her office. He is fairly nervous. Once inside her office, she tells him to close the door and sit down. He does. Professor Patrick proceeds to lecture him on the importance of preparedness. She asks him if he has a need-based scholarship and he tells her he does. She then tells him, "I can have that scholarship pulled at any time if you do not perform up to my standards, you know." She gets up from behind her desk and walks over to him seated in the chair. She places her hands on his shoulders and brings her face down right in front of his. She says, "You DO know what I mean?" Samuel, terribly nervous, says, "Yes, ma'am." She then tells him to get out of her office and to return the following week at the same time.

Samuel shows up at Professor Patrick's office the same time the following week, not sure what to expect and not sure what would happen if he did not go. She tells him to close and lock the door and to sit down on the couch. He does so. She asks him how he likes college and he tells her that he does. She asks a few more questions about school and then asks if he has a girlfriend and he responds, "No, ma'am." She asks him if he will be her research assistant. Unsure, he says, "I would have to check my schedule." She responds to him, with a smile, "You DO want to pass my class?" To which he responds, "Of course." "It's settled then, you will be my research assistant." She pulls down some books from her shelf and puts them in his lap and sits down next to him. She talks about the books and potential research. As she turns the pages in the books, she brushes his groin and says, "Does all of this interest you?" Samuel responds, "Yes, ma'am." Professor Patrick then pushes the books off of his lap and unzips his pants. Samuel is shocked and says nothing. Professor Patrick proceeds to perform oral sex on Samuel. He then gets up and leaves her office.

Samuel is humiliated. He does not tell anyone at first. He drops the history class and, when his father discovers this, he is furious with Samuel. Samuel then tells his mother what happened. His mother calls the school, threatening legal action. The school's president has heard one too many rumors and complaints about Professor Patrick at this point and turns the investigation over to the police, who charge her with sexual assault.

"Sexual assault" is defined as: "Sexual conduct with a person by forcible compulsion or threat of forcible compulsion against the will and without the consent of the person."

Assume state law has not defined any of these terms, but you have access to all of the interpretations case law has given. If you were the prosecutor in this case, how would you urge the court to read, understand and interpret the elements of the statute so that Professor

Patrick could successfully be prosecuted? As to each element, what interpretation would the defense attorney urge?

In addition, what rationale or policy reasons might support the punishment of Professor Patrick in this situation? What supports not punishing her in this situation?

CRIMINAL LAW ESSAY EXAM #5

Question #1

Michael Smith was canoeing down the Rifle River in Michigan with his wife and two children. About forty yards ahead of him, there was a group of people traveling down the river together. The group consisted of five canoes. Timothy Boomer was in one of the five canoes. Smith saw Boomer fall out of his canoe and into the river, at which point Boomer loudly uttered a stream of profanities, while slapping the river and throwing his hands into the air.

Kenneth Socia, a road patrol deputy for the Sheriff's Department, who was on duty at the Rifle River that day, heard a loud commotion and vulgar language coming from approximately one-quarter mile up the river. Socia looked up and saw Boomer chasing a group of canoes, splashing water at them with his paddle, and repeatedly swearing at them.

The river around Smith and Boomer was crowded with families and children. Smith says that Boomer would have been able to see Smith's two children, who were both under five years old. Socia issued Boomer a citation for violating the following Michigan statute:

> Any person who shall use any indecent, immoral, obscene, vulgar or insulting language in the presence or hearing of any woman or child shall be guilty of a misdemeanor.

This statute was enacted in 1897. In the one hundred year-plus history of the statute, there are no published cases addressing the statute.

At his arraignment on the misdemeanor charge, Boomer moves to dismiss the charge. What arguments can he make in support of his motion? What arguments might the prosecution make in response?

Question #2

For this question **ONLY**, refer to the following list of state statutes for all substantive crimes.

FIRST-DEGREE MURDER:

(A) A homicide which is intentionally perpetrated by any kind of premeditated and deliberated killing; or

(B) a killing which occurs in the perpetration of, or attempt to perpetrate, a felony.

SECOND-DEGREE MURDER:

Any murder which is committed recklessly under circumstances manifesting extreme indifference to the value of human life.

VOLUNTARY MANSLAUGHTER:

(A) A homicide that would otherwise be murder is committed in a sudden passion or heat of blood caused by provocation sufficient to deprive an average person of his self-control and cool reflection; or

(B) a homicide committed recklessly.

INVOLUNTARY MANSLAUGHTER:

A homicide committed negligently.

ROBBERY:

The taking of anything of value belonging to another from the person of another, or that is in the immediate control of another, by use of force or intimidation. Robbery is a felony carrying a sentence of no less than 3 and no more than 40 years in prison.

Nineteen-year-old Terry Williams was mildly mentally retarded. He read on a third-grade level and interacted with others socially at the level of someone 11 or 12 years of age. Unfortunately, he was also a crack addict. As a result, his demeanor was often both child-like and paranoid. His brother David called him "Fraidy Cat," and eventually Terry's nickname became "Cat."

One day, Terry was walking down a street when four men grabbed him, dragged him to an alley, and pinned him down. Terry recognized the four men as members of a neighborhood gang. One of them, Sid Herman, held a gun to Terry's head and told him this was the gangs' turf and they never wanted to see Terry or his brother David in their neighborhood again. Sid then spun the chamber and clicked the gun once, twice, three times against Terry's head and then let Terry go. Terry ran all of the way home.

Once home, Terry told his older brother, David, about the confrontation. David was furious and gave Terry his gun. David told Terry that Sid and his gang were vicious killers and said, "Cat, you'd better be ready to get them before they get you." As Terry was leaving, David said, just loud enough so Terry could hear him, "I swear, someone ought to rob those mother
f---ers blind and leave them for dead. I'd like to see that bi--- Sid's ring on my finger." Sid was well-known for wearing a giant rock of a diamond ring on his pinky finger.

Terry took the gun and slowly but surely worked himself into a paranoid frenzy. He cried often. For the next two days, Terry became convinced that Sid and his gang were around every corner. On the third day after his confrontation with the gang, Terry took his last $50, bought crack cocaine and smoked it. Terry became more paranoid than ever. His head felt like it was going to burst. He was terribly frightened. Sweating and frantic, he ran ten blocks into the center of Sid's neighborhood and found Sid and his gang crouched around a cardboard box gambling.

"Sid!" Terry called out. Sid turned around and Terry opened up his jacket just enough to let Sid see he had a gun. Terry said, "I just want you to know that you can't mess with me. Don't make me use this." Terry turned around to leave. Sid started to laugh, stood up and said, "Hey, Cat, wait." Terry stopped and turned around. He saw Sid walking toward him. Sid's arms swung free at his sides and his hands were empty. The ring on Sid's pinky finger glinted in the sun. Everything his brother said three days ago rang out in his head. Terry lifted his brother's gun, closed his eyes and fired it six times. When he opened his eyes, Sid was dead on the ground, another gang member named Little Moe who had been seated at the cardboard box was dead, and the rest of the gang was gone. Terry went up to Sid, took the big diamond ring off of his finger and brought it home to his brother. David took the ring, smiled at his brother and said, "Cat, my man, good work."

The police arrived at the scene within ten minutes, found Sid and Little Moe dead, and recovered guns off of both of them which had been concealed beneath their clothing. Terry and his brother David are both arrested for the deaths of Sid and Little Moe.

Discuss all possible charges that the prosecutor could bring against them and discuss all arguments the defense could make in response.

Question #3

A group of law students who live in a house

together off-campus plan to have a party at their house the upcoming weekend. The law students place signs around the law school and over at the University Center advertising the party, "Chimps and Boars." On Saturday, the students purchase three kegs of beer as well as an assortment of hard liquor. That night, their house is packed with students, many of whom they do not know. At some point during the night, a group of students are crammed onto the porch of the residence. Among them are two of the party throwers, Kip and Rocky, who are engaged in talking to two young women who have told them they do not go to school at the University, but live "in town." The young women are wearing matching plaid skirts and white shirts. Suddenly, the porch collapses and causes the students on the porch -- about twenty -- to fall two stories into the public street below. Kip and Rocky are among those lying in the street.

The police arrive within seconds to investigate. They discover that, of those who have fallen to the street, eight of them range in age from sixteen to twenty years old. Two of those are the young women in plaid, who are both sixteen. All of the rest, including Kip and Rocky, are at least twenty-one years of age. All of those on the street are exceedingly drunk.

After calling an ambulance for the injured, the police arrest Kip and Rocky and charge them with the following state criminal offenses:

1. It is unlawful for any person, other than a parent, spouse, or legal guardian, to serve any alcoholic beverage to a person under twenty-one years of age.

    Whoever violates the provisions of this Section shall be fined not more than five hundred dollars or imprisoned for not more than thirty days or both.

2. Disturbing the peace is the doing of any of the following in such a manner as would foreseeably

disturb or alarm the public:
: . . . appearing in an intoxicated condition.

Whoever commits the crime of disturbing the peace shall be fined not more than one hundred dollars or imprisoned for not more than ninety days, or both.

3. Contributing to the delinquency of juveniles is the knowing enticing, aiding, soliciting or permitting, by anyone over the age of seventeen, of any child under the age of seventeen, to:
: . . . visit any place where the consumption of beverages of alcoholic content is the principal activity.

Whoever commits the crime of contributing to the delinquency of a juvenile shall be fined not more than five hundred dollars, or imprisoned for not more than six months, or both.

Kip and Rocky state that they had no idea that anyone at the party was under twenty-one.

NOW Discuss their liability under each of the above statutes, giving both the prosecution's arguments in favor of prosecution and the defense attorney's arguments against prosecution.

CRIMINAL LAW
ESSAY EXAMS

ANSWERS

CRIMINAL LAW ESSAY EXAM #1

Question #1: Part A

I. State v. Frank

   1. First-Degree Murder, Type A

The prosecutor could charge Frank with first-degree murder, under the first prong of the statute. Thus, the prosecutor must prove that the killing was willful, deliberate and premeditated. "Willful" in this context simply means a specific intent to kill. "Deliberate" in general implies that a person has weighed the reasons for and against the action and considered the consequences. "Premeditated" generally means that it was thought about beforehand. Jurisdictions have authorized the formation of premeditation in "the blink of an eye," but others require enough time for a second look or reflection on the action before committing it. While there is no set formula for this determination, courts have provided a list of factors that could be taken into account in deciding whether a murder was premeditated, including previous ill-will between the parties, want of provocation, any statements of the defendant up to and during the crime, the brutality of the killing, the degree of planning and in the manner in which the killing was performed. In general, courts look to evidence of motive, planning activity and manner of killing.

The prosecution will point to several facts to support the charge. After Frank observed his wife and Kevin kissing, he let the air out of Kevin's tires, went back to his house and retrieved a gun. The prosecution will argue that this shows that Frank was ensuring Kevin would not leave before he got back and that he was planning to kill Kevin. Then Frank spent an hour outside the house with a gun in his pants, aware that his wife was having an affair. He had plenty of time to weigh his options, cool off, and reflect, constituting premeditation and deliberation.

The defense will counter with the facts which show that Frank's crime is the lesser crime of voluntary manslaughter (see below). Yet, the defense can also directly counter with the factors which do not support premeditation and deliberation. There was no previous ill-will between Frank and Kevin so there was no prior motive for Frank to kill Kevin before he heard Kevin and his wife having sex. Frank had made no previous statements about an intent to kill Kevin. Frank manifested a plan to stop Kevin from going until he could go back and take pictures, not a plan to kill. Frank only grabbed the gun as an afterthought. There was provocation which ultimately caused Frank to burst into the house and confront the couple, so there was no time for deliberation and premeditation. Frank shot Kevin just once, in the hip, clearly not trying to kill him. After shooting him in the hip, Frank then called the police and waited for assistance to arrive, which further evidences the fact that he had not planned to kill Kevin.

2. Second-Degree Murder

The prosecution could also charge Frank with second-degree murder, which is any killing committed recklessly under circumstances manifesting an extreme indifference to the value of human life. To be "reckless," Frank must have been aware of and disregarded a substantial and unjustifiable risk of death. "Extreme indifference" to the value of human life is meant to capture a "depraved heart", and it can be shown when there is a high probability of death or serious bodily injury occurring as a result of the conduct. There is no requirement of a specific intent to kill.

The prosecution will argue that Frank was reckless because he was aware of the risk of, at least, serious bodily injury when pointing a gun at a person and shooting. There is no indication Frank purposely shot at

Kevin's hip. To prove extreme indifference, the prosecution will say that any time you point a gun at someone and fire, as Frank did, there is a very high probability that death will occur.

The defense will counter by arguing that this is not the type of crime "extreme recklessness" murder was designed to capture, that Frank did not exhibit a depraved, or abandoned and malignant, heart or wanton disregard under the circumstances (see self-defense below). When Frank pointed the gun at Kevin's hip and fired, he was not aware of a substantial and unjustifiable risk that Kevin would die. Also, the actions of calling for help for Kevin and waiting until help arrived show he did not have a depraved heart.

3. Voluntary Manslaughter: Type A

While the prosecution can charge voluntary manslaughter, it makes more sense for the defense to argue for voluntary manslaughter as the response to first-degree murder. The defense will argue that Frank committed voluntary manslaughter, type A, or "heat of passion" manslaughter. The defense would have to show that Frank was actually acting in a heat of passion, that it occurred upon adequate provocation under circumstances in which an average person would lose self-control, and that the heat of passion was sudden upon the provocation, so that there was no time to cool.

The defense will argue that Frank was subjectively in a heat of passion as evidenced by the fact that he burst into the room upon discovering that his wife was sleeping with another man. It was also sudden in that as soon as he heard his wife and Kevin having sex, he acted. Adultery is also classic adequate provocation, considered adequate at common law. An average man of average disposition in Frank's shoes would be moved to a heat of passion upon discovering adultery.

If the defense raises voluntary manslaughter as a lesser charge to defend against first-degree murder, then the prosecution will counter with arguments that sound in first-degree murder, but also are specifically tailored to counter the claim of voluntary manslaughter. The prosecution will claim that there was no sudden heat of passion. The provocation occurred when Frank first saw his wife and Kevin kissing and he had more than adequate time to cool off and gain his self-control. He went back to his house and got a camera and a gun, evidencing that he understood that adultery was afoot, and then spent more time lying in wait outside the house.

4. Voluntary Manslaughter, Type B

The prosecution could argue that Frank committed the killing recklessly (Voluntary Manslaughter, Type B). To be "reckless," Frank must have been aware of and disregarded a substantial and unjustifiable risk of death. "Extreme indifference" to the value of human life is meant to capture a "depraved heart", and it can be shown when there is a high probability of death or serious bodily injury occurring as a result of the conduct. There is no requirement of a specific intent to kill.

The prosecution will argue that Frank was reckless because he was aware of the risk of, at least, serious bodily injury when pointing a gun at a person and shooting. There is no indication Frank purposely shot at Kevin's hip. To prove extreme indifference, the prosecution will say that any time you point a gun at someone and fire, as Frank did, there is a very high probability that death will occur.

The defense will counter by arguing that this is not the type of crime "extreme recklessness" murder was designed to capture, that Frank did not exhibit a depraved, or abandoned and malignant, heart or wanton disregard under the circumstances (see self-defense below). When Frank pointed the gun at Kevin's hip and fired, he was not aware of a substantial and unjustifiable risk that Kevin would die. Also, the actions of calling for help for Kevin and waiting until help arrived show he did not have a depraved heart.

5. Involuntary Manslaughter

To prove negligence, the prosecution would have to show that Frank, even if he was not actually aware of the risk, *should* have been aware of the substantial and unjustifiable risk that, upon firing the gun, Kevin could die or be seriously injured. In other words, the question is whether a reasonable person in Frank's position would have been aware of the substantial and unjustifiable risk of death upon firing a gun at Kevin. The prosecution will argue that a reasonable person who fires a gun in a person's direction would be aware of such a risk. The defense will argue (unpersuasively) that a reasonable person would not be aware that a person could die from a gunshot to the hip.

6. Affirmative Defense: Self-Defense

In response to any of the charges of homicide, Frank will argue that he acted in self-defense, which is an affirmative and complete defense to a charge of homicide. To prove self-defense, Frank must show that he reasonably and honestly believed: (1) there was a threat of the use of deadly force against him; (2) the threat was unlawful and immediate; (3) he was in imminent peril of death or serious bodily harm; and (4) his response was necessary to save himself.

The defense will argue that when Kevin, who was substantially larger than Frank, lunged at Frank, Frank honestly and reasonably believed that Kevin would cause him immediate serious bodily harm. Either Kevin would get the gun from his waistband and shoot him, or, at such a larger size, would beat him to a pulp. The prosecution will counter that a reasonable person would recognize that Kevin was reaching for the camera and was unaware of the presence of a gun. There was no threat of the use of deadly force, as Kevin was unarmed.

The prosecution might raise the issue of whether, even if the elements of self-defense were met, Frank had the duty to retreat. If this is a jurisdiction with a duty to retreat, then a person must retreat before using deadly force provided there is a safe manner for retreating. There is an exception in some jurisdictions if the person is in their own home. Here, if there was a duty to retreat, then Frank would have to leave before using deadly force, unless it was his home. The prosecution will argue he was living elsewhere at the time so this was not his home, while the defense will argue that it was still his home.

7. Affirmative Defense: Intoxication

Under the common law, intoxication is a defense only to specific intent crimes, and not general intent crimes. If, as a result of intoxication, the defendant did not form or was incapable of forming the specific intent, then he is not culpable. In many jurisdictions today, the defense is completely abolished. The Model Penal Code allows it as a defense if it negates the *mens rea* of the crime, unless the *mens rea* is recklessness, and then it is no defense if the reason the person was unaware of the risk was because of intoxication.

Here, under the common law, voluntary intoxication will only offer a defense to first-degree murder, the only specific intent crime discussed above. Frank will argue that after one six-pack of beer, he was too drunk to form the intent to kill, or premeditate or deliberate.

The prosecution will counter that Frank had the six-pack much earlier in the evening and then ingested only one more beer. Frank spent more than an hour in the backyard after that. He was certainly not too drunk at that point to form the intent to kill.

Question #1: Part B

I. State v. Frank

1. Insanity Defense

Frank could argue that his mental imbalance constituted insanity, which would be a complete defense to any of the charged crimes. Under the Model Penal Code, a person is not responsible for his criminal conduct if, at the time of such conduct, as a result of mental disease or defect, he lacked the substantial capacity either to appreciate the criminality [wrongfulness] of his conduct or to conform his conduct to the requirements of law. The former is a cognitive test and the latter is a volitional test. Frank's particular condition seemed to affect his volitional impulses, as both his minimal brain dysfunction and the explosive personality disorder appear to cause him to explode in stressful situations. The defense will argue that this is exactly what happened when Frank heard his wife and Kevin having sex. One of the other tests for insanity which exists at common law is the "irresistible impulse" test, where a person acted solely as the result of an irresistible and uncontrollable impulse. The defense will argue that he suffered from such an impulse at the time.

The prosecution will counter that, under the volitional test of the Model Penal Code, or under the irresistible impulse test, Frank was not insane. While his conditions may result in some impulsive behavior, that particular night, Frank seemed in control of his actions. When he saw Kevin and his wife kissing, he went back to his house and got a camera and a gun. He then waited for an hour at the house before acting. He had the capacity to conform his conduct to the law, as, after he shot Kevin, he called the police and waited for their arrival.

Furthermore, his condition would not have fulfilled either the cognitive test of the Model Penal Code, or the other tests at common law. The other tests at common law include the *M'Naghten* test: where the defendant must demonstrate that he: (1) did not know the nature and quality of the act that he was doing; or, (2) if he did know, he did not know that what he was doing was wrong. Frank would not prevail since it clear that he understood that he shot at a human being and knew that it was wrong.

Question #2

I. State v. Marty

1. Force or Threat of Force

The prosecution would charge Marty with rape. The element of sexual intercourse is not disputed. The first element that must be proven is that the sexual intercourse was achieved through force or threat of force. Arguing "force" first, in some jurisdictions the courts have held that the amount of force inherent in sexual intercourse alone is enough to constitute force (New Jersey: In re M.T.S.). Otherwise, the prosecution would argue "force" from the act of lifting her up and placing her on the bed. Easier than proving force, however, would be to prove the "threat of force." Marty's actions were designed to keep Sally from leaving when she clearly expressed her desire to leave. He stood in the way of the door and challenged her to prove she was not scared of him. Just prior to this, he had told Sally that his wife, whom he referred to as the "b—h," claimed he hit her, and that he should have hit her because she never gave him what he wanted. The implication to Sally was that a person who does not give Marty what he wanted would be hurt – this is the threat of force. The fact that Sally did not resist is of no moment since resistance is no longer required in modern statutes.

As to the element of "force," the defense will counter that most courts still interpret force as some physical force above and beyond the act of sexual intercourse (see, e.g., Rusk, Berkowitz). The fact that he stood at the doorway and carried her into the bedroom are not acts of force, as that term is intended. He did not hit her or push her. As far as a threat of force, Marty also said and did nothing to indicate he would harm her if she did not comply. The conversation about his wife had nothing to do with her. The fact that she was afraid was more likely due to her own background being abused than to Marty's words or actions. Furthermore, while resistance is not required in the statute, the defense will still point out that Sally did not resist. Courts still take lack of resistance into account when determining force or threat of force, as there is an antiquated presumption that a woman would resist if force were being used (see Berkowitz).

2. Against the Will

The prosecution will argue that the sexual intercourse took place against Sally's will. Sally's testimony to this effect will prove that the intercourse was against her will. It is supported by the fact that she did not respond physically during the act, not returning his kisses and remaining stiff and unresponsive. Some states actually require affirmative permission before proceeding (New Jersey, In re MTS) and Sally gave no such affirmative permission.

The defense will argue that Sally gave no affirmative indication that the sexual intercourse was against her will. The defense here might raise here a reasonable mistake of fact. Some jurisdictions allow a defendant to raise this as a defense to either lack of consent (not an element here) or against the will. The argument would be that, even if the sexual intercourse was against Sally's will, a reasonable person in Marty's situation would not have known that, since she gave no indication of her unwillingness to proceed. Of course, the prosecution would respond that a reasonable person would recognize the signs of an unwilling participant.

Question #3

I.   State v. Feona

    1.   Attempted Robbery

The prosecution would charge Feona with attempted robbery. Attempt lies somewhere between mere preparation and completion of the crime. Feona first must have possessed the *mens rea* for attempt. A criminal attempt involves two *mens rea*s: the actor (1) must intentionally commit the acts which constitute the *actus reus* of an attempt; and (2) must perform these acts with the specific intention of committing the target crime. The prosecution will argue she intended the acts which constituted the attempt and she intended to rob the bank. The *actus reus* of the attempt depends upon the test adopted by the jurisdiction. Many jurisdictions have adopted the Model Penal Code test, which requires a "substantial step" strongly corroborative of the actor's criminal purpose. The Model Penal Code suggests some steps which apply in this case: (1) reconnoitering the place contemplated for the commission of the crime – Feona scoped the bank earlier in the day; (2) possession of materials to be employed in the commission of the crime that are specially designed for such unlawful use or can serve no lawful purpose under the circumstances – the gun bought from the pawn shop, the scribbled layout of the bank, the wig and dark glasses. Other tests include the physical proximity test – the actor's conduct was "proximate" to the completed crime – here, the prosecution will argue, she was all the way to the bank and ready to rob it before she ran off; the dangerous proximity test – when the actor is so near the result that the danger of success is very great – here, she was dangerously close to committing the robbery; the "indispensable element" test – she appeared to have every element needed to commit the crime – map, gun, disguise; the "probable desistance" test – she had reached a point where she likely would not have desisted if she had not been interrupted; the "abnormal step" test – she had already taken the unusual steps of casing the bank, drawing a map, getting a gun and wig; and the "unequivocality" test – when a person's conduct, standing alone, unambiguously reflects her intent – here, her conduct by getting all of the way to the crime scene manifested her intent to commit the crime.

The defense would likely counter the description of Feona having fulfilled some of the tests for *actus reus* of attempt. She had not gotten inside the bank, and so had not gotten control of an "indispensable element," and neither, then was her conduct "unequivocal." She was not physically or dangerously proximate to committing the crime since the bank was not open. And under the "last act" test, she had not completed every act she thought was necessary to commit the crime.

2. Affirmative Defense to Attempt: Impossibility

The defense will also counter the charge of attempt with the defense of impossibility. The Model Penal Code has eliminated the defense of impossibility. At common law, there are two types of impossibility: legal impossibility, which is a defense, and factual impossibility, which is not a defense. This has proven to be a very murky distinction: a hunter who shoots a stuffed deer believing it to be alive has not attempted to take a deer out of season, but a person who has shot into the intended victim's bed believing he is asleep there when he is actually somewhere else is guilty of attempted murder. The defense will simply argue here that it was legally impossible for Feona to commit robbery since there was no bank to rob.

The prosecution will argue what is likely the stronger argument, that this is merely a factual impossibility. The robbery was only impossible of completion because it was closed, which was a fact, and not a legal element.

3. Affirmative Defense to Attempt: Abandonment

The defense will also counter the charge of attempt with the defense of abandonment: that Feona abandoned the crime scene with no intent of returning another day and therefore is not guilty of attempt. However, the prosecution will counter that abandonment is only a defense if it is done under circumstances manifesting a complete and voluntary renunciation of the criminal purpose: it not voluntary if it is motivated in whole or in part by circumstances not apparent at the inception of the defendant's course of conduct and that increase the probability of detection or which make more difficult the accomplishment of the criminal purpose (Model Penal Code 5.01). Here, Feona did not abandon the effort because she voluntarily decided that she no longer wanted to rob the bank, but because she had just shot at a man and killed a child across from the bank.

4. First-Degree Murder, Part B

The prosecution would charge Feona with first-degree murder based on the definition in Part B, describing a felony murder. A killing which is proximately caused in the attempted perpetration of a felony is first-degree murder. Having proven attempted robbery, the only issue is whether the killing of the child was proximately caused in the attempted robbery. One way to form the issue is to ask whether the homicide is committed within the *res gestae* of the initial felony – is the killing so closely related to the felony in time, place and causal connection as to make it part of the same criminal enterprise? The prosecution will argue that she was standing on the corner waiting to rob the bank and waved the gun in order to scare away those around her so she could complete her crime. The defense will argue that she was not attempting to perpetrate the robbery when she shot the gun. The fact that she shot the gun off at the man to scare him was entirely unrelated to the robbery of the bank. Another way to form the issue of proximate cause is to ask whether the killing of the bystander was reasonably foreseeable. The prosecution will argue that it was, since she was carrying a loaded gun to a robbery, and the defense will argue that a reasonable person in her shoes would not have foreseen injury since she reasonably thought the gun was inoperable. Whether Feona intended to kill or not is immaterial to felony-murder.

5. Second-Degree Murder

The prosecution can also charge Feona with second-degree murder, which is any murder committed recklessly under circumstances manifesting an extreme indifference to the value of human life. To be "reckless," Feona must have been aware of and disregarded a substantial and unjustifiable risk of death. "Extreme indifference" can be shown when there is a high probability of death occurring as a result of the conduct.

The prosecution will argue that when Feona shot off the weapon in the close vicinity of the young child, she was aware of the substantial and unjustifiable risk that her aim would not be true and she could hit and kill the child. Even though she was told that the gun was inoperable, she was reckless in not checking the gun herself before waving it at human beings.

The defense will respond that Feona was not aware of a substantial risk of the gun going off since she was only waving it, afraid of guns and bought it with the understanding that it was inoperable. It was as much a shock to her as to those around her that the gun went off.

[Note that the doctrine of transferred intent does not come into play. Transferred intent applies only when the *mens rea* in the crime is knowledge or purpose. In this example, at most, Feona was reckless or negligent in firing a gun in the child's direction and transferred intent is not needed to charge her with his death in that case.]

6. Voluntary Manslaughter, Type B

The prosecution could argue that Feona committed the killing recklessly. To be "reckless," Feona must have been aware of and disregarded a substantial and unjustifiable risk of death. "Extreme indifference" can be shown when there is a high probability of death occurring as a result of the conduct.

The prosecution will argue that when Feona shot off the weapon in the close vicinity of the young child, she was aware of the substantial and unjustifiable risk that her aim would not be true and she could hit and kill the child. Even though she was told that the gun was inoperable, she was reckless in not checking the gun herself before waving it at human beings.

The defense will respond that Feona was not aware of a substantial risk of the gun going off since she was only waving it, afraid of guns and bought it with the understanding that it was inoperable. It was as much a shock to her as to those around her that the gun went off.

7.   Involuntary Manslaughter

To prove negligence, the prosecution would have to show that a reasonable person in Feona's position would have been aware of the substantial and unjustifiable risk of death of killing the child. The prosecution will argue that a reasonable person who squeezes the trigger of a gun, even a gun one was told was inoperable, would be aware of such a risk. A reasonable person would certainly also check a gun to ensure it was inoperable before using it under that assumption.

The defense will argue that a reasonable person does not believe there is an unjustifiable and substantial risk of death in the circumstances here – where one is told the gun is inoperable and the trigger is not intentionally squeezed.

8.   Attempted Murder

The prosecution could charge Feona with attempted murder of the man at whom she waved the gun. However, the prosecution would have to prove that she intended to kill the man, since attempt is a specific intent crime. There is no such thing as an attempted recklessness or negligent murder, since one cannot intend to cause a result recklessly – those are two opposing states of mind as to the result. Attempted first-degree murder will be difficult to prove since there is no evidence that Feona planned to do anything but scare the man and was, at most, extremely reckless.

CRIMINAL LAW ESSAY EXAM #2

Question #1

I. State v. Joey and Chandler

1. Attempted Theft

The prosecution will charge Joey and Chandler with attempted theft. First, the prosecution must prove they had the *mens rea* to carry out the completed crime. Did Joey and Chandler intend to commit a theft? The prosecution will argue that they intended to take the espresso machine and deprive the owner of it permanently, despite any claim that it was going to be returned upon a promise to fix it. The defense will respond that they had not intended to permanently deprive the owner of it, only until he agreed to fix it. As far as the *actus reus* of attempt, the prosecution will argue that, under any test for attempt, Joey and Chandler attempted the theft. The Model Penal Code requires a "substantial step," which must be strongly corroborative of the actor's criminal purpose. By breaking into the coffee shop, they had taken a substantial step. Other tests include the physical proximity doctrine – they were inside the coffee shop; the dangerous proximity doctrine – they were dangerously close to committing the theft; the probable desistance test – they would have completed the crime if they had found the machine; the abnormal step test – they had taken a brick, thrown it through the window, and entered the coffee shop; and the unequivocality test – their conduct in getting all of the way to the crime scene and breaking in manifested their intent to commit the crime.

The defense will respond that with no espresso machine to take they were not dangerously or proximately close to committing the crime.

2. Affirmative Defense to Attempt: Impossibility

The defense will also raise the defense of impossibility. Because the espresso machine was not there, it was impossible to steal it. The Model Penal Code has eliminated the defense of impossibility. At common law, there are two types of impossibility at common law: legal impossibility, which is a defense, and factual impossibility, which is not a defense. This has proven to be a very murky distinction: a hunter who shoots a stuffed deer believing it to be alive has not attempted to take a deer out of season, but a person who has shot into the intended victim's bed believing he is asleep there when he is actually somewhere else is guilty of attempted murder. The defense will simply argue here that it was legally impossible for Joey and Chandler to commit theft since there was no espresso machine.

The prosecution will argue what is likely the stronger argument, that this is merely a factual impossibility. The theft was only impossible of completion because it was temporarily elsewhere, much like the example of the intended murder victim who just does not happen to be in his bed.

3. Burglary

The prosecution will charge Joey and Chandler with burglary. First, they were not authorized to enter the coffee shop and they entered it by way of a thrown brick. Second, the prosecution will argue they had the intent to commit a theft inside the coffee shop, as described above. Burglary does not depend upon the completion of the theft.

The defense will describe that they had no intent to commit a theft since they had no intention of permanently depriving the owner of the espresso machine.

4. First-Degree Murder, Part B

The prosecution would charge Joey and Chandler with first-degree murder based on the definition in Part B, describing a felony murder. A killing which is proximately caused in the perpetration of or attempted perpetration of a felony is first-degree murder. Provided the prosecution proves either burglary or attempted theft, then only issue is whether the death of the elderly woman was proximately caused by either of those crimes. The question to ask is whether the homicide is committed within the *res gestae* of the initial felony – is the killing so closely related to the felony in time, place and causal connection as to make it part of the same criminal enterprise? The prosecution will argue this requirement is met because the woman fell and hit her head from fear over seeing the burglary taking place.

Another way to frame the issue of proximate cause is to ask whether such an event was foreseeable. The defense will argue that the death of the elderly woman is too remote from the underlying crime in terms of causation. A death was likely unforeseeable. The woman died because she fell and hit her head, not from any action on the part of Joey and Chandler.

5. Second-Degree Murder

The prosecution can charge Joey and Chandler with second-degree murder, which is any murder committed recklessly under circumstances manifesting an extreme indifference to the value of human life. To be "reckless," they must have been aware of and disregarded a substantial and unjustifiable risk of death. "Extreme indifference" can be shown when there is a high probability of death occurring as a result of the conduct.

The prosecution has a virtually impossible case here. The defense will argue that by breaking into the coffee shop, unarmed and with intent only to take the espresso machine, they were unaware of a substantial risk that a person would be killed in the process, much less in the manner in which it occurred here.

6. Voluntary Manslaughter, Type B

The prosecution could argue that Joey and Chandler recklessly caused the elderly woman's death (Voluntary Manslaughter, Type B). To be "reckless," Joey and Chandler must have been aware of and disregarded a substantial and unjustifiable risk of death. "Extreme indifference" can be shown when there is a high probability of death occurring as a result of the conduct.

The prosecution has a virtually impossible case here. The defense will argue that by breaking into the coffee shop, unarmed and with intent only to take the espresso machine, they were unaware of a substantial risk that a person would be killed in the process, much less in the manner in which it occurred here.

7. Negligent Manslaughter

To prove negligence, the prosecution would have to show that a reasonable person in Joey and Chandler's situation would have been aware of the substantial and unjustifiable risk of death to someone. The defense has the better part of this claim since a reasonable person who breaks into a building unarmed would not be aware of a substantial risk someone would die.

II. State v. Ross

1. Accomplice Liability

Ross can only be charged with any of these crimes through accomplice liability. Ross was not at the scene of the crime, had described the idea as a bad one, and suggested that if they did commit the crime that they bring him a latte. To be guilty as an accomplice, the prosecution would have to show that the accomplice had the *mens rea* required for the underlying crime, intent to aid in the commission of the crime, and actually gave assistance. The assistance can come in the form of physical assistance (such as supplying a weapon) or psychological assistance (such as encouragement), but mere presence on the scene with knowledge of the crime is not enough. There is no evidence that Ross either had the *mens rea* for the underlying crimes or intended to assist the crimes. While he may have provided minimal encouragement to the crime by suggesting he would share in the proceeds, that minimal *actus reus* is not enough to establish accomplice liability.

III. State v. Monica

1. Accomplice Liability

Monica, on the other hand, said she liked the idea, went to the scene of the crime, and ran away yelling "Forget it!" after an alarm went off. She would appear to have possessed the *mens rea* for theft and burglary, and intended to assist and did assist by going to the scene of the crime. She would be liable for theft and burglary and felony-murder to the same extent as Chandler and Joey, unless the defense can show she abandoned the crime before its completion.

2. Affirmative Defense to Liability: Abandonment

Abandonment is only a defense if it is done under circumstances manifesting a complete and voluntary renunciation of the criminal purpose: it is not voluntary if it is motivated in whole or in part by circumstances not apparent at the inception of the defendant's course of conduct and that increase the probability of detection or which make more difficult the accomplishment of the criminal purpose (MPC 5.01). Here, Monica abandoned the effort when an alarm went off, making detection more probable. She would not likely succeed in proving abandonment.

IV. State v. Phoebe

    1. Accomplice Liability

The prosecution will argue that Phoebe is an accomplice to all of Joey and Chandler's crimes. She has the *mens rea* for the underlying crimes of theft and burglary and intended the acts which constituted the assistance. Her assistance was that she encouraged the idea and went to the scene with them, which offered further encouragement. The defense will try to argue that mere knowledge of the crime and presence at the scene of the crime is not enough to constitute accomplice liability, but her encouragement of the idea constitutes more than mere knowledge and presence.

V. State v. Rachel

    1. Accomplice Liability

Rachel's status as an accomplice is questionable because of her unspoken hope that the plan not succeed. It does not appear that she had the *mens rea* for theft or burglary since she did not want the crimes to occur. She did commit the *actus reus* of assistance, in that she encouraged its commitment by saying she would let them in with the key. However, if she did not intend the underlying crimes, then she would not be an accomplice.

Question #2

I. State v. Ally

    1. Statutory Interpretation by the Court

Ally will argue that the statute is vague (see argument below). The court must engage in the presumption that the statute is constitutional. If the court agrees that the terms are vague, then the court can look to statutory history and precedent to see whether there is a limiting interpretation of the statute. Here, statutory history shows that the legislature intended the kind of conduct involved in the two cases described – both of which involved threats of violence which would strike fear into the reasonable person. Ally would argue to the court that, in order to save the statute, the court should adopt a limiting construction which includes that the activity involve a threat of violence, as well as that the activity be such that a reasonable person would recognize it as "annoying" or "harassing." Ally would argue her conduct is not covered under such a limiting interpretation.

2. Void-for-Vagueness

Ally will argue that the statute is unconstitutionally vague. There are three claims of vagueness in this context. First, the terms employed are so vague as to leave the law-abiding person guessing as to what conduct is prohibited. For example, what "annoys"? The dictionary meaning provided – "to irritate with a nettling or exasperating effect" does not sufficiently define conduct to give the law-abiding citizen fair notice. And what is a "legitimate purpose"?

Second, the statute is overbroad in that it sweeps in innocent activity. It would seem to sweep in the moonstruck teenage boy as well as the serious stalker intended by the legislature.

Third, since the statute is so broadly worded and encompasses a wide range of activity, the statute leaves to the arresting officer too much discretion to enforce the law selectively.

3. Not Liable Under Statute

Even under the statute as written, Ally would argue that her conduct does not constitute stalking. She will argue that she only followed him once, as opposed to repeatedly. She will also argue that, to the extent she annoyed him, it was not "serious," as indicated by his comment "Oh for God's sake." Finally, she will say her purpose in her conduct was legitimate – to get the man out on a date.

Question #3

I. State v. Mad Cap

1. First-Degree Murder, Type A

The prosecutor will charge Mad Cap with first-degree murder, under the first prong of the statute. Thus, the prosecutor must prove that the killing was willful, deliberate and premeditated. While there is no set formula for this determination, courts have provided a list of factors that could be taken into account in deciding whether a murder was premeditated, including previous ill-will between the parties, want of provocation, any statements of the defendant up to and during the crime, the brutality of the killing, the degree of planning and in the manner in which the killing was performed. Jurisdictions have authorized the formation of premeditation in "the blink of an eye," but others require enough time for a second look or reflection on the action before committing it.

The prosecution will point to the fact that there was ill will between the parties giving Mad Cap a motive to kill June Bug, that June Bug did not provoke him (other than through some words), that Mad Cap had said that the next time he saw June Bug on his turf he was going to kill him, and that he shot June Bug in the abdomen, leaving him there to die. To counter any claim of provocation on the part of June Bug (see below), the prosecution will point out that Mad Cap had his gun out and was ready to shoot before June Bug said anything about his mother.

The defense will counter the charge of first-degree murder with an argument that supports a charge of voluntary "heat of passion" manslaughter. The defense would argue that Mad Cap was actually acting in a heat of passion (he flew into a rage), that it was sudden upon the provocation (no cooling period), and that it occurred upon adequate provocation (under circumstances in which an average person would act similarly). The provocation was that June Bug said that "You can't even keep your own mama off drugs," knowing that Mad Cap's mother was a heroin addict and he was very sensitive about it. In some jurisdictions, words alone are not enough to constitute adequate provocation. Even if they are, the uphill battle for the defense would be to show that the average person would lose self-control. For the average person, it is unlikely that an insult to one's mother about a vulnerable characteristic would cause the person to fly into a homicidal rage.

2. Causation

This question raises a causation issue. The issue is whether Dr. Green's actions were an intervening cause sufficient to break the chain of causation between Mad Cap's shooting and June Bug's death. If Dr. Green had performed the experimental procedure, there was a 65% chance that June Bug would have lived. Given that only by Dr. Green's intervention could June Bug have lived at all, even if Dr. Green were negligent or accelerated June Bug's death, neither affect the underlying liability of Mad Cap. The courts usually employ the following test for proximate cause, which is a test for foreseeability: if the intervening act was a coincidence (putting the victim at a certain place at a certain time, making it possible for him to be acted upon by the intervening cause), then the chain of causation will not be broken if it was foreseeable; and if the intervening act was a response to the defendant's actions (a reaction to the conditions created by the defendant), then the chain of causation is only broken if the response was abnormal. Dr. Green's intervention was a response, and his decision to forego the experimental treatment was certainly not abnormal. Hence, Dr. Green's omission did not break the chain of causation.

II. State v. Dr. Green

1. Causation

First, no matter what Dr. Green is charged with, are his actions a direct ("but for") cause of June Bug's death? But for the abandonment of the procedure, there was a 65% chance June Bug would have lived. It is questionable whether a percentage is enough to constitute a "but for" cause.

2. Actus Reus

Dr. Green did not perform an act, but an omission. He withheld care. He can be liable for an omission only if he had a duty to act. The prosecution will argue that as a doctor, he has a duty to his patient to save his life at all costs. If he knew of a treatment that gave June Bug a 65% chance of living, he should have performed it, regardless of how experimental or expensive it was. The defense will counter that a physician only has a duty to give what is necessary and proportionate and cannot be deemed to have a duty to go above and beyond ordinary care. If he is found not to have a duty, then he is not guilty of any crime.

3. Second-Degree Murder

Assuming the prosecution jumps the hurdles of

causation and *actus reus*, the prosecution could charge Dr. Green with second-degree murder, which is any murder committed recklessly under circumstances manifesting an extreme indifference to the value of human life. To be "reckless," Dr. Green must have been aware of and disregarded a substantial and unjustifiable risk of death. "Extreme indifference" can be shown when there is a high probability of death occurring as a result of the conduct.

The risk of death was 100% by foregoing the procedure, so there was clearly a substantial risk of death. Was it an unjustifiable risk? That would depend upon whether one agreed with the assessment of the doctor that, because it was experimental, expensive and no guarantee, that it was not worth doing. As far as whether the risk was extreme, while Dr. Green would seem to know his omission would cause death, the question is whether he had an "abandoned and malignant heart" in foregoing the procedure. The prosecution will argue it was a heartless choice and the defense will argue it was not.

4. Voluntary Manslaughter, Part B

This charge requires recklessness. To be "reckless," Dr. Green must have been aware of and disregarded a substantial and unjustifiable risk of death. "Extreme indifference" can be shown when there is a high probability of death occurring as a result of the conduct.

The risk of death was 100% by foregoing the procedure, so there was clearly a substantial risk of death. Was it an unjustifiable risk? That would depend upon whether one agreed with the assessment of the doctor that, because it was experimental, expensive and no guarantee, that it was not worth doing. As far as whether the risk was extreme, while Dr. Green would seem to know his omission would cause death, the question is whether he had an "abandoned and malignant heart" in foregoing the procedure. The prosecution will argue it was a heartless choice and the defense will argue it was not.

5. Involuntary Manslaughter

The prosecution will argue that Dr. Green was negligent in that a reasonable person in his shoes would have been aware of the substantial and justifiable risk of death. Of course, the risk was 100%, and the question simply becomes whether it was justifiable, as described above. Another way to state the issue in this particular case is whether Dr. Green exhibited the reasonable care of a doctor in his situation, and the same issues again arise.

Question #4

I. State v. Winston

1. Insanity

Winston could argue that his condition, Borderline Personality Disorder, was a mental disease or defect that rendered him insane at the time of the killing. Courts rarely define the term "mental disease or defect" so this will be open to interpretation by experts. If Winston is able to show that Borderline Personality Disorder is a mental disease or defect, then he will argue he was insane under one of the following tests. Many states have adopted the Model Penal Code test: a person is not responsible for criminal conduct if at the time of such conduct as a result of mental disease or defect he lacks substantial capacity either to appreciate the criminality [wrongfulness] of his conduct or to conform his conduct to the requirements of law. This test involves both a cognitive and a volitional component. Some of the characteristics of Borderline Personality Disorder seem to involve volition – difficulty controlling anger and impulsivity in areas that are potentially self-damaging. Winston could argue that he lost control over his impulses when he hit her with the bar bell. His frantic efforts to avoid abandonment and his paranoia led to his reaction. He would also argue that his condition fits the another common law test, the "irresistible impulse" test, where the person acted from an irresistible and uncontrollable impulse. The defense will argue that he suffered from such an impulse at the time.

The other tests at common law include the *M'Naghten* test: where the defendant must demonstrate that he: (1) did not know the nature and quality of the act that he was doing; or, (2) if he did know, he did not know that what he was doing was wrong. This is a purely cognitive test and one under which Winston is unlikely to prevail since there is no indication in his diagnosis that he would not know right from wrong.

The prosecution will respond that frantic efforts to avoid abandonment plus difficulty controlling anger does not make a mental disease or defect sufficient to raise the flag of insanity. There is no indication that he lacked substantial capacity to conform his conduct to the law as he lived a normal life on a daily basis and did not normally lose control like this.

2. Self-Defense

Winston will argue he was acting in self-defense. At common law, a non-aggressor is justified in using deadly force in self-protection if the actor reasonably believes that its use is necessary to prevent imminent and unlawful use of deadly force by the aggressor. "Deadly force" is force intended or likely to cause death or grievous bodily injury.

Winston's argument will be that Charlene had just employed deadly force on him – she fired a round at him and missed. He was trying to prevent her from shooting him again when he hit her over the head with the bar bell. He was therefore reasonable in his belief that deadly force was imminent and that he needed to use deadly force in response.

The prosecution will have several counterarguments. First, Winston was the first aggressor and hence lost his right of self defense. The question here turns upon whether Winston was a deadly aggressor or a non-deadly aggressor. He slapped her hard and she fell against the wall of the bedroom. The prosecution will argue that this is deadly force – enough to cause serious bodily injury to a woman. If the prosecution prevails, then the only way that Winston could have regained his right of self-defense was by withdrawing from the conflict and successfully communicating this fact. If he was a non-deadly aggressor instead, and then Charlene responded with deadly force, there are two possibilities. Some courts hold that once she responded with deadly force, he immediately regained his right to self-defense. Other courts hold that he is not entitled to use deadly force unless he retreats, if safe retreat is available. If he does, or if there is no safe retreat, then he may use deadly force. Because one cannot retreat safely from a loaded gun, if Winston is a non-deadly aggressor, then he would regain his right of self-defense. This latter point also goes to any duty to retreat. If there is a jurisdiction with a duty to retreat, and there is no exception for a man's home, then Winston still would not have to retreat since he could not do so safely with an uplifted gun.

The prosecution will also argue that at the point at which Winston hit Charlene over the head with a bar bell, he had grabbed her hand with the gun. At that moment, then, there was no imminent threat of deadly force.

Finally, the prosecution will argue that Winston could not avail himself of self-defense because he was not defending himself against an unlawful use of force.

Winston had just hit Charlene, and Charlene may have had a right to use deadly force at that point. The prosecution will argue that she believed that seriously bodily injury was imminent because he had slapped or hit her before. The prosecution might employ the battered woman's syndrome to explain how women in her position reasonably feel that grievous bodily injury is imminent. If the prosecution is successful, then Winston had no right to self-defense. However, in some jurisdictions, he might have an "imperfect" right of self-defense if he was unreasonable but honest in his belief that deadly force was necessary.

CRIMINAL LAW ESSAY EXAM #3

Question #1

I. State v. Leonard

   1. First-Degree Murder of Benny, Type A

The prosecutor will charge Leonard with first-degree murder of Benny, under the first prong of the statute. Thus, the prosecutor must prove that the killing was willful, deliberate and premeditated. "Willful" in this context simply means a specific intent to kill. "Deliberate" in general implies that a person has weighed the reasons for and against the action, considering the consequences. "Premeditated" generally means that it was thought about beforehand. Jurisdictions have authorized the formation of premeditation in "the blink of an eye," but others require enough time for a second look or reflection on the action before committing it. While there is no set formula for this determination, courts have provided a list of factors that could be taken into account in deciding whether a murder was premeditated, including previous ill-will between the parties, want of provocation, any statements of the defendant up to and during the crime, the brutality of the killing, the degree of planning and in the manner in which the killing was performed. In general, courts look to evidence of motive, planning activity and manner of killing.

The prosecution will use the fact that there was previous ill-will between Leonard and Benny, and so Leonard had a motive to kill Benny. Leonard had threatened to kill Benny when he saw him again. Leonard also had the time to reflect upon his actions, deliberate and premeditate as he did not kill him instantly upon seeing him or upon Benny shooting at him. He saw Benny shoot Ruth, and then grabbed the gun out of his hand and beat him over the head with it. Since he beat him so hard that Benny died, one can infer that the beating was particularly brutal.

2. First-Degree Murder of Benny, Type B

The prosecution would charge Leonard with first-degree murder based on the definition in Part B of the statute, describing a felony murder. A killing which is proximately caused in the perpetration of a felony is first-degree murder. The underlying felony would be child abuse. The prosecution would prove child abuse by showing that the severe beating with the gun was likely to (and did) produce great bodily harm and by doing this, Leonard willfully (intentionally or knowingly) caused Benny to suffer, as well as inflicted unjustifiable physical pain.

The defense will counter with the doctrine of merger. If the underlying felony merges with the homicide, there is no separate cause for felony-murder. Hence, if a person shoots at someone and kills them, there is no felony-murder with the underlying felony as assault with intent to kill – the assault merges with the homicide. Here, the same is true. It appears that the beating is precisely what constitutes the homicide and hence the two offenses merge.

3. Child Abuse

The prosecution would charge Leonard with child abuse. The prosecution would prove child abuse by showing that the severe beating with the gun was likely to (and did) produce great bodily harm and by doing this, Leonard willfully (intentionally or knowingly) caused Benny to suffer, as well as inflicted unjustifiable physical pain.

The defense will counter with the doctrine of merger. If the underlying felony merges with the homicide, there is no separate cause for felony-murder. Hence, if a person shoots at someone and kills them, there is no felony-murder with the underlying felony as assault with intent to kill – the assault merges with the homicide. Here, the same is true. It appears that the beating is precisely what constitutes the homicide and hence the two offenses merge.

4. Second Degree Murder

The prosecution can charge Leonard with second-degree murder, which is any murder committed recklessly under circumstances manifesting an extreme indifference to the value of human life. To be "reckless," Leonard must have been aware of and disregarded a substantial and unjustifiable risk of death. "Extreme indifference" is the equivalent to the common law notion of "depraved heart" and can be shown when there is a high probability of death occurring as a result of the conduct. There is no requirement of an intent to kill.

The prosecution will argue that since Leonard beat his son so hard that he died, he was aware of and disregarded the substantial and unjustifiable risk of death to a 15-year-old boy. The prosecution will further argue that Leonard exhibited a "depraved heart" and extreme indifference to the value of human life when he beat the young boy to death.

5. Voluntary Manslaughter, Type A

While the prosecution can charge voluntary manslaughter, it makes more sense for the defense to argue for voluntary manslaughter as a lesser charge to first-degree murder. As to Type A, or "heat of passion" manslaughter, the defense would have to show that Leonard was actually acting in a heat of passion, that it was sudden upon the provocation (no cooling period), and that it occurred upon adequate provocation (under circumstances in which an average person would lose self-control).

The defense will argue that the provocation was that his son had just shot at him and killed his wife. The average person under those circumstances would lose control as Leonard did. The manner of the killing – beating Benny to death – also tends to show that Leonard was acting in the heat of passion.

The prosecution will counter with the facts which support the charge of first-degree premeditated murder. Leonard was not reacting to the fact that Benny had just shot at him, but was acting under the previous threat that he would kill his son when he returned home.

6. Voluntary Manslaughter, Type B

The prosecution will argue that Leonard was guilty of at least recklessness in beating his son to death with the gun. To be "reckless," Leonard must have been aware of and disregarded a substantial and unjustifiable risk of death. "Extreme indifference" is the equivalent to the common law notion of "depraved heart" and can be shown when there is a high probability of death occurring as a result of the conduct. There is no requirement of an intent to kill.

The prosecution will argue that since Leonard beat his son so hard that he died, he was aware of and disregarded the substantial and unjustifiable risk of death to a 15-year-old boy. The prosecution will further argue that Leonard exhibited a "depraved heart" and extreme indifference to the value of human life when he beat the young boy to death.

7. Negligent Homicide

The prosecution will argue that at the very least Leonard was negligent. A reasonable person in Leonard's shoes would know that there was a substantial and unjustifiable risk that beating a 15-year-old boy in the head would lead to his death.

8. Affirmative Defense: Voluntary Intoxication

Under the common law, intoxication is a defense only to specific intent crimes, and not general intent crimes. If, as a result of intoxication, the defendant did not form or was incapable of forming the specific intent, then he is not culpable. In many jurisdictions today, the defense is completely abolished. The Model Penal Code allows it as a defense if it negates a mens rea. However, the exception under the Model Penal Code is for a recklessness crime, where if the reason the person is unaware of the risk is because of intoxication, it is no defense.

If it is available as a defense, then the defense would argue it as a defense to first-degree murder, that he was so drunk he could not have formed the intent to kill. The prosecution would simply argue the opposite. This would be a factual issue for a jury.

9. Affirmative Defense: Self-Defense

At common law, a non-aggressor is justified in using deadly force in self-protection if the actor reasonably believes that its use is necessary to prevent imminent and unlawful use of deadly force by the aggressor. "Deadly force" is force intended or likely to cause death or grievous bodily injury.

The defense will simply lose the argument that Leonard was facing the imminent use of deadly force when he acted upon Benny. After he grabbed the gun out of Benny's hands, the necessity disappeared.

II. State v. Billy

1. Accomplice Liability to Attempted Murder

In order to be charged as an accomplice to Benny, the prosecution has to prove the elements of accomplice liability. The required *mens rea* is that he (1) intend to assist the primary party to engage in the conduct that forms the basis of the offense; and (2) possess the mental state required for the commission of the offense. As to (2), he need not share the same mens rea as the primary party. The required *actus reus* is assistance, either by physical conduct or psychological influence (such as encouragement). Mere presence at the scene of the crime and knowledge of the crime is not enough. The assistance can be very trivial but must actually assist.

As far as the *actus reus*, Billy supplied the gun and also provided encouragement by saying "That no-good bastard" and going into the house with Benny. It would appear that Billy also has the requisite *mens rea* for murder. His words and actions tend to show that, by giving Benny the gun, he intended to assist in the underlying conduct of killing Leonard. There was clearly an attempt to kill Leonard as Benny fired at Leonard but simply missed him.

2. Accomplice Liability to First-Degree Murder, Type A (Transferred Intent)

The prosecution could try to charge Billy with the First-Degree Murder of Ruth, by using the doctrine of transferred intent. The elements of first-degree murder are set out above for Leonard. The prosecution would argue that Billy premeditated and deliberated the killing of Leonard outside of Benny's home. Once he heard of Benny's plight, he, too, wanted Benny's father dead and handed Benny the gun with every intention of seeing Benny shoot him. Benny shot him, missed him, and hit Ruth. If Benny were alive, he could be charged with first-degree murder of his mother under the doctrine of transferred intent. Transferred intent allows the intent to transfer from the intended victim (Leonard) to the actual victim (Ruth).

3. Accomplice Liability to Second-Degree Murder

Even if intent were not transferred, the prosecution could argue that Billy had the *mens rea* for extreme recklessness when it came to Ruth's killing. First, Billy would have had to have consciously disregarded a substantial and unjustifiable risk of death. That would seem clear in that Billy gave Benny a gun knowing Benny was planning to go in and shoot it. Someone was liable to get hit. The second element would require that Billy manifest extreme indifference to the value of human life. The defense would argue that Billy was acting out of a sense of protection of his friend's life and thus was not exhibiting an abandoned and malignant heart. The prosecution would argue that extreme recklessness can be shown by the high probability that the conduct would result in death, which was clear.

4. Affirmative Defense: Self Defense

If Benny could have availed himself of the defense of self-defense, then it would mean his conduct was justified and Billy, as an accomplice, would share his defense. At common law, a non-aggressor is justified in using deadly force in self-protection if the actor reasonably believes that its use is necessary to prevent imminent and unlawful use of deadly force by the aggressor. "Deadly force" is force intended or likely to cause death or grievous bodily injury.

The defense will argue that Benny was in imminent fear of death because his father had told him he would kill him and then came toward him after he entered the house. The history of abuse would mean a reasonable person in his situation would view Leonard's approach as deadly. The prosecutor would respond that deadly force was not imminent as his father was coming toward him unarmed. Further, Benny was the first deadly aggressor by coming in the house with a gun pointed at his father. As such, he loses his right to self-defense unless he completely withdraws from the affray and successfully communicates his withdrawal. The defense may try to expand the concept of self-defense here to communicate a battered-child defense, which would say that, for a battered child in Benny's situation, the threat of death is always imminent, even if not imminent in the traditional sense. This is unlikely to work, however, and self-defense is likely to fail.

III.   State v. Emma

   1.   Accomplice Liability

Again with Emma, the prosecution would have to prove accomplice liability as outlined above. It is arguable that she assisted by going in the house with Benny, as it may have encouraged and emboldened Benny. But it is fairly clear that she was merely present and did not have the requisite *mens rea* to assist or see Leonard dead. She tried to talk them out of going in and did not manifest any intention of seeing the crime completed.

Question #2

I.   State v. Conrad

   1.   Attempted Sex with a Minor

An attempt lies somewhere between mere preparation and completion of the crime. Paul Conrad first must have possessed the *mens rea* for attempt. A criminal attempt involves two *mens rea*s: the actor (1) must intentionally commit the acts which constitute the *actus reus* of an attempt; and (2) must perform these acts with the specific intention of committing the target crime. The prosecution will argue that Paul intended to commit the acts described in the *actus reus* section below, and that he had every intention of having sex with a minor. On that second issue, the prosecution will argue that his intent can be inferred from his asking "Just 14 and fun?" and, upon seeing a photo of an underage girl, asked her to come to a place where they could "talk easier."

The *actus reus* of the attempt depends upon the test adopted by the jurisdiction. Many jurisdictions have adopted the Model Penal Code test, which requires a "substantial step" strongly corroborative of the actor's criminal purpose. The Model Penal Code suggests some steps, one of which would seem to apply in this case: (1) enticing or seeking to entice the contemplated victim of the crime to go to the place contemplated for its commission. In fact, however, none of the other steps suggested by the Model Penal Code which might apply in this case were taken: he did not reconnoiter the place contemplated for the commission of the crime; and he did not enter the structure where the crime would be committed. The only other common law test for attempt which arguably was met was the "abnormal step" test, since most would consider it abnormal to entice a minor on-line and arrange a meeting place.

Most of the other tests for attempt are not met by the facts here. Other tests include the physical proximity test – the actor's conduct was "proximate" to the completed crime – here, Conrad did not come to the scene of the crime, and there was no 15 year old to commit the crime with; the dangerous proximity test – when the actor is so near the result that the danger of success is very great – here, he was neither at the scene nor was there a victim; the "indispensable element" test – he was lacking elements needed for the crime – namely, a victim; the "probable desistance" test – he actually did desist; and the "unequivocality" test – when a person's conduct, standing alone, unambiguously reflects her intent – he did not show up and sent a message that he had decided against it.

2. Defense to Attempt: Impossibility

The defense will counter with the defense of impossibility. Here, there was no victim with whom to complete the crime. The Model Penal Code has eliminated the defense of impossibility. At common law, there are two types of impossibility: legal impossibility, which is a defense, and factual impossibility, which is not a defense. This has proven to be a very murky distinction: a hunter who shoots a stuffed deer believing it to be alive has not attempted to take a deer out of season, but a person who has shot into the intended victim's bed believing he is asleep there when he is actually somewhere else is guilty of attempted murder. In general, however, when there is no victim in being, it is considered a legal impossibility. Conrad could have never committed the crime. However, courts have made exceptions in the context of police undercover work.

3. Defense to Attempt: Abandonment

The defense could claim abandonment. Abandonment is only a defense if it is done under circumstances manifesting a complete and voluntary renunciation of the criminal purpose: it is not voluntary if it is motivated in whole or in part by circumstances not apparent at the inception of the defendant's course of conduct and that increase the probability of detection or which make more difficult the accomplishment of the criminal purpose (MPC 5.01). It also does not constitute the defense of abandonment if the perpetrator merely abandons the effort with plans to continue it on another day. The defense will argue that Conrad voluntarily abandoned the crime because he was nervous about meeting her. However, fear of being found out cuts in the other direction, and, by e-mailing "J'aime14" he may be indicating a desire to pursue this again another day.

Question #3: Part A

I.   State v. Donald

   1.   Reckless Endangerment

If George does not die, the prosecution could charge Donald with recklessly endangering another human being. The question is whether he was reckless when he shot his gun. "Reckless" is defined as conscious disregard of a substantial and unjustifiable risk, in this case, of death or serious bodily injury. The prosecution will argue that it is reckless to go hunting when you are color-blind and rely on another human being to be your eyes. Even though he and Kit had a system that had worked for them in the past, the chance of error was substantial and unjustifiable. The defense will argue that the risk was not substantial since the system had worked for them in the past, and for that reason, he was not aware of the risk that Kit would not pay attention.

   2.   Attempted Murder

The prosecution cannot charge Donald with an attempted reckless or negligent homicide. An attempt requires an intent to commit the crime – by definition, one cannot intend to kill someone recklessly or negligently. The prosecution would have to charge Donald with an attempted first-degree murder, which would be impossible to prove. Donald had no intention of killing a human being. He did have an intention of killing a deer, and he thought he was shooting a deer. [The law of homicide contemplates an intention to kill a *human being*].

II. State v. Kit

   1.   Reckless Endangerment

Kit was aware that Donald was color-blind and that when he asked her whether he could shoot, she was not looking. Under these circumstances, there was a substantial and unjustifiable risk that Don would shoot at a human being. The defense would argue in response that Kit was not aware that the risk was substantial since Don had only made a mistake once before, and that was a turkey not a human being. Also, it was freezing cold out and deer hunting season so the chances of a human being taking a hike out there were low.

2. Attempted Murder

The prosecution cannot charge Kit with an attempted reckless or negligent homicide. An attempt requires an intent to commit the crime – by definition, one cannot intend to kill someone recklessly or negligently. The prosecution would have to charge Kit with an attempted first-degree murder, which would be impossible to prove. Kit had no intention of killing a human being. She did have an intention of killing a deer, and he thought he was shooting a deer. [The law of homicide contemplates an intention to kill a *human being*]. At most, Kit was reckless or extremely reckless, she did not have the intent to kill a human being.

Question #3: Part B

I. State v. Donald

1. Causation

If George's actions are a supervening cause for his death, then Don and Kit would not be liable. There are many different tests for proximate cause. The general test is one of foreseeability. The test most courts apply is as follows: if the intervening cause is coincidental, then it will not break the chain of causation unless it was unforeseeable; if the intervening cause is responsive, then it will not break the chain of causation unless it was abnormal. George crawls behind a rock and falls asleep from the cold and freezes to death in his sleep. It would seem that crawling behind the rock was responsive, as he did it as a direct result of the gunfire. Falling asleep from the cold could be seen as either responsive or coincidental. In either case, his actions will only break the chain of causation if they were unforeseeable or abnormal. It would seem that his responses to being shot and to the cold were both foreseeable and normal. Other common law issues that may come into play involve the question of whether George's actions were those of "free, deliberate, informed human intervention," which would break the chain of causation. It would not appear that George chose to crawl behind a rock and fall asleep of his own free choice, but was a result of being wounded and cold. Another issue is whether George had reached a place of apparent safety and did not avail himself of the opportunity, but it also does not appear that he was at or near a safe place.

2. Second-Degree Murder

Assuming that causation is proven, the prosecution may charge Donald with second-degree murder, which requires recklessness, and extreme indifference to the value of human life.

"Reckless" is defined as conscious disregard of a substantial and unjustifiable risk, in this case, of death or serious bodily injury. The prosecution will argue that it is reckless to go hunting when you are color-blind and rely on another human being to be your eyes. Even though he and Kit had a system that had worked for them in the past, the chance of error was substantial and unjustifiable. The defense will argue that the risk was not substantial since the system had worked for them in the past, and for that reason, he was not aware of the risk that Kit would not pay attention.

As for extreme indifference, the prosecution would argue that Donald was essentially hunting blind, with little regard for shooting into an area where a human being would be walking. The defense would argue that

Donald did not exhibit such wanton disregard since he employed Kate to be his eyes.

3. Voluntary Manslaughter, Type B

This charge would require proof of simple recklessness. "Reckless" is defined as conscious disregard of a substantial and unjustifiable risk, in this case, of death or serious bodily injury. The prosecution will argue that it is reckless to go hunting when you are color-blind and rely on another human being to be your eyes. Even though Donald and Kit had a system that had worked for them in the past, the chance of error was substantial and unjustifiable. The defense will argue that the risk was not substantial since the system had worked for them in the past, and for that reason, he was not aware of the risk that Kit would not pay attention.

4. Involuntary Manslaughter

Finally, the prosecution would argue that Donald was at least negligent. A reasonable person in Donald's situation would have realized the substantial and unjustifiable risk of death. The prosecution would argue that a reasonable person would never count on someone else to be their eyes while hunting if the other person is hunting at the same time. The defense will argue that Donald took reasonable precautions and a person in his situation would have reasonably assumed that Kit was watching where he was pointing his weapon.

II. State v. Kit

1. Second-Degree Murder

Assuming the requirement of causation is met, the case is a bit stronger against Kate as she knew she was not looking when she told Donald to go ahead and shoot. The recklessness issue would be repeated as described above for reckless endangerment. Assuming she was reckless, did she exhibit extreme indifference to the value of human life? Again, the prosecution would say yes, by allowing an essentially blind man to shoot into the forest. The defense will argue that she did not exhibit wanton disregard for human life as she relied on the fact that Donald had not made such a mistake before.

2. Voluntary Manslaughter, Type B

The argument under reckless homicide will be the same as the argument under reckless endangerment. "Reckless" is defined as conscious disregard of a substantial and unjustifiable risk, in this case, of death or serious bodily injury. The prosecution will argue that it is reckless to go hunting when you are color-blind and rely on another human being to be your eyes. Even though he and Kit had a system that had worked for them in the past, the chance of error was substantial and unjustifiable. The defense will argue that the risk was not substantial since the system had worked for them in the past, and for that reason, he was not aware of the risk that Kit would not pay attention.

3. Involuntary Manslaughter

The prosecution would prove negligence by showing that a reasonable person in Kit's situation would have known there was a substantial and unjustifiable risk of death by not looking to confirm that Donald did not have a human being in his sights. The prosecution and defense will debate whether the risk was substantial dependent upon the frequency of seeing other human beings in the area.

Question #4

I. State v. Josephine

1. Statute One

As to the first statute, Josephine's attorney must argue that a *mens rea* should be read into the statute. Both at common law and under the Model Penal Code, every crime is presumed to have an accompanying *mens rea*, and, if none is provided, that *mens rea* must be at least recklessness. The rationale for the argument is that it would be unfair to punish a person for acts that they did not somehow intend, or have some reason to know about. People cannot be deterred unless they are aware their conduct is wrongful. Furthermore, in this case the statute carries 90 days of potential jail time, a not insignificant amount of time, therefore cutting against the notion that the statute should be construed as a strict liability statute.

Therefore, if the *mens rea* the government has to prove is at least recklessness, then Josephine was not consciously aware of the substantial and unjustifiable risk that she was distributing medication without a license because she had no idea her license was suspended. Another form of this argument is to say that Josephine made a mistake of fact as to whether she had a license, believing wrongly that she did, and her mistake was reasonable, since she did not appear to know about the licensing rules, and therefore it should be a defense to this general intent crime.

The prosecutor would argue that this statute is clearly a strict liability statute. It carries little jail time and is a public welfare offense, exactly the type of *malum prohibitum* offense that is designated as a strict liability offense, putting the risk of learning the circumstances on those who are in the best position to avoid the distribution of dangerous materials or devices, such as drugs or weapons. Therefore, Josephine's mental state with regard to the license is irrelevant, as she is strictly liable.

2. Statute Two

Josephine's attorney will argue that she did not "knowingly distribute" controlled substances to a minor. "Knowingly" should be deemed to modify not only "distribute" but also the attendant circumstance of minor, since that is the social harm the statute is attempting to prohibit and since, otherwise, absurd results would occur. The Model Penal Code also supports this result, because it states that if there is one *mens rea* term generally appearing in the statute, then it is deemed to modify each and every element of the crime. Therefore, Josephine is not guilty of knowingly distributing to a minor because she did not know that the girl was a minor. Although she looked at the girl's identification, she did not look at her age and was not focused on the girl's age as much as her identity. See Nations (where defendant did not actually "know" the girl's age, even though she may have suspected or been reckless, she was not guilty of contributing to the delinquency of a minor).

The prosecutor will argue that "knowingly" only modifies "distribute" and not the attendant circumstance of the girl's minor status, as this is the common law rule of statutory interpretation. It also makes sense, since, like a statutory rape strict liability statute, the emphasis is on the protection of minors, and those who run the risk of distributing to minors will pay the price. However, even if "knowingly" did modify the attendant circumstance, Josephine was "willfully blind" to the girl's minor age. The girl looked to be in high school and Josephine looked right at her identification. If Josephine chose to ignore the girl's age, she can nonetheless be deemed with knowing the girl's age if she was aware of a "high probability" that the girl was a minor. Given that the girl looked to be in high school and was picking up for her mother, Josephine had to be aware of a high probability that the girl was under 18.

CRIMINAL LAW ESSAY EXAM #4

Question #1

I. State v. Martin

1. First-Degree Murder

The prosecution could charge Martin with first-degree murder if it can prove he premeditated and deliberated killing Mildred. The first time it appears clear that this may be in Martin's head is when he grabs hold of Mildred's wheelchair and pushes it toward the front door. That he wanted her dead by his action of pushing her out the door is clear by his phrase, "I hope you die too, then!" The prosecution will argue that he knew he wanted to kill her when he took hold of her wheelchair and that, since premeditation (to think about beforehand) and deliberation (to turn over in one's mind) can occur, at the least, in the "blink of an eye", and at the most, with enough time to reflect on his actions, the time from grabbing her wheelchair to pushing her out the door was sufficient to take a second look. If one takes the <u>Forrest</u> factors, the prosecution could argue that there was no provocation on the part of the accused (meaning that her statement that his wife was dead was not enough to provoke this reaction), the statement of the defendant that he wanted her dead indicated his desire, the ill-will just prior to the killing indicates his motivation.

The defense will argue that this is not a first-degree murder by any stretch. There is no certainty that he intended to kill her when he shoved her out the door. It might have been a whim, but not his conscious object. Part of this argument goes to support that, if anything, this intent was borne out of the heat of passion. The killing was not done in a brutal manner, there were not multiple blows, and there was provocation, in that Mildred gave him information that upset him deeply.

2. Voluntary Manslaughter

The defense will argue that if this killing was considered intentional, it was done in the heat of passion, making it voluntary manslaughter. First, Martin was in fact in a heat of passion when he sent Mildred wheeling out the door. He got "madder and madder" until he was "thoroughly" distraught. Second, the heat of passion was "sudden" upon the heels of the provocation. The argument occurred and then he wheeled her out the door in a heat of passion. Third, the provocation was adequate such that it would "deprive an average person of his self-control and cool reflection." In this case, Martin was just told that his wife was dead. While he should have known that his wife had been dead for years, he, in fact, was suffering from a bout of dementia and did not know this. The defense's argument depends upon the jury being able to look at the reasonable person "in the actor's situation." The defense will argue that "his situation" was that he suffered from bouts of senility. The defense would point to the Model Penal Code's suggestion of what qualifies for the "actor's situation" and argue that senility is like "blindness" or "extreme grief." Indeed, this was, from his perspective, extreme grief. While words alone may not be enough in some jurisdictions, the words here are more like "informational words", such as informing a person that they saw his wife in bed with another man.

The prosecution will retort that while Martin was in the heat of passion and it was sudden, that the provocation was not "adequate to deprive an average person of his self-control and cool reflection." The reasonable person is, by definition, not senile. A reasonable person in his situation would have known his wife had been dead. The senility is more like drunkenness – just an aspect of a person's character that causes them to have less self-control, and therefore should not be taken into account. Even if the information given by Mildred were the first time Martin had heard it, his reaction was extreme. The ordinary person does not react to news about a loved one's death by killing the messenger.

3. Second-Degree Murder

The prosecution will argue that Martin is guilty of second-degree murder. First, he was reckless in that he was consciously aware of a substantial and unjustifiable risk that Mildred might be hit by a car in the street. Indeed, one knows he was aware because he yelled after her that he hoped she would die. That statement also supports the "extreme indifference to human life." Pushing someone out into the street and yelling after them, "I hope you die, too!" manifests this indifference; it shows a depraved heart. Martin clearly hoped she would die.

The defense will argue that there was not a "substantial risk" that she would be hit by a car, given that it was a side street and that the chance of a car coming along and not being able to stop was minimal. Also, he was suffering from a bout of senility, so it is hard to say that he was "aware" of anything. Second, his statement that he hoped she would die was a statement borne of anger and not a true sentiment of his beliefs. We all say things like that when we are angry without meaning them.

4. Reckless or Negligent Manslaughter

The prosecution could also charge Martin with reckless homicide. At the very least, the prosecution will argue that Martin was guilty of negligent homicide, in that he should have been aware of the substantial and unjustifiable risk that Mildred would be hit by a car. A reasonable person would have been aware of the risk. Again, here, the defense will argue that the reasonable person in his situation is senile and is not much aware of anything.

5. Causation

For all crimes, the defense will argue that Martin's actions were not a proximate cause of Mildred's death. First, under the foreseeability test used in many states, Walter hitting Mildred was a coincidence. It was not foreseeable, however, that Mildred would get hit, since this was a quiet side street, where the chance of a car coming along at just that time was minimal, and, in any case, it was unforeseeable that a car would not be able to stop in time for a wheelchair crossing the street. Additionally, the defense will raise the "apparent safety" doctrine, since Mildred could have been safe if she had simply turned her wheelchair but she chose not to (like Preslar, where the woman who was chased out of her home chose to sleep outside and froze to death). Also, her not turning her wheelchair was a "free, deliberate human intervention" in that she chose not to save herself, hence breaking the chain of causation.

The prosecution will retort that what she did was fail to act, that her not saving herself was an omission, and therefore, no omission can break the chain of causation. She simply traveled along at the speed and the direction that Martin pushed her in. Also, Walter hitting her was a coincidence, but it was entirely foreseeable that a car would come along and hit her (as Martin indeed hoped), and it would be hard to stop since no one is expecting or looking for a wheelchair to suddenly enter the road.

6. Affirmative Defense -- Insanity

Martin could argue that his senility constituted insanity, which would be a complete defense to any of the charged crimes. Under the Model Penal Code, a person is not responsible for his criminal conduct if, at the time of such conduct, as a result of mental disease or defect, he lacked the substantial capacity either to appreciate the criminality [wrongfulness] of his conduct or to conform his conduct to the requirements of law. The former is a cognitive test and the latter is a volitional test. Senility usually affects the cognitive function. It is unlikely that senility will fulfill either the cognitive test of the Model Penal Code, or the *M'Naghten* test: where the defendant must demonstrate that he: (1) did not know the nature and quality of the act that he was doing; or, (2) if he did know, he did not know that what he was doing was wrong. While Martin was confused about some facts, he knew that he was pushing Mildred out into the street in her wheelchair.

II. State v. Walter

1. Reckless or Negligent Homicide

In connection with Walter's act of hitting Mildred, the prosecution will charge Walter with either reckless homicide or negligent homicide. To prove reckless homicide, the prosecution will have to show that Walter was aware of a substantial and unjustifiable risk that he would hit someone, and chose to disregard that risk. The prosecution will argue that anyone who drives the roads is aware that, if they take their eyes off the road, the risk is high that they will cause an accident. The defense will argue that Walter was not aware of such a risk. He was on a quiet side street with no expectation of a wheelchair entering the road, and reached down for just a second. Also, the risk that Mildred would enter the street at that time was not substantial. His reaching down for a CD was not a gross deviation from the conduct of the average law-abiding citizen.

The prosecution will argue that he was negligent in that, even if he did not know of the risk, he should have known. The defense will argue that the reasonable person in his situation would never have anticipated such a risk, for all of the reasons argued in the above paragraph.

If the prosecution cannot prove recklessness or

negligence in the act of hitting Mildred, he may pursue an omission theory. Because Walter hit Mildred, he created the risk that caused her injury and he owed her a duty of care, which he neglected by driving away. The omission can be said to have accelerated her death: but for his leaving she would not have died *when* she did. The prosecution can argue that he was reckless in that he aware of the risk she would die if he left her there and leaving her there was a gross deviation from the standard of care of the law-abiding person. Even if he was not aware because he panicked and did not know how seriously injured she was, a reasonable person would know of the risk she would die if left without care.

Question #2

I. State v. Mary Beth

The prosecutor would charge Mary Beth with "child abuse," under either section (1) or section (2) of the statute, and would charge her with "child neglect" under either section of the statute.

   1. Child Abuse, Section (1)

As to Abuse, section 1, the prosecutor will <u>not</u> be charging Mary Beth for any infliction of physical injury since she did not knowingly or purposefully inflict physical injury -- her husband did. However, the prosecutor will charge Mary Beth for knowing or purposeful infliction of mental injury. While mental injury is undefined, the prosecution will argue that verbal insults to a child such as calling a child "stupid" or "bad" are clearly harmful to a child's sense of well-being. Such name-calling would satisfy the *actus reus* of the statute. As for *mens rea*, the statute calls for either a knowing or purposeful *mens rea*. Since the prosecution will only have to prove the lesser *mens rea*, the issue if whether Mary Beth was "practically certain" of the result, i.e., mental injury. The prosecution will argue that Mary Beth was well aware of the consequences of her actions. Calling a child "stupid" or "bad" or telling a child to "shut up" for childish infractions she knows is practically certain to hurt the child's feelings.

The defense would argue that calling your child "stupid" or "bad" is not mental injury but simply legitimate discipline (unless after challenging the statute, the legislature has wiped out his argument), and will argue that Mary Beth did not knowingly inflict mental injury. She was not practically certain that mental injury would result from calling her child "bad" or "stupid." She would tell the jury that she was simply disciplining her child and had no intention of causing any harm. Furthermore, she was actually taking steps to protect her child from her husband's wrath, who would surely punish Annie for making too much noise.

2. Child Abuse – Section (2)

As to Abuse, section 2, this would be charged in the alternative to section 1 as it would be easier to prove. Here, Mary Beth's name-calling was a knowing or purposeful act, which here does not mean that she knows the consequences (because now we are talking about the "act" not the "result"), but simply that she is aware that her conduct is of that nature (i.e., name-calling). From there, the prosecutor must prove that it "could reasonably be expected to result" in mental injury, which means the prosecutor does not have to prove that Mary Beth knew that it would but that, in the abstract, a person could reasonably expect name-calling to result in mental injury. Here, the prosecutor's proof could involve a social worker or psychologist who could tell the jury that name-calling "injures" a child mentally, or the prosecutor could just call on the good sense of the jury to understand that name-calling and "shut up" can hurt a child's feelings (the definition of "injury" that the prosecutor will urge upon the court).

The defense will argue that while her act was knowing, it could not reasonably be expected to result in mental injury. This argument would mimic the arguments in Section (1).

3. Child Abuse – Section (3)

The prosecutor will not charge Mary Beth with section 3 because she did not actively encourage her husband to commit acts that caused her child physical injury nor did she encourage anyone else to inflict mental injury.

4. Neglect – Section (1)

As for Neglect section 1, this allows Mary Beth to be prosecuted for her omissions, as opposed to acts. The statute designates the care giver with a duty of care. Mary Beth, as the mother of Annie, is clearly her care giver. The prosecutor will argue that she failed to provide Annie with the care or services necessary to maintain her physical health (and mental health could be pursued in that it is likely the physical injury is also damaging Annie mentally). A reasonable care giver in Mary Beth's situation would recognize that Annie needed to be protected from physical injury by Kenneth and would provide the care needed to protect her. Mary Beth did nothing to provide her child with the necessary care.

As for a defense of Child Neglect, the issue for either section 1 or 2 is whether Mary Beth was negligent in not taking more steps to protect her child. Here, the defense will argue that she made all of the efforts that a reasonable person in Mary Beth's situation would have. The defense attorney will hope to put on evidence of Mary Beth's situation as one of a battered spouse, or perhaps one suffering from battered woman's syndrome (BWS). The point will be to explain to the jury that a reasonable person in her situation would be frightened of her spouse and feel unable to escape, even to protect the child. Kenneth regularly beat Mary Beth so that she was in a state of "learned helplessness" and when she tried to protect her child once she was told not to intervene or she would be "sorry." A reasonable person in Mary Beth's situation would know that meant if she intervened she would be beaten. Reasonable steps for her were just to yell at Annie to keep her quiet and keep her from incurring the wrath of Kenneth.

The prosecution will have a response to this defense. First, the prosecutor will argue that BWS syndrome should not be taken into account -- that negligence is an objective standard to and take BWS into account for "the actor's situation" would be to subjectivize the standard beyond recognition. Second, the prosecutor will argue, perhaps, that being hit by one's husband 12 times in two years does not qualify her for the syndrome (unsavory argument). Finally, along those same lines, even if the jury can take into account she was beaten twelve times, he or she will argue to the jury that a reasonable woman in that situation would STILL seek out help and protection for her child.

5. Neglect – Section (2)

Even more fitting for this situation is Neglect section 2, which describes the situation in this case. The issue is that Mary Beth did not take reasonable steps to protect Annie from abuse. A reasonable parent would know that Annie would need to be taken out of the home, or Kenneth would have to be stopped, in one way or another, to protect Annie from abuse. Mary Beth failure was, at least, negligent. Indeed, her *mens rea* is "knowing", in that she could be practically certain that her omission would mean further injury to Annie.

5. Affirmative Defense – Void for Vagueness

The defense attorney for Mary Beth will attack the

constitutionality of the statute itself. First, as to the statute itself, the defense attorney will argue that it is constitutionally vague in its use of the term "mental injury." The term does not put people on notice as to what activity will be proscribed and thus fails due process. The term is vague in several ways. It is overbroad in that it encompasses innocent activity: indeed, Mary Beth's case provides such an example. Parents, out of ordinary human nature, gets frustrated with their children and call them "bad" or tell them to "shut up." Whether legitimate exercise of discipline or simple, ordinary frustration, this is activity that is not criminal. If the statute was designed to get at verbal abuse that does in fact cause injury that is greater than "hurt feelings" then the legislature must go back to the drafting board and attempt to write such a statute. Another way in which the term is vague is that the very term itself is susceptible to numerous definitions. As the court described in In re Banks, if "men of common intelligence must necessarily guess at its meaning and differ as to its application," then it is does not satisfy the demands of due process. What is "mental injury"? Is it hurt feelings? Is it a recognizable mental disorder? Finally, the statute is vague in that it allows the police unfettered discretion in making arrests. There would be a fear that such a statute could be used to discriminate and target families from cultures who are stricter disciplinarians, or, in any case, allow the police to pick an choose among their arrestees, going into poor homes to make the arrests.

Question #3

I. State v. Professor Patrick

   1. Forcible Compulsion or Threat of Forcible Compulsion

   The prosecutor would urge the following

interpretations of the terms on the court. (Note: The definition of "sexual conduct" is not an important issue). "Forcible compulsion" must be defined broader than physical force (as Rusk defined it). Rather, it can be "mental coercion," as discussed in Berkowitz. While, in a different case the prosecutor may want mental coercion to cover cases of persons in the same age and peer group as in Berkowitz (the defendant and prosecutrix were both college sophomores so that the court did not find that their situation met the narrow definition of "mental coercion"), in this case, the professor-student status relationship meets the qualifications for "mental coercion." The age disparity was significant (48 to 18); the atmosphere and physical setting were coercive (professor's office); the defendant was in a position of authority over the victim (professor to student) and the victim was under duress/imposed stress (he was both naive and threatened with his academic livelihood). The mental coercion here, or "threat" of mental coercion (it appears that mental coercion and threat of mental coercion would coincide somewhat) are that Professor Patrick threatened to pull his scholarship and not pass him in the class, which, when coupled with her suggestive actions (pulling her face down close to his with her hands on his shoulders, and then having him lock the door and sitting next to him asking him if he has a girlfriend and brushing his groin) all suggest that he would have to comply with her sexual desires or potentially fail out of her class or not be able to continue college. The threats should be measured from a subjective point of view, or at least, the reasonable person in Samuel's situation. As a naive farm boy, this situation is far from titillating, but frightening. Should there be a requirement that the mental coercion be such that it would overcome the reasonable person's ability to resist, the prosecutor would argue that requirement was fulfilled here due to the threats to his academic survival, her overbearing demeanor and his contrasting naive demeanor. The prosecutor will urge, however, that resistance not be required (as was in Rusk and, in so many words continued to be operative in Berkowitz) as that forces victims into dangerous situations where threats of force become force. Likewise with mental coercion, Samuel should not have to choose between resisting or possibly failing or losing his scholarship.

The requirement of "forcible compulsion" could also be defined as it was in MTS. In MTS, the sexual act itself (in that case intercourse) was deemed sufficient to be the "force" needed to satisfy the statute. Here, the sexual act of oral sex would be enough to constitute the force. In addition, she exhibited the threat of that physical force by having Samuel lock the door and brushing his groin prior to this act.

The defense attorney will argue that "forcible compulsion" means physical force (Rusk) and nothing less. In this case, as in Berkowitz there was no force that rose to the level of physical force. In Berkowitz, the defendant leaned into the alleged victim and here, Professor Patrick sat next to Samuel and brushed his groin. Neither situation is the kind of physical force contemplated by the rape statute (see Rusk, where physical force is manifested by bruises, scrapes and other signs of injury). Furthermore, there was no threat of such physical force, in that locking the door from the inside is not such a threat (Berkowitz). Also, to constitute a threat of force, if no physical force was actually used, or even if we use the mental coercion model, the alleged victim must have resisted or the threat was so great that the victim could not resist (Rusk). Here, there is no attempt on the part of Samuel to resist. He comes willingly to her office, despite rumors and innuendo, locks the door as she says, and does not protest when she performs oral sex on him. Indeed, one can assume Samuel was adequately aroused for the act to be completed. Furthermore, the threat of physical force was nonexistent and the threat of mental coercion was not so great that a person would not resist. There were many ways out for Samuel, he could have refused to participate and not reaped any consequences by dropping her class and reporting her threat of pulling his scholarship to the appropriate office. Professor Patrick did not have that kind of control over his situation. In any case, there is no sign he even tried to resist.

2. Against the Will

Against the will has traditionally been defined as a purely subjective factor so that here, in fact, Samuel would testify that the act was against his will. The prosecutor would urge that resistance not be required.

The defense will argue that it is the government's burden to prove he did not consent and it should be defined traditionally, not as "affirmative permission." First, Samuel said, "yes ma'am," which can be construed as consent, and second, he did nothing to manifest non-consent, such as by verbally saying "no," or resisting in any way. His silence cannot be deemed non-consent (Rusk I and Berkowitz demonstrate these two principles). In addition, even if the jury believes that Samuel did not consent as a matter of fact, then Professor Patrick has an excellent mistake of fact claim. As the court in Sherry suggested, but did not decide, a reasonable mistake of fact should be a defense to this general intent crime. Her mistake was reasonable here in that he came to her office willingly, said "yes ma'am," and then did not struggle with her or stop the oral sex, where his pleasure was manifested physically. The defense could retort that "without consent" (as well as "against the will") is an attendant circumstance and, as such, should traditionally be read as strict liability, leaving Professor Patrick with no *mens rea* defense, since none is required.

3. Without Consent

As for "consent," the prosecutor will urge that consent be defined much as it was in MTS, where the court defined it as "affirmative permission," which could be manifested through words or actions indicating the free will of the victim. While it is true that Samuel in this case responded to a question, "Does all of this interest you?", which could have been seen as suggestive, with "Yes, ma'am," the prosecutor will argue that this exchange in no way indicated affirmative permission. The very notion of the requirement is that it is clear to both parties that the victim freely consents to the act of sex. Here, Samuel's response can be seen as either a response to the question about research and not sex, or a compelled response given her power over him at that point. His silence during the act itself indicates more fully his lack of willingness (as in Rusk, where her actions in lying still and not moving because she froze did not necessarily indicate consent).

As far as "against the will" and "without consent," the defense will argue that it is the government's burden to prove he did not consent and it should be defined traditionally, not as "affirmative permission." First, Samuel said, "yes ma'am," which can be construed as consent, and second, he did nothing to manifest non-consent, such as by verbally saying "no," or resisting in any way. His silence cannot be deemed non-consent (Rusk I and Berkowitz demonstrate these two principles). In addition, even if the jury believes that Samuel did not consent as a matter of fact, then Professor Patrick has an excellent mistake of fact claim. As the court in Sherry suggested, but did not decide, a reasonable mistake of fact should be a defense to this general intent crime. Her mistake was reasonable here in that he came to her office willingly, said "yes ma'am," and then did not struggle with her or stop the oral sex, where his pleasure was manifested physically. The defense could retort that "without consent" (as well as "against the will") is an attendant circumstance and, as such, should traditionally be read as strict liability, leaving Professor Patrick with no *mens rea* defense, since none is required.

4.   Rationales for and Against Punishment

Professor Patrick should be punished for several reasons. First, the utilitarian purpose would be to deter both women and those in positions of authority from presuming they are immune from prosecution. Society should become aware as a whole that unwanted sexual pressure from women is just as unacceptable as from men. In addition, many of the cases involving authority figures are never prosecuted – students and employees are afraid of failing school or losing their jobs and need to be encouraged to come forward with these claims. Only then will those in positions of authority know that they cannot get away with such acts with impunity. As for specific deterrence, of course, Professor Patrick needs to be stopped. She apparently terrorizes male students repeatedly, or in any case takes advantage of them, and she must learn that society will not condone her behavior. From a retributive standpoint, what she did, taking advantage of a Kansas farm boy, was morally repugnant and she should be condemned for her immoral acts.

Professor Patrick should not be prosecuted in this scenario. To stretch out the meaning of sexual assault to include prosecution of persons who engage in sexual acts with seemingly willing partners, who manifest at least partial consent, and in no way give the reasonable person a reason to believe they are not consenting, would be extremely harmful to society. Such prosecutions will send a message to society that sexual freedom is vastly limited by requirements of confirmations of consent and that if a boyfriend and girlfriend should forego such a requirement, then the boyfriend is subject to a rape claim. The social utility of prosecuting her is outweighed by the social utility of ensuring freedom of sexual activity without the threat of prosecution. Furthermore, retributionists would say that there is nothing morally wrong with proceeding to have sex with a seemingly willing partner. That the partner may have regrets later is not a reason to prosecute.

CRIMINAL LAW ESSAY EXAM #5

Question #1

I.   State v. Boomer

   1.   Void for Vagueness

Timothy Boomer will argue that the Michigan statute violates the due process clause of the U.S. Constitution because it is void for vagueness. A statute can be void for vagueness in one of three ways: (1) the statute is so unclear that ordinary persons have to guess at its meaning; (2) the statute is overly broad in that it includes innocent conduct; (3) the statute allows for unfettered police discretion.

Boomer will argue that the words "indecent," "immoral," "obscene," "vulgar," and "insulting" are so unclear that a law-abiding human being would not know what behavior was precluded. For example, words that are "insulting" to one person may be simply humorous to another. If a person told a joke involving a rabbi and a priest, for example, some might find that "indecent" or "immoral," while others would find it normal humor. The meaning of the words turns too much on the sensibilities of the individual. They do not have common meanings to which all agree.

Mr. Smith will also argue, for many of the same reasons already stated, that the language of the statute is overly broad. Purely innocent commentary can be taken as "insulting" or "vulgar" depending upon the listener. Also for the same reasons, the statute allows for unfettered police discretion on whom to arrest, since the arrests will turn on the own individual officer's definition of what is "insulting" or "indecent." This is not unlike the unfettered discretion given to officers in <u>Chicago v. Morales</u> in defining when a person is loitering "with no apparent purpose."

While in 1897, it might have been clear to the framers of the statute what would be "insulting" or "vulgar" to say in the presence of women and children, we do not have that statutory history available, and, in any case, as times have changed dramatically since then, it would be a violation of due process to hold persons liable for making statements that no longer carry that meaning.

The prosecution may respond to this argument that the average person understands what would be insulting to a woman or children, just as the dissent argued in Chicago v. Morales that the average person knows when they are loitering with no apparent purpose. For example, in this case, when Timothy Boomer fell into the water and cussed, these words are universally unacceptable in mixed company. However, this argument will be problematic since Smith will be arguing that the statute is void on its face and not just in application to his case.

2. Mens rea as to attendant circumstance

Boomer can argue that he had no idea there were women and children around. To do this, however, he needs to argue that the statute contains some sort of *mens rea* that applies to "in the present or hearing of any woman or child." This will be impossible, since, at the most, he may be able to argue that the common law dictates that a crime carry a *mens rea* of at least recklessness, but that *mens rea* would apply only to the nature of conduct element of the crime, which is "using" the indecent language. Clearly, he was not only reckless about using vulgar language, but purposeful. However, the common law presumes that *mens rea* does <u>not</u> apply to the attendant circumstance of "in the presence of . . .". This presumption makes sense here since the law was meant to prohibit offending women and children and so a person would be at their own risk, if they used offensive language, to be sure there were no women or children present. If this statute were strict liability (which could be argued in that it is a misdemeanor offense dealing with an issue of public welfare), the attendant circumstance would obviously still be strict liability.

Question #2

I. State v. Terry Williams

   1. Robbery

The only debate surrounding this charge might be that the victim is actually dead when Terry steals the ring. The prosecutor will argue that this should not matter since Terry formed the *mens rea* to commit the crime of robbery of the ring and then shot Sid to carry it out. The intent to commit the crime will be proven by the fact that Terry's brother suggested the robbery within Terry's hearing, and then Terry saw the ring as Sid approached him, thought of everything his brother had said, which would include the ring, and then shot Sid and stole the ring. The defense attorney may argue that there is insufficient evidence that Terry had stealing the ring in mind when he shot Sid. If stealing the ring were only an afterthought, after Sid was dead, then the elements of robbery are not met. The statute clearly intends that the taking of anything of value by force or intimidation be perpetrated on a <u>live</u> human being. The issue here, then, is when the crime of robbery began.

   2. First-Degree Murder of Sid, Type B

The only question for the jury is whether the murder occurred "in the perpetration of" the felony. Most states construe this requirement as a limitation on the felony murder doctrine to ensure that the murder is a proximate cause of the felony, or occurs "in furtherance of" the felony. Assuming the prosecutor is successful in his argument that there was a robbery (because the robbery began before the murder), then it is clear that the murder occurred "in furtherance of" the felony. The robbery was complete upon the killing of Sid and the carrying away of his ring. The defense could argue the same point that it did on the robbery charge – the robbery started and ended after the killing. The killing was motivated by provocation by Sid and the robbery was an afterthought. Therefore, the murder did not occur in "furtherance of" the robbery since the robbery had not begun.

3. First-Degree Murder of Sid, Type A

The prosecutor could also charge Terry with premeditated and deliberated murder. The following facts could be marshaled in favor of proof that Terry premeditated and deliberated the killing of Sid. He had a motive to kill Sid before Sid killed him, as expressed to him by his brother David. He brought a gun to Sid's neighborhood and sought Sid out. Although he appeared to be leaving the scene at one point, in the next instant he was facing Sid, who was unarmed (from Terry's point of view, who could only see empty hands swinging at Sid's sides). He thought about everything his brother told him which included killing Sid before Sid killed him (a pre-emptive strike rather than self-defense), and then he shot six times. According to the factors in <u>Forrest</u>, Terry's conduct also meets the requirements of premeditation and deliberation: (1) want of provocation on the part of the deceased (Sid had no weapon in his hands); (2) conducts and statements of defendant before and after (Terry showed him his gun just before, saying not to mess with him, and stole Sid's ring after, showing remorselessness); (3) threats and declarations of the defendant before and during the course of the occurrence (same); (4) ill-will or previous difficulty between the parties (Sid had threatened Terry); (5) dealing of lethal blows after the deceased has fallen (six shots, and stole ring after dead); (6) evidence that the killing done in a brutal manner (same); (7) nature and number of the victim's wounds (same).

The defense will argue that Terry did not premeditate or deliberate the killing. Terry brought the weapon to the scene with no intent to use it. It was only when suddenly come upon by Sid that he shot. The prosecution can counter that premeditation can be formed in the blink of an eye, although there is case law to the contrary that premeditation and deliberation require time for second thoughts, which the defense may be able to argue that Terry did not have.

4. Voluntary Manslaughter, Sid, Type A

On some level, defense arguments against premeditation and deliberation will look like arguments for voluntary manslaughter. The prosecution could try to prove voluntary manslaughter in this case (although he or she would likely try to prove first-degree murder and it would be the defense who might ask for this as a lesser charge). The requirements for heat-of-passion manslaughter at common law were: (1) there must have been adequate provocation; (2) the killing must have been in the heat of passion; (3) it must have been a sudden heat of passion – before a reasonable opportunity for the passion to cool; (4) there must have been a causal connection between the provocation, the passion and the act. The prosecution will argue that all of the elements were met here. Terry's days prior to the shooting reveal an anguished man. Having had his life threatened, Terry is crying and fearful. Then, on the day of the killing, Terry is high on cocaine and in a paranoid frenzy. His ultimate act of shooting is caused by the provocation of Sid calling out his name and coming toward him. The question would be whether this is the type of provocation that would cause an "average person" to lose his power of self-control. If the prosecution were arguing against this charge (and for first-degree), she would argue that the "average person" should not include one high on cocaine. While that argument may be successful, the defense will argue that the "average person" should include one who is mildly mentally retarded with their life previously threatened. Some courts have held that a jury should be able to take into account age and gender on the issue of self-control -- it would seem by analogy that mental retardation (which puts an older person in a younger age bracket -- here, that of a child of 11 or 12) should be taken into account.

5. Second-Degree Murder of Sid

A prosecutor could charge Terry with second-degree murder. Clearly, by closing his eyes and firing a gun toward Sid, he exhibited "extreme indifference to the value of human life." The requirement of extreme indifference can be demonstrated by showing the probability that the conduct involved will cause death – clearly true of the act of firing at a man. The other requirement is either that Terry be aware of the risks of the conduct. By firing a weapon, he consciously disregarded a substantial and unjustifiable risk that Sid would be killed.

6. Voluntary Manslaughter, Sid, Type B

The prosecutor could charge Terry with reckless manslaughter, which would simply involve a claim of recklessness. The claim would be that by firing a weapon, he consciously disregarded a substantial and unjustifiable risk that Sid would be killed

7. Negligent Manslaughter, Sid

The prosecution could argue that, at the least, Terry was negligent in that a reasonable person would be aware of the substantial and unjustifiable risk of death when firing a weapon.

8. Affirmative Defense: Self-Defense

The elements of self-defense are that Terry reasonably believe that unlawful deadly force is imminent and that deadly force is a necessary response. The defense attorney will argue that the "reasonable person in the defendant's situation" should take into account events occurring prior to the fateful encounter that bear on that belief. In this case, Sid had threatened Terry three days prior by pointing a gun to his head and clicking it three times and telling him not to come around. Next, the defense attorney will move the window of time to the moments just before the shooting. Sid was moving toward Terry. And, while Sid was not visibly armed, a reasonable person in Terry's situation, facing a known and violent gun-carrying gang member, would assume he was armed (which, as it was borne out by investigation, he was). Therefore, given all that Terry honestly and reasonably believed about Sid, Sid calling out to him just as Terry was going to leave and coming toward him could have been perceived as a deadly threat. Terry was therefore justified in pulling his gun and shooting Sid.

The prosecution has several arguments against the application of self-defense. First, Terry cannot claim self-defense because he was the first aggressor and forfeited his right of self-defense. The prosecution will argue that Terry arrived on the scene armed and showing Sid his gun, clearly demonstrating himself to be the "deadly aggressor" – an unlawful act reasonably likely to elicit a deadly response. The defense will argue in response that when Terry turned to walk away, he had clearly and unequivocally communicated to Sid that he was withdrawing from the conflict, that he had concluded his purpose in coming, and had therefore regained his right of self-defense. Terry only turned around because Sid called him. Further, the defense may try to characterize Terry's actions in carrying a gun as not a threat (which would be unlawful) but an attempt to protect and arm himself against an unlawful danger. However, the prosecution will respond to these points as follows: first, turning to walk away is not a clear communication of a withdrawal from the conflict, especially after a threat was just delivered.

Second to the aggressor issue, the prosecution will also argue that a reasonable person in Terry's situation would not see Sid as a deadly threat. Sid was not readily armed and was merely approaching Terry with empty hands. Terry was unjustified in seeing a threat from an unarmed man and was merely taking advantage of his opportunity to shoot Sid before he shot him. Thus far, the law of self-defense does not allow pre-emptive strikes (except, to some extent, by battered women). Here, there was no "immediate" threat from an unarmed man.

Finally, the prosecutor may argue, if this is a jurisdiction where retreat is required, that Terry did not retreat as he should have. The success of this argument will depend entirely upon the success of the arguments above. If the argument is successful that Terry reasonably believed that Sid was an immediate deadly threat (with a gun), then complete and safe retreat to an area known by Terry would not be possible. There is rarely any safe retreat from a gun, and especially here, where Terry is on a gang's turf.

Should the prosecutor win the argument (i.e., convince the jury) that Terry's belief that Sid was about to use deadly force on him was unreasonable, but the defense was still convincing that Terry genuinely held this belief, the jury could find Terry had an imperfect self-defense and therefore find him guilty of voluntary manslaughter.

9. Affirmative Defense: Insanity

The defense may try to plead Terry not guilty by reason of insanity, but this claim is likely to fail. Under any definition of insanity, Terry must be suffering from a "mental disease or defect" at the time of his act. The two potential contributing factors to Terry's paranoid state of mind appear to be mild mental retardation and crack addiction. Narcotics addiction, although listed in the DSM IV as a mental health condition, has been rejected by the courts as a "mental disease or defect" for insanity purposes. The reason is largely policy-based: courts are not going to exonerate defendants who are high on drugs, often considered by courts to be a situation of the defendant's own making. Even if mental retardation is considered a "mental disease or defect," Terry's mild condition probably will not meet any of the definitions of insanity. Under the Model Penal Code, Terry must lack substantial capacity to appreciate the wrongfulness/criminality of his actions OR to conform his conduct to the requirements of the law. This is the most liberal of the tests and so Terry's condition will have the most success, if any, meeting this test. The defense will have to prove (usually by a preponderance of the evidence) either prong, and it will be difficult since mild mental retardation does not usually interfere substantially with either appreciation of what is right and what is wrong or with impulse control. Nonetheless, it will be a jury question. The other tests are harsher -- the *M'Naghten* test requires that Terry not know the nature and quality of his action or, if he does, that he not know that it is wrong (whether legally or morally) -- this cognitive test is harsher than the MPC's since it requires complete lack of knowledge on Terry's part, which will be difficult to prove. If supplemented with the irresistible impulse test, Terry's condition does not appear to be volitionally based and therefore this test has little chance of success. Under the product (or *Durham*) test, Terry will have to show that his actions were the result of mental disease or defect. That may be difficult again because his actions appear to have rational independent motivations, whether for robbery or for a pre-emptive strike.

10. First-Degree Murder of Little Moe, Type B

The prosecution will first look to charge Terry with first-degree felony-murder. Once again, the prosecution will prove robbery and then the question is whether the killing of Moe occurred in the perpetration of the felony. The killing of Moe is a bit more remote than the killing of Sid, but the prosecution will argue that the rule anticipates the application to a killing that would not have occurred but for the felony. The killing of Little Moe was reasonably foreseeable as an associate of Sid's in the near proximity caught in the crossfire.

11. First-Degree Murder of Little Moe, Type A

The prosecution can charge Terry with first degree premeditated murder through a transferred intent theory. At common law, intent cannot be used up, so that even though the harm caused (two deaths) was greater than the harm intended, the intent to kill Sid can still transfer to Little Moe.

As to the felony underlying the felony-murder — the robbery — the only debate surrounding this charge might be that the victim is actually dead when Terry steals the ring. The prosecutor will argue that this should not matter since Terry formed the *mens rea* to commit the crime of robbery of the ring and then shot Sid to carry it out. The intent to commit the crime will be proven by the fact that Terry's brother suggested the robbery within Terry's hearing, and then Terry saw the ring as Sid approached him, thought of everything his brother had said, which would include the ring, and then shot Sid and stole the ring. The defense attorney may argue that there is insufficient evidence that Terry had stealing the ring in mind when he shot Sid. If stealing the ring were only an afterthought, after Sid was dead, then the elements of robbery are not met. The statute clearly intends that the taking of anything of value by force or intimidation be perpetrated on a <u>live</u> human being. The issue here, then, is when the crime of robbery began.

As to the felony-murder, the only question for the jury is whether the murder occurred "in the perpetration of" the felony. Most states construe this requirement as a limitation on the felony murder doctrine to ensure that the murder is a proximate cause of the felony, or occurs "in furtherance of" the felony. Assuming the prosecutor is successful in his argument that there was a robbery (because the robbery began before the murder), then it is clear that the murder occurred "in furtherance of" the felony. The robbery was complete upon the killing of Sid and the carrying away of his ring. The defense could argue the same point that it did on the robbery charge –

the robbery started and ended after the killing. The killing was motivated by provocation by Sid and the robbery was an afterthought. Therefore, the murder did not occur in "furtherance of" the robbery since the robbery had not begun.

In addition, the defense will argue the transfer of Terry's self-defense claim. Terry was not shooting at Little Moe, but at Sid, and in self-defense. Therefore, if Terry's self-defense claim against Sid is allowed, then some states will allow it to transfer to his shooting of Little Moe, which was by accident. However, some states follow the Model Penal Code, in that if Terry were reckless or negligent about the killing of an innocent bystander, then he can be charged with a negligent or recklessness crime.

> 12. Second-Degree Murder, Voluntary Manslaughter, Type B, and Negligent Homicide, Moe

The prosecution will argue in any case that Terry was extremely reckless when he closed his eyes and fired six times. Terry was aware that others were in the near vicinity when he fired the gun and therefore he was aware of an unjustifiable and substantial risk that his firing with his eyes closed would result in the killing of another person. If the defense can convince the jury that he was somehow not aware (in that he has the mental age of an 11 or 12 year old and genuinely was unaware of the risks), then the prosecutor will argue he was at least negligent, in that a reasonable person would have been aware of the risk. Again, reasonable person turns on whether the jury will consider the reasonable mentally retarded adult with the mental age of 11 or 12, and whether such a person would be aware of the risk. The prosecutor will argue that even an 11 or 12 year old understands such risks.

II. State v. David

1. Accomplice Liability, Robbery

David's liability as an accomplice is derivative in nature and depends upon the guilt of his brother. If Terry did not commit robbery, for example, because the defense is successful that the formulation of the intent to take the ring occurred after the death of Sid and hence did not fit the meaning of the statute, then no offense of robbery was committed and David therefore could not be convicted of robbery. However, if Terry did commit robbery, was David an accomplice? First, did David have the intent to assist Terry in the conduct that constituted the crime? The prosecution will argue that he did, as illustrated by his words to his brother indicating a desire that a robbery occur and that he get to wear Sid's ring on his finger, especially just after he had told his brother that he had better be ready to get Sid. The defense will argue that is a stretch, that it only indicates a whimsical desire that someone rob Sid, not that his brother commit a robbery. The prosecution will point to the fact that his brother accepted the ring and congratulated his brother as an indication of his intent. Second, did David have the *mens rea* for the crime? Robbery requires intent (although it would be understandable if you stated "at least recklessness" here since no *mens rea* is stated, and the argument is stronger that he was at least reckless about his brother committing a robbery), and again, the same issues as above recur here. If the *mens rea* of accomplice liability is satisfied, then the question is whether David "assisted" in the crime, the requisite *actus reus* for accomplice liability. His assistance does not need to be necessary but must be effective. It can be psychological, in the form of encouragement. The prosecution will argue that his statements to his brother about a robbery in fact encouraged his brother to commit the crime, as Terry recalled his brother's words at the time of the crime and did indeed take the ring. The defense will argue that these comments were not what encouraged Terry, and, again, will focus on the argument that what happened was a self-defense killing, followed by a decision to take the ring.

2. First-Degree Murder, Type B

If David was an accomplice in the robbery, the prosecution would argue that he was liable for felony-murder for both Sid and Little Moe. David is strictly liable for the killings perpetrated during the course of the felony, regardless of whether he anticipated them. An agent is responsible for the acts of his agent in furtherance of the felony. Thus, for the same reasons Terry would be liable for felony-murder, David would be. An alternative path to this same result is to say that David, as an accomplice in the robbery, is responsible for the natural and probable consequences of the felony. As his brother set out with his gun, it was "reasonably foreseeable" that Terry would use the gun to carry out the robbery, especially on violent gang members. Hence, once again, David would be liable to the same extent as David.

3. Accomplice Liability, First-Degree Murder, Type A

David is potentially liable as an accomplice to the killing of at least Sid directly (as opposed to through robbery). The prosecution will argue that David had the *mens rea* for an accomplice because he (1) intended to assist in the conduct that constituted the crime; and (2) had the *mens rea* for the substantive crime of first-degree murder. As to the first, he intended to encourage Terry to engage in a homicide. The prosecution will argue that his words revealed that intent, as well as giving the gun, and then, after the fact, his congratulations also revealed what he intended to have happen. As for (2), the prosecution could argue that David premeditated and deliberated the killing because he gave his brother the gun ahead of time, knowing his brother's excited state of mind and then by his words, encouraged the killing. The defense will argue that he only intended to help his brother protect himself.

4. Accomplice Liability, Lesser Charges

The prosecution will argue that David had at least the *mens rea* of recklessness, if not extreme recklessness, toward the murder. He gave his brother a gun when his brother was in an agitated mental state and then told him he had better be ready to kill then first, contributing to his brother's paranoia -- that is at least reckless, in that he was consciously aware of a substantial and unjustifiable risk that his conduct would result in a homicide by his brother.

5. Accomplice Liability – Self-Defense

If the defense is successful in its self-defense claim for Terry, then David cannot be found guilty as accomplice. If the principal is acquitted on the basis of a justification defense then it is as if no crime occurred.

6. Accomplice Liability – Insanity

However, if Terry were acquitted on the basis on insanity, then David may still be liable as an accomplice. Acquittal of the principal under an excuse defense means that a wrong has still occurred in the eyes of society and hence David can still be liable for that wrong, as he has no excuse. In addition, if Terry is truly insane (which is doubtful), then David can also be charged as a principal for first-degree premeditated murder, on an innocent agent theory. The theory is that David wanted Sid killed and manipulated his brother, an innocent dupe, into killing Sid by working him into a paranoid frenzy and giving him a gun. This will only work if Terry was truly duped and manipulated – David's mere encouragement of a paranoid crack addict will only make him an accomplice.

7. Crimes Associated with Death of Little Moe

As for the death of Little Moe, the prosecution could argue that David intended to encourage the premeditated and deliberated murder of any of the gang members as his comments about getting "them" were directed at the gang in general. In any case, sending his brother off with a weapon with the words he spoke could again be argued as at least negligence and at most extreme recklessness that gang members would get shot.

Question #3

I. State v. Kip & Rocky

1. Statute One

The prosecution is going to argue that this is a strict liability offense and mistake of fact or lack of knowledge as to the age of the persons served is no excuse. The prosecution will argue that this is a strict liability offense from several factors: (1) this is a *malum prohibitum* offense, not a *malum in se* offense. In other words, this offense is a creature of statute. As such, we can more readily presume that when the legislature wrote it, they meant to leave out a *mens rea*; (2) this is a public welfare offense. It involves a dangerous substance, alcohol, and its consumption by minors. The law might well have chosen to put the burden of knowledge on those in charge of the substance; (3) it carries little jail time, only thirty days, making it more likely to be a strict liability offense. Obviously, the state's rationale for having this as a strict liability offense is as a protection of minors, putting the burden on those in a position to know better.

The defense will argue that the rule at common law is that a *mens rea* applies to every offense. Further, that *mens rea* is at least "recklessness." The prosecution may respond that also at common law, even if a *mens rea* is presumed, it is not presumed to apply to attendant circumstances, which "under twenty-one years of age" appears to be. If for any reason, a court decided that the mental state should apply to the attendant circumstances for fairness purposes, then the prosecution would have to prove that Kip and Rocky were aware of a substantial and unjustifiable risk that the persons at the party drinking alcohol were under twenty-one. This is discussed in relation to Statute 3.

2. Statute Two

The prosecution will argue that the two students clearly appeared in an intoxicated condition in public and that it would have been foreseeable to any reasonable person that such as appearance would disturb or alarm the public. Obviously, to suddenly plunge to the earth in an intoxicated condition would disturb the public – it is scary, noisy and disruptive. The prosecution will argue that they do now have to show that the appearance itself was foreseeable, just that it was foreseeable that the appearance would be alarming.

The defense will argue first of all that there was no voluntary act in this case. A part of the *actus reus* of any crime is that there have been a voluntary act. A voluntary act is a bodily movement that is the product of the effort or determination of the actor, whether conscious or habitual (Model Penal Code 2.01(2)). This case is exactly like Martin, where Martin, who was intoxicated, was carried into public by the police and therefore did not commit the voluntary act of appearing in public. Here, the students were on a private porch in an intoxicated condition, and only ended up in public by the fact that the balcony fell. Their bodies falling to the street were not the result of their own effort or determination, but was an involuntary movement.

As to whether their appearance drunk would

foreseeably alarm the public, the defense would argue that it was not their drunken condition that was alarming, but the fall to the earth. Furthermore, the defense will try to argue that appearing in the "manner" that they did was not foreseeable – there was no indication or warning that the balcony was going to fall under their weight. Of course, the prosecution would disagree, saying it is obvious to any reasonable person that a balcony would not be designed to hold twenty students.

3. Statute Three

The prosecution will argue that the *mens rea* term, "knowing," applies only to the nature of conduct elements and not the attendant circumstances. Therefore, the prosecution only need prove that Rocky and Kip knew they were "enticing, aiding, soliciting, or permitting" and that they need not prove that Rocky and Kip knew the age of those they were "enticing, etc." Of course, by advertising the party, where it is clear the main activity was the consumption of alcohol, Rocky and Kip "knew" (were aware that the nature of their conduct was of this nature) that they were enticing and soliciting.

The defense might argue that while as a technical matter at common law this might be true, it would seem unfair to not apply the *mens rea* term to the attendant circumstance in this case, since the crime seems to turn on one's state of mind toward enticing juveniles. In that case, Kip and Rocky did not know the ages of those at the party and therefore were not guilty of the offense.

The prosecution would respond that as long as Kip and Rocky were "willfully blind" to the ages of those at the party, then they will be deemed to have had the knowledge. Willful blindness can be defined as seem in the Model Penal Code, as being aware of a "high probability" that there were people at the party under seventeen (amounting to a "recklessness" standard).

Willful blindness suggests that a person does not actually know of the circumstances simply because he or she refuses to know. Here, Kip and Rocky not only put up signs for the party at the University Center, which might well attract a younger crowd, but were talking to two girls in high school-type uniforms who said they did not go to the University . The only reason they did not know their age is because they never asked. It would appear there was a "high probability" that these two girls were under age.

CRIMINAL LAW
MULTIPLE CHOICE

100 QUESTIONS

ANSWER SHEET

Print or copy this answer sheet to answer all multiple choice questions.

1. A B C D	26. A B C D	51. A B C D	76. A B C D
2. A B C D	27. A B C D	52. A B C D	77. A B C D
3. A B C D	28. A B C D	53. A B C D	78. A B C D
4. A B C D	29. A B C D	54. A B C D	79. A B C D
5. A B C D	30. A B C D	55. A B C D	80. A B C D
6. A B C D	31. A B C D	56. A B C D	81. A B C D
7. A B C D	32. A B C D	57. A B C D	82. A B C D
8. A B C D	33. A B C D	58. A B C D	83. A B C D
9. A B C D	34. A B C D	59. A B C D	84. A B C D
10. A B C D	35. A B C D	60. A B C D	85. A B C D
11. A B C D	36. A B C D	61. A B C D	86. A B C D
12. A B C D	37. A B C D	62. A B C D	87. A B C D
13. A B C D	38. A B C D	63. A B C D	88. A B C D
14. A B C D	39. A B C D	64. A B C D	89. A B C D
15. A B C D	40. A B C D	65. A B C D	90. A B C D
16. A B C D	41. A B C D	66. A B C D	91. A B C D
17. A B C D	42. A B C D	67. A B C D	92. A B C D
18. A B C D	43. A B C D	68. A B C D	93. A B C D
19. A B C D	44. A B C D	69. A B C D	94. A B C D
20. A B C D	45. A B C D	70. A B C D	95. A B C D
21. A B C D	46. A B C D	71. A B C D	96. A B C D
22. A B C D	47. A B C D	72. A B C D	97. A B C D
23. A B C D	48. A B C D	73. A B C D	98. A B C D
24. A B C D	49. A B C D	74. A B C D	99. A B C D
25. A B C D	50. A B C D	75. A B C D	100. A B C D

CRIMINAL LAW QUESTIONS

1. Joe is prosecuted under an old statute that prohibits the crime of battery. Which of the following elements are likely to be included in this common law crime?

   I. The elements of an intent to touch offensively, and of an offensive touching of a victim.

   II. The elements of an intent to injure or criminal negligence, and of a bodily injury of a victim.

   III. The elements of criminal negligence, and of an offensive touching of a victim.

   IV. The elements of an intent to put a victim in fear, and of the putting of a victim in fear.

   A. I, II

   B. I, II, III

   C. I, II, IV

   D. I, II, III, IV

2. Sam is prosecuted for aggravated battery under a modern statute. In addition to the elements of common law battery, which additional elements are likely to be included as "aggravating" factors in the aggravated battery statute?

   I. The element of intent to commit another crime such as murder, rape, or robbery.

II. The element of the use of a deadly or dangerous weapon.

III. The element of the infliction of serious bodily harm.

IV. The element of a particular type of victim, such as a police officer.

A. I, II, IV

B. II, III

C. I, II

D. I, II, III, IV

3. Jill is prosecuted under an old statute that prohibits the crime of assault. Which of the following elements are likely to be included in this common law crime?

I. The element of an attempt to commit a battery.

II. The element of a present ability to commit a battery.

III. The element of an attempt to place another in fear.

IV. The element of an intent to cause a battery.

A. III

B. I, II

C. I, II, IV

D. I, II, III, IV

4. Larry is prosecuted under a modern statute that prohibits the crime of assault. Which of the following elements are likely to be included in this crime?

   I. The element of conduct that reasonably causes another to fear immediate bodily harm.

   II. The element of an intent to cause apprehension of immediate bodily harm.

   III. The element of the result of a person experiencing fear of immediate bodily harm.

   IV. The elements of an attempt to commit a battery and an intent to cause a battery.

   A. I, II, III, IV

   B. I, II

   C. I, II, III

   D. IV

4. Elly buys a keychain that has a laser light attached to it. There is no warning label concerning the use of the laser. When the "on" button is pushed on the laser, a beam of light is emitted that appears as a red dot. Elly brings the keychain to school and one of her classmates, Vic, asks her about how the laser works. Elly says, "I don't know, really. Hold still and see if you feel anything." Elly then points the laser light at Vic's face, and Vic feels

a stinging sensation in his eye. He also "sees red." The next day when Vic's eye is examined by a doctor, it is found to have "heavy irritation." Elly is charged with battery under an old common law statute and convicted.

On appeal, what are the strongest arguments that Elly's defense lawyer can make in order to persuade the trial judge to reverse the conviction on the grounds that there is insufficient evidence of the elements of the crime?

    I. There was no bodily injury or offensive touching caused to the victim.

    II. There was no criminal negligence.

    III. There was no mental state of intent to touch offensively.

    IV. There was no mental state of intent to cause bodily injury.

A. III, IV

B. I, II

C. I, II, III

D. I, III, IV

4. Elly buys a keychain that has a laser light attached to it. There is no warning label concerning the use of the laser. When the "on" button is pushed on the laser, a beam of light is emitted that appears as a red dot. Elly brings the keychain to school and one of her classmates, Vic, asks her about how the laser works. Elly says, "Hold still and see if you feel anything." Elly then points the laser light at Vic's face, and Vic feels a stinging sensation in his eye. He also "sees red." Elly is later convicted of

battery under an old common law statute.

On appeal, what policy arguments will the prosecutor make in order to persuade the trial judge to affirm the conviction on the grounds that there is sufficient evidence of the elements of the crime?

    I. The battery crime is based on the need to punish behavior that may lead to a breach of the peace or harm to the sacredness of the person.

    II. The offensive touching definition of battery receives widespread support in state statutes and this justifies the expansion of this form of battery in the context of an intangible force.

    III. The battery crime should protect against harms to the person caused by either tangible or intangible forces.

    IV. It is within common knowledge that a laser has the potential to touch offensively or to cause bodily injury.

A. I, II, III

B. I, II

C. I, III, IV

D. I, IV

7. Dan is prosecuted and convicted under a modern statute that prohibits the crime of assault. The evidence at Dan's trial showed that Dan and Mike are patients in the same ward at a hospital for veterans. Dan obtained possession of a knife, and Dan decided to use it to scare Mike so that Dan could take Mike's food away from him.

Dan waved the knife in Mike's face at the dinner table and then took Mike's food from him. However, Dan did not realize that Mike is almost blind and could not see the knife. On appeal, Dan's lawyer argues that the evidence is insufficient to convict Dan of assault.

Which of the following reasons will the appellate court give for the decision it makes in Dan's case?

    I. The lack of a frightened victim means that the conviction must be reversed.

    II. The lack of Dan's intent to injure Mike means that the conviction must be reversed.

    III. The lack of actual injury to Mike means that the conviction must be reversed.

    IV. The fact that Dan got very close to the point where he could cause an injury to Mike means that the conviction should be affirmed.

A. I, II, III

B. I, II

C. I

D. IV

8. Jake is prosecuted under an old statute that prohibits the crime of larceny. Which of the following elements are likely to be included in this common law crime?

    I. The element of a taking of the property of another.

II. The element of the intent to permanently deprive the owner of the property.

III. The element of a taking from the possession of the owner.

IV. The element of asportation of the property taken.

A. I, II, III, IV

B. I, II, III

C. I, II, IV

D. I, III, IV

9. Harriet is prosecuted under an old statute that prohibits the crime of embezzlement. Which of the following elements are likely to be included in this common law crime?

I. The element of a taking from the possession of the owner.

II. The element of an entrustment of the property by the owner.

III. The element of the intent to convert the property.

IV. The element of a taking of the property of another.

A. I, II, IV

B. I, III, IV

C. I, II, III, IV

D. II, III, IV

10. Cate is an employee of an armored truck service that delivers money and valuables. A bank hires the service company to deliver bags of money that belong to the bank to various branches throughout the city. Cate is the employee who is assigned to drive the truck that contains the money bags belonging to the bank. Soon after she starts driving to the first branch, she parks the truck, goes to the back door, gets the money bags, opens them, and removes the money. She takes the money home. Cate is charged with larceny and convicted. On appeal, Cate's lawyer argues that her conviction should be reversed because there is insufficient evidence of the elements of larceny.

Which of the following reasons will the appellate court give for the decision it makes in Cate's case?

   I. The fact that Cate was given only temporary custody of the money means that the conviction should be reversed.

   II. The fact that Cate qualifies as a bailee means that the conviction should be affirmed.

   III. The fact that Cate had instructions for delivery of the money means that the conviction should be affirmed.

   IV. The fact that Cate took the money while it was in the custody of the service company means that the conviction should be reversed.

A. II

B. II, III

C. I

D. I, IV

11. Ali was employed by a casino to refill the coins in the hoppers inside the slot machines. He was given a card that he could use to gain access to the inside of the machines. The card also identified him as the employee who was opening the door of each machine. Ali was told that he was not to touch the component of the slot machines where the paper currency was kept, called the bill validator. If Ali discovered that a particular bill validator component was causing a problem, he was instructed to call his supervisor, who would arrange for an employee in charge of currency to deal with the problem. Ali was instructed to open the machine door for these other employees, who were authorized to refill the bill validator and to give cash refunds to customers when necessary. After some months it appears that the machines serviced by Ali have large shortages of cash, and that Ali has been gambling and losing large sums. He is charged with embezzlement and convicted. On appeal, Ali's lawyer argues that his conviction should be reversed because there is insufficient evidence of the elements of embezzlement.

Which of the following reasons will the appellate court give for the decision it makes in Ali's case?

I. The fact that Ali was told not to touch the currency means that the conviction must be reversed.

II. The fact that Ali was given a card that gave him access to the coins and currency means that the conviction should be affirmed.

III. The fact that Ali was supposed to give access to other employees to the bill validator in any machine (where the cash posed a problem of some kind) means that the conviction should be reversed.

IV. The fact that Ali was required to contact a supervisor if he noticed a problem with a bill validator means that the conviction should be reversed.

A. I, III

B. II

C. I, III, IV

D. I, IV

12. Gary is prosecuted under an old statute that prohibits the crime of obtaining property by false pretenses. Which of the following elements are likely to be included in this common law crime?

I. The element of a victim who passes title to property to the defendant in reliance on a false representation.

II. The element of the intent to defraud the victim.

III. The element of a false representation of a material fact or promise.

IV. The element of knowledge that the representation is false.

A. II, III

B. I, II, III, IV

C. I, II, IV

D. II, III, IV

13. A security guard saw Rhoda take the sales tag off a red dress that was on sale and switch it with the tag of a blue dress that was not on sale. So the guard believed that Rhoda was planning to try to pay a sale price for the blue dress that was not on sale. The guard notified the cashier that a suspicious person meeting Rhoda's description was coming through the check out line, and told the clerk to charge Rhoda the price on the tag, unless Rhoda asked the clerk to check the correctness of the price. In that case, the clerk should do as Rhoda asked. Soon thereafter, Rhoda came through the check out line. When the cashier took the blue dress from Rhoda, the cashier noticed that the price tag had been removed and reinserted, but the cashier could not tell whether the price tag was the original one or a different one. Therefore, the cashier was unsure about whether the price on the sales tag on the blue dress was erroneous. Given the guard's instruction, the cashier decided that she should charge Rhoda the sale price as indicated on the tag. Rhoda left the store and the police were called to the scene to arrest her. Rhoda was charged with the modern crime of theft by deception, which provides that the crime is "obtaining by deception control over property." The element of "deception" is defined as "knowingly making a false statement or representation, express or implied, pertaining to a present or past existing fact." Rhoda testified at trial that she did not switch the tags, but the jury did not believe her and she was convicted. On appeal, Rhoda's defense counsel argues that there is insufficient evidence of the elements

of theft by deception.

Which of the following reasons will the appellate court give for the decision it makes in Rhoda's case?

    I. The fact that the statute does not require that the victim must rely on a false representation means that the conviction should be affirmed.

    II. The fact that the cashier remained unsure about whether the sales tag was erroneous means that the conviction should be affirmed.

    III. The common law element of victim reliance on the false representation should be read into the statute, and this means that the conviction should be reversed.

    IV. The security guard saw the defendant switch the tags and so the store as owner of the property could not be deceived by the switch; therefore, the conviction should be reversed.

    A. III, IV

    B. III

    C. II

    D. I

14. Sara is a paralegal at a large law firm in New York. The firm represents plaintiffs in a class action case, for which the lawyers prepared a 400-page trial plan that includes deposition excerpts, summaries of trial strategy, and lists of anticipated trial exhibits. Sarah is working on the case as a paralegal, and so she was able to obtain access to the trial plan in the form of a document on a

law firm computer. She contacts the defendant's attorney, who is a member of a large law firm in New Jersey. Sara offers to sell the plan for two million dollars to the defendant's attorney, and she sends a sample excerpt of 80 pages of the plan to the attorney via an email attachment. The defendant's attorney contacts the FBI, and an FBI agent, who is posing as the defendant's attorney, sends Sara an email agreeing to buy the rest of the trial plan. When Sara arrives at the meeting where she expects to receive the two million dollars, she is arrested and charged under a modern federal statute that provides as follows: "Whoever transports, transmits, or transfers in interstate commerce any goods, wares, merchandise, securities, or money, of the value of $5,000, knowing the same to have been stolen, shall be guilty of dealing in stolen property." Sara is convicted at trial. On appeal, Sara's defense counsel argues that some of the elements of the statute were not proved at trial to exist beyond a reasonable doubt.

What are the strongest arguments that the prosecutor can make to persuade the appellate court that the facts establish sufficient evidence of the elements of the crime?

   I. That the term "transmits" implies that Congress intended the crime to include the electronic transmission of emailed information.

   II. That the term "goods" appears in a group of terms, "goods, wares and merchandise," which implies that Congress intended the statute to cover any property that is the subject of commerce.

   III. That the term "goods" should be interpreted in light of the more specific statutory terms, "securities" and "money."

IV. That the absence of a specific limitation of the crime to tangible property implies that Congress intended the crime to include intangible property.

A. I, II, IV

B. III, IV

C. I, II

D. I, III, IV

15. Sara is a paralegal at a large law firm in New York. The firm represents plaintiffs in a class action case, for which the lawyers prepared a 400-page trial plan that includes deposition excerpts, summaries of trial strategy, and lists of anticipated trial exhibits. Sarah is working on the case as a paralegal, and so she was able to obtain access to the trial plan in the form of a document on a law firm computer. She contacts the defendant's attorney, who is a member of a large law firm in New Jersey. Sara offers to sell the plan for two million dollars to the defendant's attorney, and she sends a sample excerpt of 80 pages of the plan to the attorney via an email attachment. The defendant's attorney contacts the FBI, and an FBI agent, who is posing as the defendant's attorney, sends Sara an email agreeing to buy the rest of the trial plan. When Sara arrives at the meeting where she expects to receive the two million dollars, she is arrested and charged under a modern federal statute that provides as follows: "Whoever transports, transmits, or transfers in interstate commerce any goods, wares, merchandise, securities, or money, of the value of $5,000, knowing the same to have been stolen, shall be guilty of dealing in stolen property." Sara is convicted at trial. On appeal, Sara's defense counsel argues that some of the

elements of the statute were not proved at trial to exist beyond a reasonable doubt.

Which of the following policy reasons will the appellate court give for the decision it makes in Sara's case?

> I. The information in the trial plan is transferable, accessible, and salable, and therefore should be covered by the statute.
>
> II. It is common for goods like dollars or documents to travel electronically, and therefore it will unduly restrict the scope of the statute to read a "tangible goods" requirement into the text.
>
> III. The email version of the trial plan is similar to photocopies of documents that should be covered by the statute.
>
> IV. The trial plan should not be covered by the statute because information communicated in telephone conversations should not be covered.

A. I, II

B. IV

C. I, II, III

D. I

16. Darlene is prosecuted under an old statute that prohibits the crime of receiving stolen property. Which of the following elements are likely to be included in this common law crime?

> I. Concealing and withholding stolen property.

II. Believing the property is probably stolen.

III. Knowing the property to be stolen.

IV. Having the intent to deprive the owner permanently of the property.

A. I, II, III, IV

B. III, IV

C. II, III, IV

D. I, III, IV

17. Hanna is arrested for the modern crime of receiving stolen property. Hanna and her friend Max got a ride to a late night party and fell asleep there at their friend's house. They woke up early and they had no ride home. They tried hitchhiking for 30 minutes, and they walked slowly along the highway without getting any rides. As they walked by a gas station, Max spotted an empty truck with its engine running. Presumably, its owner was inside the station. Max jumped in the truck and drove it away. The owner chased Max and couldn't catch him. About 20 minutes later, after Hanna had walked further down the road, Max suddenly appeared, driving the truck, and offered to give Hanna a ride. Max drove Hanna home, which took about 20 minutes. Just as Hanna got out of the truck, the police appeared on the scene. They had been able to trace the truck based on eyewitness reports. Max was charged with a variety of crimes and Hanna was charged with receiving stolen property. This crime is defined as applying to a person who "purposely receives, retains, or disposes of movable property of another knowing that it has been stolen." The term "receiving" is defined as "acquiring possession, control or

title." Hanna is convicted, and on appeal, her defense counsel, Zeb, argues that there is insufficient evidence of the elements of the crime to affirm the conviction.

Which of the following policy reasons will the appellate court give for the decision it makes in Hanna's case?

    I. Hanna's role as a passenger should not subject her to liability because she did not share joint possession or control of the truck.

    II. Hanna's presence in the truck should not demonstrate control or possession of the truck because she was not the driver.

    III. Hanna should not be deemed to have been in control or possession of the truck because she did not use the truck for her own benefit and enjoyment.

    IV. Hanna should not be liable because she did not have the capacity to influence Max's control and possession of the truck.

A. II, IV

B. I, IV

C. I, III

D. III, IV

18. Karl is prosecuted under an old statute that prohibits the crime of robbery. Which of the following elements distinguish this common law crime from larceny?

I. A taking and carrying away of property.

II. A taking by means of force or fear

III. A taking from the person or presence of another

IV. A taking with the intent to permanently deprive another of property.

A. III, IV

B. II, IV

C. I, II

D. II, III

19. Harvey, Maude and Jen are going to be prosecuted, and the prosecutor is trying to decide which crime to charge in each case, and whether it is possible to convict any of the three defendants of robbery as well as theft. There are three victims, Hen, Maurey, and Jerome. The three victims were standing together, chatting on the sidewalk, when the trio of defendants approached them. At first, the three victims did not notice the three defendants because the sidewalk was very crowded and the defendants were indistinguishable from others in the crowd. Harvey creeps up behind Hen and picks her wallet out of her large purse, which is hanging open. Hen does not notice Harvey's act. At the same time, Maurey is gesturing in the air, holding a $100 bill in his hand, waving it around, and talking to the other two victims about how happy he is that he just won the $100 in a bet with his best friend. As Maurey continues to wave the bill around, Maude steps up behind him and asks, "Sir, do you know what time it is?" Maurey turns to look at her and Maude unexpectedly reaches out and takes the $100

bill from Maurey, who simply lets go of it without having time to grab it back. At the same time, Jen approaches Jerome and starts to pull on his briefcase, which he is holding by its handle, down at his side. Jerome sees Jen pulling and so Jerome pulls back hard on his briefcase for five seconds. After a brief struggle, Jen yanks it away from Jerome. The theft statute prohibits the "taking of the property of another with the purpose to deprive that person of the property." The robbery statute prohibits the "taking of the property of another with the purpose to deprive that person of the property, when in the course of the taking there is the use of force or violence."

Which of the defendants, Harvey, Maude, and Jen may be prosecuted successfully for robbery, and which for theft?

    I. All three defendants of theft, Jen of robbery.

    II. All three defendants of theft, only Maude and Jen of robbery.

    III. All three defendants of theft, all three defendants of robbery.

    IV. All three defendants of theft, no defendant of robbery.

    A. III

    B. II

    C. I

    D. IV

20. Kim is prosecuted under an old statute that prohibits the crime of burglary. Which of the following

elements are likely to be included in this common law crime?

I. The breaking into a dwelling.

II. The entering into a dwelling.

III. Entry at nighttime.

IV. Entry with the intent to steal.

A. I, III, III, IV

B. I, II, III

C. II, III, IV

D. I, III, IV

21   Thuy is prosecuted under a statute that defines burglary as follows: "Burglary is knowingly and without authority entering into or remaining within any building, manufactured home, mobile home, tent, or other structure which is not a dwelling, with the intent to commit a felony therein." Thuy was arrested when Hal found him, after midnight, in Hal's lean-to structure that provides sheltered parking next to Hal's enclosed workshop at the back of Hal's house. Hal sells handmade crafts at his workshop. The lean-to has three walls (one of which is actually a wall of Hal's house), and is open on the fourth side. The lean-to has a roof and a dirt floor. Hal has installed an alarm system all around the lean-to, and Hal found Thuy in the lean-to because the alarm system went off when Thuy entered the lean-to. Hal keeps old furniture, garden tools, and auto supplies in the lean-to. Hal also parks his car in the lean-to every night. The lean-to has two extra car spaces that Hal's

customers can use when they come to buy items at his workshop. Thuy claims that he was looking for a car jack to fix a flat car. Thuy's car was parked a few blocks away with no flat tire. Thuy was convicted of burglary, and on appeal, Thuy's defense counsel argues that the conviction should be reversed because a lean-to is not a "structure" under the statute.

Which of the following arguments will be the prosecutor's strongest ones to persuade the appellate court to affirm the conviction by finding that a lean-to qualifies as a "structure" under the statute?

> I. The lean-to should be a "structure" under the statute because the statute uses a broad definition of structures that can be burglarized, including any building and structures that are not dwellings.
>
> II. The lean-to should be a "structure" under the statute because the statute includes the example of a tent, which is similar to a lean-to because it is often open and cannot be secured effectively from entry.
>
> III. The lean-to should be a "structure" under the statute because Hal installed an alarm system to detect intruders around it, and thereby made the lean-to a secured portion of the workshop.
>
> IV. The lean-to should be a "structure" under the statute because the lean-to contains possessions that are closely associated with the possessions of a dwelling, and which are a target of those who burglarize dwellings.

A. I, II, IV

B. I, III, IV

C. I, II, III, IV

D. I, IV

22. Thuy is prosecuted under a statute that defines burglary as follows: "Burglary is knowingly and without authority entering into or remaining within any building, manufactured home, mobile home, tent, or other structure which is not a dwelling, with the intent to commit a felony therein." Thuy was arrested when Hal found him, after midnight, in Hal's lean-to structure that provides sheltered parking next to Hal's enclosed workshop at the back of Hal's house. Hal sells handmade crafts at his workshop. The lean-to has three walls (one of which is actually a wall of Hal's house), and is open on the fourth side. The lean-to has a roof and a dirt floor. Hal has installed an alarm system all around the lean-to, and Hal found Thuy in the lean-to because the alarm system went off when Thuy entered the lean-to. Hal keeps old furniture, garden tools, and auto supplies in the lean-to. Hal also parks his car in the lean-to every night. The lean-to has two extra car spaces that Hal's customers can use when they come to buy items at his workshop. Thuy claims that he was looking for a car jack to fix a flat car. Thuy's car was parked a few blocks away with no flat tire. Thuy was convicted of burglary, and on appeal, Thuy's defense counsel argues that the conviction should be reversed because a lean-to is not a "structure" under the statute.

Which of the following reasons will the appellate court give for reversing the conviction in Thuy's case?

   I. The lean-to is not intended to be a "structure" under the statute because it is not an occupied structure that is adapted for overnight accommodation or for carrying on business.

II. The lean-to is not intended to be a "structure" under the statute because it is not an enclosed space for the security of persons or property.

III. The lean-to is not intended to be a "structure" under the statute because it does not have a barrier to entry.

IV. The lean-to is not intended to be a "structure" under the statute because it does not share the attributes of the other examples of enumerated structures in the statute.

A. II, III, IV

B. I, II, III, IV

C. I, III

D. I, III, IV

23. Vera is prosecuted under an old statute that prohibits the crime of murder. Which of the following types of murder were included originally in this common law crime?

I. Deliberated and premeditated murder.

II. Felony murder.

III. Depraved heart murder.

IV. Intent to kill murder.

A. II, IV

B. I, II, III, IV

C. I, II, IV

D. II, III, IV

24. Tina is prosecuted under a modern first degree murder statute that prohibits the crime of deliberate and premeditated murder with intent to kill. Which of the following definitions of the crime may be used in jury instructions concerning the meaning of this mens rea?

   I. Deliberation and premeditation may exist when the act of killing follows soon after the formulation of an intent to kill.

   II. Deliberation requires a cool mind that is capable of reflection.

   III. Premeditation requires that a person did actually reflect upon the decision to kill.

   IV. Deliberation and premeditation may exist when the intention to kill and the act of killing are as instantaneous as successive thoughts in the mind.

A. I, IV

B. I, II, III, IV

C. II, III

D. I, II, III

25. Liam is prosecuted under an old statute that

prohibits the crime of voluntary manslaughter. Which of the following elements are likely to be included in this common law crime?

   I. Provocation that will cause a reasonable person to lose self-control.

   II. Malice aforethought.

   III. No cooling time for the heat of passion to cool.

   IV. Heat of passion.

   A. I, II

   B. I, II, III

   C. I, III, IV

   D. I, II, III, IV

26.   Ian is prosecuted under a statute that prohibits the crime of reckless manslaughter. Which of the following elements are likely to be included in this common law crime?

   I. Adequate provocation that would cause a reasonable person to kill.

   II. Conscious disregard of a substantial and unjustifiable risk of death.

   III. Conscious disregard that is a gross deviation from a law-abiding person standard.

   IV. Heat of passion.

A. I, III, IV

B. I, II, III, IV

C. I, III

D. II, III

27. Belle and Jock had a stormy relationship, and they had a fight and decided to stop seeing each other. After a few hours passed, Jock decided he wanted to reconcile with Belle. So that night, he went to Belle's house and knocked on the front door. There was no answer. He went around to the back yard and looked in the bedroom window. He saw Belle on the bed with another man and both were naked. Jock ran back around to the front door and kicked it in. Then he ran back to his car that was parked by the curb near the front door, and he retrieved a loaded handgun from the glove compartment. Then he ran straight up the front walk and into the house. He kept running, and when he got to the bedroom door, he kicked it down, ran into the bedroom, and confronted Belle and the unknown man. Belle screamed at Jock and Jock yelled at the man to "get out of this house!" The man raced out of the bedroom with Jock in pursuit; Jock kept holding out the gun and pointing it at the man, as he chased the man through the house. The man was about to make his escape through the front door when Jock tripped over a bump in the carpet and fell to the ground. The gun went off, and fired a bullet that hit the man in the upper thigh. It was an unusual wound that hit a vein, and the man, Vic, quickly bled to death. Jock was arrested soon afterwards because Belle called the police. The prosecutor is considering a variety of homicide charges and expects that Jock will be convicted of at least one homicide crime.

Which of the following charges may produce a conviction?

I. Depraved heart murder.

II. Voluntary manslaughter.

III. Reckless manslaughter.

IV. Deliberated and premeditated murder.

A. I, III

B. II

C. I, II, III

D. I, IV

28. Belle and Jock had a stormy relationship, and they had a fight and decided to stop seeing each other. After a few hours passed, Jock decided he wanted to reconcile with Belle. So that night, he went to Belle's house and knocked on the front door. There was no answer. He went around to the back yard and looked in the bedroom window. He saw Belle on the bed with another man and both were naked. Jock ran back around to the front door and kicked it in. Then he ran back to his car that was parked by the curb near the front door, and he retrieved a loaded handgun from the glove compartment. Then he ran straight up the front walk and into the house. He kept running, and when he got to the bedroom door, he kicked it down, ran into the bedroom, and confronted Belle and the unknown man. Belle screamed at Jock and Jock yelled at the man to "get out of this house!" The man raced out of the bedroom with Jock in pursuit; Jock kept holding out the gun and pointing it at the man, as he chased the man through the house. The man ran through the front door space, jumped over the broken door, and started running down the street. Jock followed

right behind the man and kept chasing him for three blocks. Suddenly, the man jumped into an empty car that was parked at the side of the road. Jock screamed, "No you don't!" and pointed the gun at the windshield. Then Jock fired through the windshield. The bullet hit the man, Vic, in the head and he died instantly. Jock was arrested soon afterwards because Belle called the police. The prosecutor is considering a variety of homicide charges and expects that Jock will be convicted of at least one homicide crime.

Which of the following charges may produce a conviction?

I. Depraved heart murder.

II. Reckless manslaughter.

III. Felony murder.

IV. Deliberated and premeditated murder.

A. I, III

B. I, II, III, IV

C. I, II, III

D. I, IV

29. Belle and Jock had a stormy relationship, and they had a fight and decided to stop seeing each other. After a few hours passed, Jock decided he wanted to reconcile with Belle. So that night, he went to Belle's house and knocked on the front door. There was no answer. He went around to the back yard and looked in the bedroom window. He saw Belle on the bed with another man and both were naked. Jock ran back around to the front door

and kicked it in. Then he ran back to his car that was parked by the curb near the front door, and he retrieved a loaded handgun from the glove compartment. Then he ran straight up the front walk and into the house. He kept running, and when he got to the bedroom door, he kicked it down, ran into the bedroom, and confronted Belle and the unknown man. Belle screamed at Jock and Jock yelled at the man to "get out of this house!" The man raced out of the bedroom with Jock in pursuit; Jock kept holding out the gun and pointing it at the man, as he chased the man through the house. The man ran through the front door space, jumped over the broken door, and started running down the street. Jock followed right behind the man and kept chasing him for three blocks. Suddenly, the man jumped into an empty car that was parked at the side of the road. Jock screamed, "No you don't!" and pointed the gun at the windshield. Then Jock fired through the windshield. The bullet hit the man, Vic, in the head and he died instantly. Jock was arrested soon afterwards because Belle called the police. Assume that the prosecutor charges Jock with murder and that the mens rea for this crime is defined as purposely or knowingly causing death. Jock's defense counsel, Amy, persuades the trial judge to instruct the jury that voluntary manslaughter is also an appropriate verdict option. Jock is convicted of murder. On appeal, his defense counsel Amy argues that the murder conviction should be reversed and that the verdict should be reduced to voluntary manslaughter.

Which of the following arguments will be made by Jock's defense counsel to show that there is sufficient evidence for a verdict of voluntary manslaughter?

> V. When Jock shot through the windshield, he did not know that his bullet would kill Vic.
>
> VI. During the interval between the time that Jock saw Vic and Belle through the window and

the time that Jock fired his gun, there was no cooling time.

VII. The sight of Vic and Belle through the window was adequate provocation.

VIII. Evidence of heat of passion is shown by Jock's conduct in kicking down two doors, screaming, and chasing Vic for three blocks.

A. I, II, IV

B. II, III, IV

C. I, III, IV

D. I, II, III

30. Belle and Jock had a stormy relationship, and they had a fight and decided to stop seeing each other. After a few hours passed, Jock decided he wanted to reconcile with Belle. So that night, he went to Belle's house and knocked on the front door. There was no answer. He went around to the back yard and looked in the bedroom window. He saw Belle on the bed with another man and both were naked. Jock ran back around to the front door and kicked it in. Then he ran back to his car that was parked by the curb near the front door, and he retrieved a loaded handgun from the glove compartment. Then he ran straight up the front walk and into the house. He kept running, and when he got to the bedroom door, he kicked it down, ran into the bedroom, and confronted Belle and the unknown man. Belle screamed at Jock and Jock yelled at the man to "get out of this house!" The man raced out of the bedroom with Jock in pursuit; Jock kept holding out the gun and pointing it at the man, as he chased the man through the house. The man ran

through the front door space, jumped over the broken door, and started running down the street. Jock followed right behind the man and kept chasing him for three blocks. Suddenly, the man jumped into an empty car that was parked at the side of the road. Jock screamed, "No you don't!" and pointed the gun at the windshield. Then Jock fired through the windshield. The bullet hit the man, Vic, in the head and he died instantly. Jock was arrested soon afterwards because Belle called the police. Assume that the prosecutor charges Jock with first degree murder and that the mens rea for this crime is defined as an intentional killing with deliberation and premeditation. The trial judge instructs the jury that the other verdict option is second degree murder, which is an intentional killing with no deliberation and premeditation. Jock is convicted of first degree murder. On appeal, his defense counsel Amy argues that the conviction should be reversed, and that the verdict should be reduced to second degree murder.

What are the strongest arguments that the defense counsel can make to demonstrate the insufficiency of the evidence to support the conviction for first degree murder?

    I. Jock shot only once, which indicates that he did not use a method of killing that demonstrated a plan to kill.

    II. Jock did not know the victim, which suggests that he lacked a motive that would demonstrate a plan to kill.

    III. Jock had no plan to shoot Vic when he did, because he chased Vic and then shot at him impulsively.

    IV. Jock's provocation by Belle and Vic shows that Jock was acting under the influence of an extreme emotional disturbance, which is inconsistent with the formulation of a plan to kill.

    i. II, IV

    ii. I, II, III, IV

    iii. I, III

    iv. I, II, III

31. Belle and Jock had a stormy relationship, and they had a fight and decided to stop seeing each other. After a few hours passed, Jock decided he wanted to reconcile with Belle. So that night, he went to Belle's house and knocked on the front door. There was no answer. He went around to the back yard and looked in the bedroom window. He saw Belle on the bed with another man and both were naked. Jock ran back around to the front door and kicked it in. Then he ran back to his car that was parked by the curb near the front door, and he retrieved a loaded handgun from the glove compartment. Then he ran straight up the front walk and into the house. He kept running, and when he got to the bedroom door, he kicked it down, ran into the bedroom, and confronted Belle and the unknown man. Belle screamed at Jock and Jock yelled at the man to "get out of this house!" The man raced out of the bedroom with Jock in pursuit; Jock kept holding out the gun and pointing it at the man, as he chased the man through the house. The man ran through the front door space, jumped over the broken door, and started running down the street. Jock followed right behind the man and kept chasing him for three blocks. Suddenly, the man jumped into an empty car that was parked at the side of the road. Jock screamed, "No you don't!" and pointed the gun at the windshield. Then Jock fired through the windshield. The bullet hit

the man, Vic, in the head and he died instantly. Jock was arrested soon afterwards because Belle called the police. Assume that the prosecutor charges Jock with first degree murder and that the mens rea for this crime is defined as an intentional killing with deliberation and premeditation. The trial judge instructs the jury that the other verdict option is second degree murder, which is an intentional killing with no deliberation and premeditation. Jock is convicted of first degree murder. On appeal, his defense counsel Amy argues that the conviction should be reversed, and that the verdict should be reduced to second degree murder.

What are the strongest arguments that the prosecutor can make to demonstrate the sufficiency of the evidence to support the elements of first degree murder?

  I. Jock retrieved the gun from his car, which act supplies evidence of planning.

  II. Jock waited until he had a clear shot at Vic, instead of shooting him during the chase, which provides evidence of a strategic choice by Jock.

  III. Jock's conduct in shooting an unarmed victim by hunting him down is heinous and supplies evidence of wantonness.

  IV. The provocation that Jock received by the sight of Belle and Vic through the window supplies evidence of motive.

  A. I, II, IV

  B. I, II, III

  C. I, III, IV

  D. I, IV

32. Jacob was charged with depraved heart murder for the killing of his wife. Jacob testified at trial that he had been "fooling around" with his loaded shotgun, as he sat on the floor of the living room watching TV, when the shotgun went off and the shot killed his wife in the kitchen. Jacob admitted that he knew that his wife was in the kitchen at the time when the shotgun went off. He testified that he knew how to operate the shotgun, and admitted that he had been drinking beer all afternoon. He also admitted that he occasionally "dry-fired" the shotgun by aiming it at different items in the room without pulling the trigger. Jacob denied that he was dry-firing the shotgun at the time when his wife was killed. At Jacob's trial, the jury was instructed on the elements of depraved heart murder, and on the elements of involuntary manslaughter as an alternative verdict option. Jacob was convicted of depraved heart murder. On appeal, his lawyer, Jill, argues that there is insufficient evidence of the elements of depraved heart murder to affirm Jacob's conviction, and that his conviction should be reduced to involuntary manslaughter.

What are the strongest arguments that the prosecutor can make to demonstrate the sufficiency of the evidence to support the conviction for depraved heart murder?

  I. Jacob's extremely reckless conduct resembles that of defendants who intentionally kill.

  II. Jacob consciously disregarded an extremely high risk of death and his conduct was an extremely gross deviation from that of a law-abiding person.

  III. Jacob's conduct resembles that of defendants who drive cars into crowds of pedestrians, set off bombs in train stations, and throw logs off the top of buildings when there are people in the street below.

IV. Jacob's conduct shows evidence of depravity and wantonness in its disregard for human life.

A. I, II, IV

B. I, II, III, IV

C. II, III, IV

D. I, IV

33. Carl was driving his van down a crowded street at 45 miles per hour, which speed was five miles over the speed limit. His van collided with two twelve-year-old children, who were standing in the middle of the traffic stripe that separated the traffic on the two-lane road. It appeared that the children were waiting until the traffic cleared, in order to cross to the other side of the street. Carl could have stopped his van in order to let the children cross safely in front of him, as he had a clear view of their presence in the street from some distance away, and plenty of time to stop. Carl's van did slow down to 35 miles per hour as it approached the children, but it did not stop. The street was narrow with parked cars on both sides, and Carl's van was unusually large and wide. There was no evidence that the children moved from their spot on the traffic stripe before Carl's van collided with them. Both children were killed. The prosecutor charges Carl with negligent homicide.

What elements does the prosecutor have to prove in order to obtain a conviction for negligent homicide?

I. That Carl's conduct was a gross deviation from a reasonable person's conduct.

II. That Carl consciously disregarded a risk of death.

III. That Carl should have been aware of a risk of death.

IV. That the risk of death was substantial and unjustifiable.

A. I, IV

B. I, II, IV

C. I, III, IV

D. I, II, III, IV

34. Carl was driving his van down a crowded street at 45 miles per hour, which speed was five miles over the speed limit. His van collided with two twelve-year-old children, who were standing in the middle of the traffic stripe that separated the traffic on the two-lane road. It appeared that the children were waiting until the traffic cleared, in order to cross to the other side of the street. Carl could have stopped his van in order to let the children cross safely in front of him, as he had a clear view of their presence in the street from some distance away, and plenty of time to stop. Carl's van did slow down to 35 miles per hour as it approached the children, but it did not stop. The street was narrow with parked cars on both sides, and Carl's van was unusually large and wide. There was no evidence that the children moved from their spot on the traffic stripe before Carl's van collided with them. Both children were killed. The

prosecutor is considering a variety of homicide charges and expects that Carl will be convicted of at least one homicide crime.

Which of the following charges may produce a conviction?

I. Reckless murder with extreme indifference to human life.

II. Reckless manslaughter.

III. Negligent homicide.

IV. Felony murder.

A. II, III

B. I, II

C. I, II, III, IV

D. I, II, III

35. Rufus is charged with felony murder under a modern statute. What sort of limitation on the scope of this traditional strict liability crime is likely to be found in a modern statute or in modern case law?

I. If the killing is an act of a co-felon and not the defendant's act, there is no felony murder liability.

II. There is a strict interpretation of proximate cause required for felony murder liability.

III. Felony murder liability exists only when a particular felony is inherently dangerous to human life.

IV. The time period when the death must occur in relationship to the commission of a felony is narrowly defined for felony murder liability.

A. I, II, III, IV

B. I, III

C. II, IV

D. II, III, IV

36. One evening in Salt Lake City, Sol and Todd were working together as dishwashers in the kitchen of a restaurant called The Rib House, while their co-workers prepared the meals for the customers. Sol and Todd got along well together, but on this particular night, Todd was joking around and poking fun at Sol for about twenty minutes. Sol did not respond to Todd's joking, and Sol appeared to be in a bad mood. So Todd told Sol to "lighten up" and started snapping a wet dishtowel on Sol's forearm, hitting him with it once or twice without causing anything more than a quick sting. Then Todd snapped the wet dishtowel so that it hit Sol hard on his nose. Sol became enraged, took off his dishwashing gloves and started toward Todd. Todd, still teasing, said, "Ooo, he's taking his gloves off." Then Sol took a knife from his pocket and stabbed Todd in the neck. As Todd fell to the floor, Sol also stabbed Todd in the arm. Todd looked up and cried, "Man, I was just kidding around." Sol responded: "Well, man, you should have never hit me in my nose." Then Sol ran to the front of the restaurant and asked the manager to call an ambulance for Todd.

When the police arrived at the restaurant, Todd was dead from his neck wound because of blood loss. Sol told the police that he usually carried his lock blade knife for skinning rabbits and squirrels during hunting season. It happened to be hunting season at this time. Before his trial, Sol's defense counsel, Mira, discovers that Sol suffers from an obsession with his nose. Sol's father explains to Mira that when Sol was 17 years old, he started asking his parents for assurances that his nose was not too big. During the following ten years, Sol's obsession was expressed through his constant glances in the mirror to examine his nose in profile views, dozens of times a day. Assume that the prosecutor charges Jock with first degree murder and that the mens rea for this crime is defined as an intentional killing with deliberation and premeditation. The trial judge instructs the jury that the other verdict option is second degree murder, which is an intentional killing with no deliberation and premeditation. Sol is convicted of first degree murder. On appeal, his defense counsel Mira argues that the conviction should be reversed, and that the verdict should be reduced to second degree murder.

Which of the following facts will help the defense counsel to create arguments to demonstrate the insufficiency of the evidence to support the elements of first degree murder?

    I. That Sol only carried a knife at the time of the killing because it was hunting season.

    II. That Sol ran to the restaurant manager and asked for an ambulance to be called for Todd.

    III. That Sol suffered from his nose obsession, and that this obsession is evidence of a mental abnormality.

    IV. That Sol didn't know that Todd was going to hit Sol in the nose.

A. I, II, IV

B. I, II

C. III, IV

D. II, III

37. One evening in Salt Lake City, Sol and Todd were working together as dishwashers in the kitchen of a restaurant called The Rib House, while their co-workers prepared the meals for the customers. Sol and Todd got along well together, but on this particular night, Todd was joking around and poking fun at Sol for about twenty minutes. Sol did not respond to Todd's joking, and Sol appeared to be in a bad mood. So Todd told Sol to "lighten up" and started snapping a wet dishtowel on Sol's forearm, hitting him with it once or twice without causing anything more than a quick sting. Then Todd snapped the wet dishtowel so that it hit Sol hard on his nose. Sol became enraged, took off his dishwashing gloves and started toward Todd. Todd, still teasing, said, "Ooo, he's taking his gloves off." Then Sol took a knife from his pocket and stabbed Todd in the neck. As Todd fell to the floor, Sol also stabbed Todd in the arm. Todd looked up and cried, "Man, I was just kidding around." Sol responded: "Well, man, you should have never hit me in my nose." Then Sol ran to the front of the restaurant and asked the manager to call an ambulance for Todd. When the police arrived at the restaurant, Todd was dead from his neck wound because of blood loss. Sol told the police that he usually carried his lock blade knife for skinning rabbits and squirrels during hunting season. It happened to be hunting season at this time. Before his trial, Sol's defense counsel, Mira, discovers that Sol suffers from an obsession with his nose. Sol's father explains to Mira that when Sol was 17 years old, he

started asking his parents for assurances that his nose was not too big. During the following ten years, Sol's obsession was expressed through his constant glances in the mirror to examine his nose in profile views, dozens of times a day. Assume that the prosecutor charges Jock with first degree murder and that the mens rea for this crime is defined as an intentional killing with deliberation and premeditation. The trial judge instructs the jury that the other verdict option is second degree murder, which is an intentional killing with no deliberation and premeditation. Sol is convicted of first degree murder. On appeal, his defense counsel Mira argues that the conviction should be reversed, and that the verdict should be reduced to second degree murder.

Which of the following facts will help the prosecutor to create arguments to demonstrate the sufficiency of the evidence to support the elements of first degree murder?

> I. That Sol was teased for 20 minutes by Todd before Todd hit Sol on the nose.
>
> II. That Sol took his gloves off before striking Todd with the knife.
>
> III. That Sol stabbed Todd twice.
>
> IV. That Sol and Todd reportedly got along before the killing.

A. I, II, III

B. II, III

C. I, III, IV

D. I, II, IV

38. One evening in Salt Lake City, Sol and Todd were working together as dishwashers in the kitchen of a restaurant called The Rib House, while their co-workers prepared the meals for the customers. Sol and Todd got along well together, but on this particular night, Todd was joking around and poking fun at Sol for about twenty minutes. Sol did not respond to Todd's joking, and Sol appeared to be in a bad mood. So Todd told Sol to "lighten up" and started snapping a wet dishtowel on Sol's forearm, hitting him with it once or twice without causing anything more than a quick sting. Then Todd snapped the wet dishtowel so that it hit Sol hard on his nose. Sol became enraged, took off his dishwashing gloves and started toward Todd. Todd, still teasing, said, "Ooo, he's taking his gloves off." Then Sol took a knife from his pocket and stabbed Todd in the neck. As Todd fell to the floor, Sol also stabbed Todd in the arm. Todd looked up and cried, "Man, I was just kidding around." Sol responded: "Well, man, you should have never hit me in my nose." Then Sol ran to the front of the restaurant and asked the manager to call an ambulance for Todd. When the police arrived at the restaurant, Todd was dead from his neck wound because of blood loss. Sol told the police that he usually carried his lock blade knife for skinning rabbits and squirrels during hunting season. It happened to be hunting season at this time. Before his trial, Sol's defense counsel, Mira, discovers that Sol suffers from an obsession with his nose. Sol's father explains to Mira that when Sol was 17 years old, he started asking his parents for assurances that his nose was not too big. During the following ten years, Sol's obsession was expressed through his constant glances in the mirror to examine his nose in profile views, dozens of times a day. Assume that the prosecutor charges Sol with murder and that the mens rea for this crime is defined as purposely or knowingly causing death. Sol's defense counsel, Mira, persuades the trial judge to instruct the jury that voluntary manslaughter is also a verdict option. Jock is convicted of murder. On appeal, Mira argues that Sol's murder conviction should be

reversed and that the verdict should be reduced to voluntary manslaughter.

Which of the following facts will help the defense counsel to create arguments to demonstrate the sufficiency of evidence of the elements of voluntary manslaughter?

I. Sol was enraged at the time of the killing.

II. Todd hit Sol on the nose with the towel.

III. Sol suffered from his nose obsession, and this obsession is evidence of a mental abnormality.

IV. Very little time elapsed between the time that Todd hit Sol on the nose and the time that Sol stabbed Todd.

A. I, II, III, IV

B. I, II, IV

C. I, II, III

D. I, III, IV

39. One evening in Salt Lake City, Sol and Todd were working together as dishwashers in the kitchen of a restaurant called The Rib House, while their co-workers prepared the meals for the customers. Sol and Todd got along well together, but on this particular night, Todd was joking around and poking fun at Sol for about twenty minutes. Sol did not respond to Todd's joking, and Sol appeared to be in a bad mood. So Todd told Sol to "lighten up" and started snapping a wet dishtowel on Sol's forearm, hitting him with it once or twice without causing anything more than a quick sting. Then Todd

snapped the wet dishtowel so that it hit Sol hard on his nose. Sol became enraged, took off his dishwashing gloves and started toward Todd. Todd, still teasing, said, "Ooo, he's taking his gloves off." Then Sol took a knife from his pocket and stabbed Todd in the neck. As Todd fell to the floor, Sol also stabbed Todd in the arm. Todd looked up and cried, "Man, I was just kidding around." Sol responded: "Well, man, you should have never hit me in my nose." Then Sol ran to the front of the restaurant and asked the manager to call an ambulance for Todd. When the police arrived at the restaurant, Todd was dead from his neck wound because of blood loss. Sol told the police that he usually carried his lock blade knife for skinning rabbits and squirrels during hunting season. It happened to be hunting season at this time. Before his trial, Sol's defense counsel, Mira, discovers that Sol suffers from an obsession with his nose. Sol's father explains to Mira that when Sol was 17 years old, he started asking his parents for assurances that his nose was not too big. During the following ten years, Sol's obsession was expressed through his constant glances in the mirror to examine his nose in profile views, dozens of times a day. Assume that the prosecutor charges Sol with murder and that the mens rea for this crime is defined as purposely or knowingly causing death. Sol's defense counsel, Mira, persuades the trial judge to instruct the jury that extreme emotional disturbance manslaughter is also a verdict option. Jock is convicted of murder. On appeal, Mira argues that Sol's murder conviction should be reversed and that the verdict should be reduced to extreme emotional disturbance manslaughter.

Which of the following facts will help the defense counsel to create arguments to demonstrate the sufficiency of evidence that supports the elements of extreme emotional disturbance manslaughter?

I. Sol was enraged at the time of the killing.

II. Todd hit Sol on the nose with the towel.

III. Sol suffered from his nose obsession, and this obsession is evidence of a mental abnormality.

IV. Very little time elapsed between the time that Todd hit Sol on the nose and the time that Sol stabbed Todd.

A. I, II, III, IV

B. I, III

C. I, II, IV

D. I, II, III

40. Two boys, Larry (age 10) and Max, (age 8) were waiting at a school bus stop at 8:00 a.m. in Portland, Oregon, when two Rottweiler dogs in a fenced enclosure around Donna's house across the street caught sight of the boys. The dogs started digging at one of the fence posts of the enclosure. Soon enough, the dogs had loosened the fence post, and then they were able to squeeze through the gate in the enclosure by pushing on the loose post. When the dogs ran toward the boys, Larry climbed a tree and escaped. But Max was attacked and killed by the dogs. When the school bus arrived, the driver radioed for the police. When the police arrived at Donna's house to ask her about her actions that morning, she told them that she let the dogs into the yard at 6:30 a.m. and then took a sleeping pill. When the police told her that the dogs had attacked and killed a neighborhood boy, Donna replied, "They must have killed either Larry or Max, because those boys are always teasing my dogs whenever they come around my property." Donna was charged with reckless murder under a modern statute.

At Donna's trial, the evidence showed that her neighbors had frequently complained to the police about her dogs getting out of the fenced enclosure and running loose in the neighborhood. In response to the frequent escapes of the dogs, Donna put a padlock on the gate to the fenced enclosure, the day before the dogs escaped and killed Max. The evidence also showed that the neighbors corroborated Donna's statement to the police that Larry and Max had teased the dogs on several occasions, by throwing rocks at them when the dogs were in the fenced enclosure. A dog trainer testified that she had been hired to train Donna's dogs and that she had accompanied Donna to sessions of a Schutzhund club in Portland. Schutzhund is a dog sport developed in Germany that involves tracking, obedience, retrieving and protection work. In protection work the dog attacks an "agitator" who wears a protective suit and padded sleeve. The dog is taught to bite the sleeve and hold on, even while being hit with a stick, until the handler gives the dog a command to release the sleeve. The president of the club testified that Donna had been rejected for membership after several months of attendance because her handling of her dogs was poor, because she focused exclusively on protection work and ignored obedience and tracking, and because she ignored the club's requirements that Shutzhund-trained dogs, especially Rottweilers, should be socialized to many different people and surroundings in order to decrease the risk that the dogs will act out aggressively beyond the control of their handler. The trial judge instructs the jury as to the elements of reckless murder, and Donna's defense counsel, Sam, persuades the trial judge to instruct the jury that reckless manslaughter is also a verdict option. Assume that Donna is convicted of reckless murder, and that on appeal, Sam, argues that there is insufficient evidence of the elements of reckless murder to affirm Donna's conviction, and that her conviction should be reduced to reckless manslaughter.

Which of the following facts will help the defense

counsel to create arguments to demonstrate the insufficiency of the evidence of the elements of reckless murder?

    I. Donna knew that Max and Larry had teased the dogs.

    II. Donna put a padlock on the gate to the fenced enclosure.

    III. Donna hired a dog trainer and attended dog training sessions at the club.

    IV. Donna's dogs had not bothered anyone in the past when they were running loose in the neighborhood.

A. II, IV

B. I, II, III

C. II, III, IV

D. I, II, III, IV

41. Two boys, Larry (age 10) and Max, (age 13) were waiting at a school bus stop at 8:00 a.m. in Portland, Oregon, when two Rottweiler dogs in a fenced enclosure around Donna's house across the street caught sight of the boys. The dogs started digging at one of the fence posts of the enclosure. Soon enough, the dogs had loosened the fence post, and then they were able to squeeze through the gate in the enclosure by pushing on the loose post. When the dogs ran toward the boys, Larry climbed a tree and escaped. But Max was attacked and killed by the dogs. When the school bus arrived, the driver radioed for the police. When the police arrived at

Donna's house to ask her about her actions that morning, she told them that she let the dogs into the yard at 6:30 a.m. and then took a sleeping pill. When the police told her that the dogs had attacked and killed a neighborhood boy, Donna replied, "They must have killed either Larry or Max, because those boys are always teasing my dogs whenever they come around my property." Donna was charged with reckless murder under a modern statute. At Donna's trial, the evidence showed that her neighbors had frequently complained to the police about her dogs getting out of the fenced enclosure and running loose in the neighborhood. In response to the frequent escapes of the dogs, Donna put a padlock on the gate to the fenced enclosure, the day before the dogs escaped and killed Max. The evidence also showed that the neighbors corroborated Donna's statement to the police that Larry and Max had teased the dogs on several occasions, by throwing rocks at them when the dogs were in the fenced enclosure. A dog trainer testified that she had been hired to train Donna's dogs and that she had accompanied Donna to sessions of a Schutzhund club in Portland. Schutzhund is a dog sport developed in Germany that involves tracking, obedience, retrieving and protection work. In protection work the dog attacks an "agitator" who wears a protective suit and padded sleeve. The dog is taught to bite the sleeve and hold on, even while being hit with a stick, until the handler gives the dog a command to release the sleeve. The president of the club testified that Donna had been rejected for membership after several months of attendance because her handling of her dogs was poor, because she focused exclusively on protection work and ignored obedience and tracking, and because she ignored the club's requirements that Shutzhund-trained dogs, especially Rottweilers, should be socialized to many different people and surroundings in order to decrease the risk that the dogs will act out aggressively beyond the control of their handler. The trial judge instructs the jury as to the elements of reckless murder, and Donna's defense counsel, Sam, persuades the trial judge to instruct the jury that reckless manslaughter is also a verdict option. Assume that Donna is convicted of reckless murder, and that on appeal, Sam, argues that there is insufficient evidence of the elements of reckless murder to affirm Donna's conviction, and that her conviction should be reduced to reckless manslaughter.

Which of the following facts will help the prosecutor to create arguments to demonstrate the sufficiency of the evidence to support the elements of reckless murder?

   I. Donna was rejected for membership in the Schutzhund club.

   II. Donna told the police that she expected that the dogs had killed either Larry or Max because they had teased the dogs.

   III. Donna took a sleeping pill after letting the dogs out on the morning that Max was killed.

   IV. The dogs were Rottweilers.

A. I, III, IV

B. I, II, III, IV

C. I, II, IV

D. I, II, III

42. Joe is a single father with a six-year-old son named Gabe and they live in the mountains of Arizona. One day Gabe becomes ill and Joe takes the boy to the emergency room. The emergency room doctors bring in a specialist named Dr. Krug, but none of the doctors can figure out why Gabe is ill. In fact, Gabe has an advanced case of hantavirus with very unusual symptoms. Gabe is

transferred to the intensive care unit of the hospital, and as the nurses tend to his needs, Joe keeps watch. Joe stays by his son's bedside all night, as the boy grows weaker by the hour and medications do not seem to help. Joe is frustrated by the fact that Dr. Krug seems to be ignoring Gabe and never comes to his room. When Dr. Krug briefly makes one appearance at Gabe's door, Joe asks the doctor what is wrong with Gabe, and Dr. Krug brusquely turns on his heel and leaves. When a nurse enters the room immediately afterwards, Joe mutters to her, "If that doctor doesn't start doing his job, I'm gonna kill the guy." As the next night passes, Joe notices that Gabe's condition continues to deteriorate. Finally, just after sunrise, Gabe starts to tremble and shake, says, "Goodbye, Papa," and dies in his father's arms. At this point, the nurses arrive and send Joe away to the cafeteria to compose himself, while they put in a call for Dr. Krug to come and pronounce Gabe dead. However, Joe lingers in the ICU nursing station, and when he sees Dr. Krug coming down the hall to Gabe's room, Joe accosts him and accuses him of ignoring Gabe. Joe demands to know why Dr. Krug could not prevent Gabe's death. Dr. Krug's facial muscles start to twitch, and Joe thinks that Dr. Krug is laughing. Joe screams at Dr. Krug, picks up a nearby heavy metal chair, holds it high in the air, and then crashes it down on top of Dr. Krug's head. Dr. Krug dies of head injuries as a result of this blow. Assume that the prosecutor charges Joe with first degree murder and that the mens rea for this crime is defined as an intentional killing with deliberation and premeditation. The trial judge instructs the jury that the other verdict option is second degree murder, which is an intentional killing with no deliberation and premeditation. Joe is convicted of first degree murder. On appeal, his defense counsel Lisa argues that the conviction should be reversed, and that the verdict should be reduced to second degree murder.

Which of the following facts will help the prosecutor to create arguments to demonstrate the sufficiency of the evidence to support the elements of first degree murder?

    I. Joe muttered a threat to kill Dr. Krug to one of the nurses.

    II. Joe lingered in the nursing station and waited for Dr. Krug to appear.

    III. Joe killed Dr. Krug by hitting him in the head with the chair.

    IV. Joe killed Dr. Krug some hours after Dr. Krug appeared in Gabe's door and then brusquely walked away.

A. I, II, III, IV

B. I, III, IV

C. II, III, IV

D. I, II, IV

43.   Joe is a single father with a six-year-old son named Gabe and they live in the mountains of Arizona. One day Gabe becomes ill and Joe takes the boy to the emergency room. The emergency room doctors bring in a specialist named Dr. Krug, but none of the doctors can figure out why Gabe is ill. In fact, Gabe has an advanced case of hantavirus with very unusual symptoms. Gabe is transferred to the intensive care unit of the hospital, and as the nurses tend to his needs, Joe keeps watch. Joe stays by his son's bedside all night, as the boy grows weaker by the hour and medications do not seem to help. Joe is frustrated by the fact that Dr. Krug seems to be ignoring Gabe and never comes to his room. When Dr. Krug briefly makes one appearance at Gabe's door, Joe

asks the doctor what is wrong with Gabe, and Dr. Krug brusquely turns on his heel and leaves. When a nurse enters the room immediately afterwards, Joe mutters to her, "If that doctor doesn't start doing his job, I'm gonna kill the guy." As the next night passes, Joe notices that Gabe's condition continues to deteriorate. Finally, just after sunrise, Gabe starts to tremble and shake, says, "Goodbye, Papa," and dies in his father's arms. At this point, the nurses arrive and send Joe away to the cafeteria to compose himself, while they put in a call for Dr. Krug to come and pronounce Gabe dead. However, Joe lingers in the ICU nursing station, and when he sees Dr. Krug coming down the hall to Gabe's room, Joe accosts him and accuses him of ignoring Gabe. Joe demands to know why Dr. Krug could not prevent Gabe's death. Dr. Krug's facial muscles start to twitch, and Joe thinks that Dr. Krug is laughing. Joe screams at Dr. Krug, picks up a nearby heavy metal chair, holds it high in the air, and then crashes it down on top of Dr. Krug's head. Dr. Krug dies of head injuries as a result of this blow. Assume that the prosecutor charges Joe with first degree murder and that the mens rea for this crime is defined as an intentional killing with deliberation and premeditation. The trial judge instructs the jury that the other verdict option is second degree murder, which is an intentional killing with no deliberation and premeditation. Joe is convicted of first degree murder. On appeal, his defense counsel Lisa argues that the conviction should be reversed, and that the verdict should be reduced to second degree murder.

Which of the following facts will help the defense counsel to create arguments to demonstrate the insufficiency of the evidence pf the elements of first degree murder?

> I. Joe picked up the chair when he saw what he thought was Dr. Krug's facial expression of laughter.

II. Joe was angry because he believed that Dr. Krug had been ignoring Gabe.

III. When Gabe died, Joe had been up for at least 48 hours without sleep.

IV. When Joe accosted Dr. Krug after Gabe's death, he demanded to know why Dr. Krug could not prevent Gabe's death.

A. I, II, III

B. I, III, IV

C. II, IV

D. I, IV

44. Joe is a single father with a six-year-old son named Gabe and they live in the mountains of Arizona. One day Gabe becomes ill and Joe takes the boy to the emergency room. The emergency room doctors bring in a specialist named Dr. Krug, but none of the doctors can figure out why Gabe is ill. In fact, Gabe has an advanced case of hantavirus with very unusual symptoms. Gabe is transferred to the intensive care unit of the hospital, and as the nurses tend to his needs, Joe keeps watch. Joe stays by his son's bedside all night, as the boy grows weaker by the hour and medications do not seem to help. Joe is frustrated by the fact that Dr. Krug seems to be ignoring Gabe and never comes to his room. When Dr. Krug briefly makes one appearance at Gabe's door, Joe asks the doctor what is wrong with Gabe, and Dr. Krug brusquely turns on his heel and leaves. When a nurse enters the room immediately afterwards, Joe mutters to her, "If that doctor doesn't start doing his job, I'm gonna kill the guy." As the next night passes, Joe notices that

Gabe's condition continues to deteriorate. Finally, just after sunrise, Gabe starts to tremble and shake, says, "Goodbye, Papa," and dies in his father's arms. At this point, the nurses arrive and send Joe away to the cafeteria to compose himself, while they put in a call for Dr. Krug to come and pronounce Gabe dead. However, Joe lingers in the ICU nursing station, and when he sees Dr. Krug coming down the hall to Gabe's room, Joe accosts him and accuses him of ignoring Gabe. Joe demands to know why Dr. Krug could not prevent Gabe's death. Dr. Krug's facial muscles start to twitch, and Joe thinks that Dr. Krug is laughing. Joe screams at Dr. Krug, picks up a nearby heavy metal chair, holds it high in the air, and then crashes it down on top of Dr. Krug's head. Dr. Krug dies of head injuries as a result of this blow. Assume that the prosecutor charges Joe with murder and that the mens rea for this crime is defined as purposely or knowingly causing death. Joe's defense counsel, Lisa, persuades the trial judge to instruct the jury that extreme emotional disturbance manslaughter is also a verdict option. Jock is convicted of murder. On appeal, Lisa argues that Joe's murder conviction should be reversed and that the verdict should be reduced to extreme emotional disturbance manslaughter.

Which of the following facts will help the defense counsel to create arguments to demonstrate the sufficiency of evidence that supports a conviction for extreme emotional disturbance manslaughter?

  I. Joe was angry and grieving over the death of his son Gabe.

  II. The killing of Dr. Krug happened very soon after the Gabe's death.

  III. Joe thought Dr. Krug ignored Gabe and laughed at Joe's loss.

IV. When Gabe died, Joe had been up for at least 48 hours without sleep.

A. I, III, IV

B. I, III

C. I, II, III, IV

D. I, II, III

45. Joe is a single father with a six-year-old son named Gabe and they live in the mountains of Arizona. One day Gabe becomes ill and Joe takes the boy to the emergency room. The emergency room doctors bring in a specialist named Dr. Krug, but none of the doctors can figure out why Gabe is ill. In fact, Gabe has an advanced case of hantavirus with very unusual symptoms. Gabe is transferred to the intensive care unit of the hospital, and as the nurses tend to his needs, Joe keeps watch. Joe stays by his son's bedside all night, as the boy grows weaker by the hour and medications do not seem to help. Joe is frustrated by the fact that Dr. Krug seems to be ignoring Gabe and never comes to his room. When Dr. Krug briefly makes one appearance at Gabe's door, Joe asks the doctor what is wrong with Gabe, and Dr. Krug brusquely turns on his heel and leaves. When a nurse enters the room immediately afterwards, Joe mutters to her, "If that doctor doesn't start doing his job, I'm gonna kill the guy." As the next night passes, Joe notices that Gabe's condition continues to deteriorate. Finally, just after sunrise, Gabe starts to tremble and shake, says, "Goodbye, Papa," and dies in his father's arms. At this point, the nurses arrive and send Joe away to the cafeteria to compose himself, while they put in a call for Dr. Krug to come and pronounce Gabe dead. However, Joe lingers in the ICU nursing station, and when he sees

Dr. Krug coming down the hall to Gabe's room, Joe accosts him and accuses him of ignoring Gabe. Joe demands to know why Dr. Krug could not prevent Gabe's death. Dr. Krug's facial muscles start to twitch, and Joe thinks that Dr. Krug is laughing. Joe screams at Dr. Krug, picks up a nearby heavy metal chair, holds it high in the air, and then crashes it down on top of Dr. Krug's head. Dr. Krug dies of head injuries as a result of this blow. Assume that the prosecutor charges Joe with murder and that the mens rea for this crime is defined as purposely or knowingly causing death. Joe's defense counsel, Lisa, persuades the trial judge to instruct the jury that voluntary manslaughter is also a verdict option. Jock is convicted of murder. On appeal, Lisa argues that Joe's murder conviction should be reversed and that the verdict should be reduced to voluntary manslaughter.

Which of the following facts will help the prosecutor to create arguments to persuade the appellate court to affirm the murder conviction, by demonstrating the insufficiency of evidence to supports a voluntary manslaughter verdict?

    I. Dr. Krug never spoke to Joe and only appeared to laugh.

    II. The nurse heard Joe threaten Dr. Krug after the doctor brusquely walked away from him.

    III. Some time elapsed between the time Dr. Krug brusquely walked away from Joe and the time of Gabe's death.

    IV. Joe lingered in the nursing station instead of going to the cafeteria.

    A. II, III

    B. I, II, III

C. I, II, III, IV

D. II, III, IV

46. On the last day of ski season in New Hampshire, Hal was working as a ski lift operator at a resort in the White Mountains. After the lifts closed, he skied down toward the base of the mountain and found that the slopes were not crowded. As Hal was skiing down the lower part of the slopes, he was moving very fast. His ski tips were in the air, his weight was back on his skis, and his arms were out to the side. When a knoll appeared in front of him, Hal flew off the knoll into the air. He saw people below him, but he was unable to stop or slow down as he landed and kept skiing down the slope, over the moguls (bumps) in the trail. Then Hal collided with Lee, who had been skiing on the slope below Hal. This collision caused head injuries to Lee and killed her immediately. Hal's blood alcohol level was .009, which is less than the limit for driving while intoxicated. Hal was charged with reckless manslaughter under a modern statute. At trial the prosecutor presented evidence that Hal was a former ski racer trained in skier safety. According to witnesses, Hal was skiing straight down a steep and bumpy slope and appeared to be out of control for some distance and some period of time. At the time of the collision, Hal was traveling at such a high speed that the force of the impact fractured the thickest part of the Lee's skull. Hal was not turning from side-to-side while traversing the slope; instead, he was skiing straight down the trail on the mountain. He was bounding off the bumps as he went. A deputy sheriff testified that during the past decade two other collisions had resulted in the deaths of skiers on the same slope. Hal testified that he did not intend to ski fast down the mountain, and that he was trying to slow down but wasn't able to stop because of the bumps. The jury convicted Hal of reckless manslaughter and on appeal, Hal's defense counsel,

Marsha, argues that that there was insufficient evidence for conviction and that Hal should have been acquitted.

Which of the following facts will help the prosecutor to create arguments to persuade the appellate court to affirm the conviction, by demonstrating that there is sufficient evidence of the elements of reckless manslaughter?

   I. Two other collisions had caused deaths during the prior decade.

   II. Hal had been drinking.

   III. Hal was not turning from side to side while skiing.

   IV. Hal was a former ski racer trained in skier safety.

A. I, II, III

B. II, III, IV

C. I, II, III, IV

D. II, III

47. On the last day of ski season in New Hampshire, Hal was working as a ski lift operator at a resort in the White Mountains. After the lifts closed, he skied down toward the base of the mountain and found that the slopes were not crowded. As Hal was skiing down the lower part of the slopes, he was skiing very fast. His ski tips were in the air, his weight was back on his skis, and his arms were out to the side. When a knoll appeared in front of him, Hal flew off the knoll into the air. He saw people below him, but he was unable to stop or slow

down as he landed and kept skiing down the slope, over the moguls (bumps) in the trail. Then Hal collided with Lee, who had been skiing on the slope below Hal. This collision caused head injuries to Lee and killed her immediately. Hal's blood alcohol level was .009, which is less than the limit for driving while intoxicated. Hal was charged with reckless manslaughter under a modern statute. At trial the prosecutor presented evidence that Hal was a former ski racer trained in skier safety. According to witnesses, Hal was skiing straight down a steep and bumpy slope and appeared to be out of control for some distance and some period of time. At the time of the collision, Hal was traveling at such a high speed that the force of the impact fractured the thickest part of the Lee's skull. Hal was not turning from side-to-side while traversing the slope; instead, he was skiing straight down the trail on the mountain. He was bounding off the bumps as he went. A deputy sheriff testified that during the past decade two other collisions had resulted in the deaths of skiers on the same slope. Hal testified that he did not intend to ski fast down the mountain, and that he was trying to slow down but wasn't able to stop because of the bumps. The jury convicted Hal of reckless manslaughter and on appeal, Hal's defense counsel, Marsha, argues that that there was insufficient evidence for conviction and that Hal should have been acquitted.

Which of the following facts will help the defense counsel to create arguments to persuade the appellate court to reverse the reckless manslaughter conviction because there is insufficient evidence of the elements of the crime?

    I. Hal tried to slow down but could not stop because of the bumps.

    II. Hal's blood alcohol level was less than the limit for driving while intoxicated.

III. Hal was skiing with his ski tips in the air and his weight on the back of his skis.

IV. The slopes were not crowded when Hal skied toward the base of the mountain.

A. I, IV

B. I, III, IV

C. I, II, IV

D. I, II, III, IV

48. Al, Bob, and Cat are three teenagers who agreed to burglarize a house in their neighborhood. They waited until the family who lived in the house left for an evening outing. The teenagers did not realize that an old friend of the family, Vicky, had arrived for a visit, and that she was staying in an upstairs guest bedroom in the house. Al had given Bob a knife a few days before the burglary, but neither Al nor Cat knew that Bob planned to bring the knife with him during the crime. After the three teenagers entered the house, Cat and Al went through the rooms on the first floor, selecting objects to steal. Bob went upstairs and encountered Vicky, who had been awakened from a nap by Bob making noise. Bob stabbed and killed Vicky, and Cat and Al ran upstairs and were shocked to see Vicky's body. Then the three teenagers fled the house and were soon apprehended. The prosecutor charged all three teenagers with felony murder, and the murder statute provides that felony murder liability is established when a death occurs during the course of the felony of burglary. All three defendants are convicted of felony murder. On appeal, Cat's lawyer, Mike, argues that under felony murder doctrine, Cat should not have been convicted.

What facts will the defense counsel use to create a policy argument that the scope of felony murder liability should be limited so that Cat will not be liable?

  I. Cat was not armed with a deadly weapon.

  II. Cat did not know that Bob was armed with the knife.

  III. Cat did not know that Bob planned to use the knife against any surprise eyewitness on the scene of the burglary.

  IV. Cat did not participate in the conduct of stabbing and killing Vicky.

A. I, III, IV

B. I, II, IV

C. II, III, IV

D. I, II, III, IV

49. Al, Bob, Cat and Dan are four teenagers who agreed to burglarize a house in their neighborhood. They waited until the family who lived in the house left for an evening outing. The teenagers did not realize that an old friend of the family, Vicky, had arrived for a visit, and that she was staying in an upstairs guest bedroom in the house. Before the family left the house, the parents showed Vicky the location of a gun in the bureau drawer of the guest bedroom, and encouraged her to use it for her protection if necessary. Each of the four teenagers was armed with a gun at the scene of the burglary. After the four teenagers entered the house, Dan, Cat and Al went through the rooms on the first floor, selecting objects to

steal. Bob went upstairs and encountered Vicky, who had been awakened from a nap by Bob making noise. Vicky grabbed the gun from the bureau and ran downstairs, heading for the front door. Bob ran downstairs after her, firing his gun. Cat heard the shot and ran to the stairs, just as Bob fired again at Vicky and missed. Bob's bullet hit Cat and killed her. Just before Vicky ran out the front door, she turned to fire her gun at Al. A bullet from Vicky's gun hit and killed Al. Then Vicky made good her escape. Dan and Bob fled the house and were soon apprehended. The prosecutor charged both Dan and Bob with two counts of felony murder for the deaths of Cat and Al. The murder statute provides that felony murder liability is established when a death occurs during the course of the felony of burglary. Dan and Bob are convicted of both counts of felony murder. On appeal, the defense counsel for each defendant argues that felony murder liability is inappropriate, and that each conviction should be reversed.

How should the appellate court resolve the appeals of Dan and Bob, in order to conform to the norms of felony murder jurisprudence?

    I. Affirm the conviction of both for the death of Al.

    II. Reverse the conviction of both for the death of Cat.

    III. Reverse the conviction of both for death of Al.

    IV. Affirm the conviction of both for the death of Cat.

    A. III, IV

    B. I, II

    C. I, IV

D. II, III

50. Bob, Cat and Dan are three teenagers who agreed to burglarize a house in their neighborhood. They waited until the family who lived in the house left for an evening outing. The teenagers did not realize that an old friend of the family, Vicky, had arrived for a visit, and that she was staying in an upstairs guest bedroom in the house. Each of the three teenagers was armed with a gun at the scene of the burglary. After the teenagers entered the house, Dan and Cat went through the rooms on the first floor, selecting objects to steal. Bob went upstairs and encountered Vicky, who had been awakened from a nap by Bob making noise. Vicky ran downstairs, heading for the front door. Bob ran downstairs after her, firing his gun, but then he tripped and fell on the stairs and was knocked unconscious. Vicky ran out the front door and into the arms of Dan, who had dashed out of the house as soon as he heard Bob firing his gun on the stairs. Cat had also run out of the house with Dan. As soon as Dan grabbed Vicky, police officer Eve dashed across the front lawn toward him; Eve had been alerted to the burglary because a neighbor had seen the teenagers enter the house, and had called the police. When Dan saw Eve, he put Vicky in front of his own body as he moved toward Cat's escape vehicle across the street. Dan kept pointing his own gun at officer Eve, as Eve ran toward Dan in an attempt to rescue Vicky. Eve attempted to aim her gun at Dan and fired. But Eve's aim was inaccurate and her bullet hit and killed Vicky. This caused Dan to fall down and drop his gun. Eve turned to see Cat racing toward her escape vehicle, and Eve fired a warning shot. Cat shot back at Eve and missed; Even then shot and killed Cat. Dan was immediately apprehended and Bob was discovered in the house and arrested. The prosecutor charged both Dan and Bob with two counts of felony murder for the deaths of Vicky and Cat. The murder statute provides that felony murder liability is established

when a death occurs during the course of the felony of burglary. Dan and Bob are convicted of both counts of felony murder. On appeal, the defense counsel for each defendant argues that felony murder liability is inappropriate, and that both convictions should be reversed for each defendant.

How should the appellate court resolve the appeals of Dan and Bob, in order to conform to the norms of felony murder jurisprudence?

    I. Reverse the conviction of both for the death of Vicky.

    II. Affirm the conviction of both for the death of Vicky.

    III. Reverse the conviction of both for the death of Cat.

    IV. Affirm the conviction of both for the death of Cat.

A. I, III

B. II, III

C. II, IV

D. I, IV

51. Gavin is prosecuted under an old statute that prohibits the crime of rape. Which of the following elements are likely to be included in this common law crime?

    V. Genital penetration through sexual intercourse.

VI. An act of sexual intercourse by a man with a woman who is not his wife.

VII. The use of force or threat of force by the man.

VIII. The woman's resistance to the acts of the man.

A. I, III, IV

B. I, II, IV

C. I, II, III, IV

D. I, II, III

52. Len is prosecuted under a modern statute that prohibits the crime of sexual assault. Which of the following elements are commonly included in this modern crime?

I. Anal or oral penetration, or penetration by fingers or objects.

II. The lack of the consent of the victim.

III. The use of force, threat of force, or fear.

IV. A gender neutral definition of the prohibited conduct.

A. I, III, IV

B. I, III

C. II, III, IV

D. I, II, III, IV

53. Mel is prosecuted under a modern statute that prohibits the crime of sexual assault. At trial, Mel's defense counsel, Celia, is prohibited from cross-examining the victim on certain subjects because of a "rape shield" provision in the evidence code. Which of the following types of evidence are likely to be excluded under the prohibitions of a rape shield statute?

   I. Prior sexual intercourse of the victim with the defendant.

   II. Prior sexual intercourse of the victim with persons other than the defendant.

   III. The prior sexual reputation of the victim.

   IV. Prior sexual activity of the victim with persons other than the defendant.

   A. II, III, IV

   B. I, II, III

   C. II, III

   D. II, IV

54. Mel is prosecuted under a modern statute that prohibits the crime of sexual assault. At trial, Mel's defense counsel, Celia, is prohibited from cross-examining the victim on certain subjects because of a "rape shield" provision in the evidence code. Which of the following subjects are likely to be treated as an exception to the rape shield ban, either as provided in a statute or

in case law doctrine interpreting a statute, so as to allow Mel's defense counsel to ask cross-examine the victim on particular subjects?

    I. Prior sexual intercourse of the victim with the defendant.

    II. Prior sexual intercourse of the victim with persons other than the defendant to explain the source of semen, injury or disease.

    III. Prior sexual intercourse of the victim with persons other than the defendant to establish bias, motive, or a history of false claims.

    IV. A distinctive pattern of sexual behavior by the victim with persons other than the defendant, which pattern so closely resembles defendant's version of the encounter that it tends to prove the victim consented.

A. I, II, III

B. I, II, III, IV

C. I, II, IV

D. I, III, IV

55. If Max were prosecuted under an old common law rape statute, what requirements would be likely to have been imposed on the prosecutor?

    I. The requirement that the victim must be chaste.

    II. The requirement of corroboration of the testimony of the rape victim.

III. The requirement of giving the jury the Lord Hale instruction.

IV. Proof of the victim resisting the acts of the defendant to the utmost.

A. I, II, III

B. I, III, IV

C. II, III, IV

D. I, II, IV

56. If Andy were prosecuted under an old common law rape statute, what proof of mens rea would be likely to be required?

I. No proof of mens rea was required.

II. General intent.

III. The intent to have sexual intercourse without the consent of the victim.

IV. A reasonable belief in consent would be a defense.

A. I

B. II

C. III

D. IV

57. Nat is a doctor who was charged with the crime of sexual assault under a modern statute that defines the crime as: "an act of sexual intercourse that is accomplished against a person's will by means of force, violence, or fear of immediate and unlawful bodily injury on the person of another." Two other co-defendants, also doctors, were convicted of rape at the same trial. Nat hosted an evening holiday party at his house in Plainville, Virginia, for all the doctors and nurses who worked on the second floor of the city hospital. Vicki is a nurse at the hospital and she was invited to the party, even though she knew Nat and his two co-defendants only slightly. As the party was ending, Nat invited Vicki to accompany him and the two co-defendants to his beach house in Virginia Beach after the party, about an hour away from Plainville by car. Vicki said, "No, thanks," but she stayed at the party. Soon thereafter, the last few guests started to leave around midnight. As Vicki was walking out the door, Nat announced, "We're going to Virginia Beach," picked Vicki up, and carried her out to his car, followed by the two co-defendant doctors. Vicki protested, saying, "Put me down, guys," and the other partygoers heard this comment but did nothing. Vicki later testified that she did not physically resist because she thought the three men were "just horsing around."

En route to Virginia Beach, Vicki engaged in superficial conversation with Nat and the two other doctors. Once they arrived at the beach house, Nat gave the group a tour of his house. When they got to the bedroom on the second floor, all three men took off their clothes, and Vicki later testified that she became frightened at this point. She asked the men to leave her alone. As Nat walked toward her, she backed away, and then fell backwards down on to the bed because she wasn't looking where she was going. Nat lifted up Vicki's skirt, pulled down her underwear, and had sexual intercourse with her. The other two doctors watched while Nat did this, and then each of them had sexual intercourse with Vicki in the same manner. Vicki later testified that she did not physically resist any of the men at this point because she felt humiliated and disgusted. Finally, Nat announced that he was on call at the hospital and needed to return to Plainville. Vicki and the men got into Nat's car and Vicki was driven to where she had parked her car outside Nat's house in Plainville, and dropped off. She drove herself to her apartment and then called the police. The police arrested Nat for rape and he was convicted. On appeal, Nat's lawyer, Jana, argues that the evidence is insufficient to affirm the conviction.

What are the strongest arguments that the prosecutor may use to persuade the appellate court to affirm the conviction because the evidence is sufficient to prove the elements of the crime?

   I. Vicki was reasonably frightened by the three naked men, who had the physical power to overpower her and cause her bodily injury if she resisted.

   II. The prosecution need not prove that Vicki's fear was reasonable, only that Vicki was afraid when she was in the bedroom with Nat and the two men.

   III. Vicki was afraid of bodily injury because Nat had ignored her earlier protest at being physically forced to accompany them, and ignored her earlier refusal to go to the beach house.

   IV. Resistance is not required by the statute and its absence may be inferred to be a legislative policy choice to abandon this common law requirement.

   A. I, II, III

   B. I, II, III, IV

C. I, II, IV

D. I, III, IV

58. Nat is a doctor who was charged with the crime of sexual assault under a modern statute that defines the crime as: "an act of sexual intercourse that is accomplished against a person's will by means of force, violence, or fear of immediate and unlawful bodily injury on the person of another." Two other co-defendants, also doctors, were also convicted of rape. Nat hosted an evening holiday party at his house in Plainville, Virginia, for all the doctors and nurses who worked on the second floor of the city hospital. Vicki is a nurse at the hospital, and she was invited to the party, even though she knew Nat and his two co-defendants only slightly. As the party was ending, Nat invited Vicki to accompany him and the two co-defendants to his beach house in Virginia Beach after the party, about an hour away from Plainville by car. Vicki said, "No, thanks," but she stayed at the party. Soon thereafter, the last few guests started to leave around midnight. As Vicki was walking out the door, Nat announced, "We're going to Virginia Beach," picked Vicki up, and carried her out to his car, followed by the two co-defendant doctors. Vicki protested, saying, "Put me down, guys," and the other partygoers heard this comment but did nothing. Vicki later testified that she did not physically resist because she thought the three men were "just horsing around."

En route to Virginia Beach, Vicki engaged in superficial conversation with Nat and the two other doctors. Once they arrived at the beach house, Nat gave the group a tour of his house. When they got to the bedroom on the second floor, all three men took off their clothes, and Vicki later testified that she became frightened at this point. She asked the men to leave her alone. As Nat walked toward her, she backed away, and then fell backwards down on to the bed because she wasn't looking where she was going. Nat lifted up Vicki's skirt, pulled down her underwear, and had sexual intercourse with her. The other two doctors watched while Nat did this, and then each of them had sexual intercourse with Vicki in the same manner. Vicki later testified that she did not physically resist any of the men at this point because she felt humiliated and disgusted. Finally, Nat announced that he was on call at the hospital and needed to return to Plainville. Vicki and the men got into Nat's car and Vicki was driven to where she had parked her car outside Nat's house in Plainville, and dropped off. She drove herself to her apartment and then called the police. The police arrested Nat for rape and he was convicted. On appeal, Nat's lawyer, Jana, argues that the evidence is insufficient to affirm the conviction.

What are the strongest arguments that may be used by the defense counsel to persuade the appellate court to reverse the conviction because the evidence is not sufficient to prove the elements of the crime?

I. There is insufficient proof of lack of consent because Vicki did not physically resist the actions of Nat and the other men after she fell on the bed.

II. There is insufficient proof of fear because Vicki was not threatened with bodily injury by Nat or the other men at any time.

III. There is insufficient proof of force because force should not be defined to include merely the removal of clothing or the act of penetration.

IV. There is insufficient proof of lack of consent because Vicki did not physically resist Nat when she was carried to the car.

A. I, II, IV

B. I, II, III

C. I, II, III, IV

D. II, III, IV

59. Zena and Ty are college students. They happen to meet at a fraternity party where neither one has a date. Ty invites Zena to come upstairs and talk to him in his room, as he lives in the fraternity. Zena tells him that she doesn't have time to come up because she has to get some notes from a friend to study for the big Geology final the next day. Ty tells her that he has some notes he can give her. So Zena comes up to his room to get the notes. Once they arrive in his room, Ty locks his door but Zena doesn't notice. Ty gives Zena the notes and then starts telling her about his old girlfriend Gia. Zena sits down on the bed to listen to the story -- it is the only place to sit down other than the floor. Ty tells Zena that Gia once claimed that he hit her and called the police, so that Ty ended up in jail, although he managed to get the assault charge dropped because Gia had no corroborating evidence. Ty becomes visibly angry as he tells this story, and he ends by saying, "I should have taught that girl a lesson, given the fact that she was nothing but trouble." Zena remains silent during Ty's story and does not tell him about her prior abusive relationships in college with two other men. Zena gets up to leave and Ty says, "Hey wait, why not stay and maybe we can try study Geology? And anyway, I like you." Zena says, "I really should be going." Ty looks at her and says, "You're acting scared." Zena says, "No, I'm not. I just think I should be studying." Ty blocks the door to his room and as Zena comes closer, Ty reaches out and kisses her. Zena pulls away and Ty says, "Prove to me you're not scared." Zena says nothing, and Ty keeps kissing her and then pulls her

down to the floor. Ty takes off Zena's clothes and even though Zena is unresponsive, Ty gets on top of her and has sexual intercourse with her. Afterwards, Zena goes immediately to the campus police and says that Ty raped her. She tells the police that she felt frozen with fear because she was afraid that Ty would hurt her. Ty is charged with rape under an old statute that provides: "Rape is sexual intercourse with another person by force or threat of force against the will of that person." Ty is convicted at trial and on appeal, his defense counsel, Melli, argues that the conviction should be reversed because of insufficient evidence to prove all the elements of the crime.

Which of the following facts will help the prosecutor to create arguments to demonstrate the sufficiency of the evidence to support the elements of the crime?

   I. Ty told Zena a story about being accused of physical violence by Gia.

   II. Ty locked Zena in his room.

   III. Ty noticed that Zena was acting scared.

   IV. Ty pulled Zena to the floor and took off her clothes.

   A. I, II, III

   B. I, II, III, IV

   C. I, III, IV

   D. I, IV

60. Zena and Ty are college students. They happen to meet at a fraternity party where neither one has a date.

Ty invites Zena to come upstairs and talk to him in his room, as he lives in the fraternity. Zena tells him that she doesn't have time to come up because she has to get some notes from a friend to study for the big Geology final the next day. Ty tells her that he has some notes he can give her. So Zena comes up to his room to get the notes. Once they arrive in his room, Ty locks his door but Zena doesn't notice. Ty gives Zena the notes and then starts telling her about his old girlfriend Gia. Zena sits down on the bed to listen to the story -- it is the only place to sit down other than the floor. Ty tells Zena that Gia once claimed that he hit her and called the police, so that Ty ended up in jail, although he managed to get the assault charge dropped because Gia had no corroborating evidence. Ty becomes visibly angry as he tells this story, and he ends by saying, "I should have taught that girl a lesson, given the fact that she was nothing but trouble." Zena remains silent during Ty's story and does not tell him about her prior abusive relationships in college with two other men. Zena gets up to leave and Ty says, "Hey wait, why not stay and maybe we can try study Geology? And anyway, I like you." Zena says, "I really should be going." Ty looks at her and says, "You're acting scared." Zena says, "No, I'm not. I just think I should be studying." Ty blocks the door to his room and as Zena comes closer, Ty reaches out and kisses her. Zena pulls away and Ty says, "Prove to me you're not scared." Zena says nothing, and Ty keeps kissing her and then pulls her down to the floor. Ty takes off Zena's clothes and even though Zena is unresponsive, Ty gets on top of her and has sexual intercourse with her. Afterwards, Zena goes immediately to the campus police and says that Ty raped her. She tells the police that she felt frozen with fear because she was afraid that Ty would hurt her. Ty is charged with rape under an old statute that provides: "Rape is sexual intercourse with another person by force or threat of force against the will of that person." Ty is convicted at trial and on appeal, his defense counsel, Melli, argues that the conviction should be reversed because of insufficient evidence to prove all the elements of the crime.

Which of the following facts will help the defense counsel to create arguments to demonstrate the insufficiency of the evidence to support the elements of the crime?

    I. Zena said nothing when Ty asked her to prove she was not scared.

    II. Zena sat down on Ty's bed.

    III. Zena told Ty she was not scared.

    IV. Zena was unresponsive when Ty got on top of her on the floor.

A. I, II, III, IV

B. I, III

C. I, II, IV

D. I, II, III

61. Kirk is charged with sexual assault, and during his trial, an expert witness for the prosecution testifies concerning rape trauma syndrome. Assume that the two purposes of the testimony were to assist the jury in evaluating the evidence, and to respond to the arguments by Kirk's defense counsel, Kay, that the victim's behavior after the rape was inconsistent with how a victim of rape might be expected to behave. During the expert's testimony, the defense counsel objects to various subjects covered by the expert in answering the prosecution's questions. The trial judge overrules the objections and Kirk is convicted. On appeal, Kay argues that Kirk should receive a new trial because some of the expert's

testimony was inadmissible.

What type of testimony would the appellate court be likely to view as inadmissible?

    I. Testimony that the expert's opinion is that the victim suffered from rape trauma syndrome, based on the expert's examination of the victim.

    II. Testimony about the common behavior of rape victims.

    III. Testimony that rapists commonly claim consent.

    IV. Testimony about data on the issue of false reporting of rape, to explain that virtually all rapes that are reported actually occurred.

A. I, III, IV

B. III, IV

C. I, III

D. I, II, IV

62. Zak is being prosecuted for the rape of Dee in Florida, and the crime is defined by the Florida statute as: "an act of sexual intercourse accomplished against the person's will by means of force, violence, duress, menace, or fear of immediate and unlawful bodily injury, without the consent of the person." "Penetration" is defined as "vaginal penetration when the male sex organ penetrates the female sex organ." During the course of the jury deliberations, the jury sends a note to the trial judge with the following question: "If, after penetration, the female changes her mind and says, 'stop,' and the male continues, is this still rape?" Assume that the facts of

Zak's case make the jury's question a plausible one. At this point, the trial judge asks the defense counsel and the prosecutor to meet in chambers, in order to argue their positions on the question asked by the jury.

What are the strongest arguments that the prosecutor can make to support the position that the answer to the jury's question is, "Yes"?

> I. It should not be difficult for a defendant to determine whether consent is revoked in the middle of sexual intercourse.
>
> II. The essential harm done to a rape victim is the outrage to her person and feelings, which can happen whenever a victim's revoked consent is ignored by the defendant.
>
> III. When a victim withdraws her consent during a sexual act, then this means that force is used to continue the act, and the completion of the act is without her consent.
>
> IV. Changes in modern rape law support the concept that a victim's verbal resistance counts as being equivalent to physical resistance, which provides evidence that the sex act was done with force and without consent.

A. I, II, III

B. II, III, IV

C. I, III, IV

D. I, II, IV

63. Zak is being prosecuted for the rape of Dee in

Florida, and the crime is defined by the Florida statute as: "an act of sexual intercourse accomplished against the person's will by means of force, violence, duress, menace, or fear of immediate and unlawful bodily injury, without the consent of the person." "Penetration" is defined as "vaginal penetration when the male sex organ penetrates the female sex organ." During the course of the jury deliberations, the jury sends a note to the trial judge with the following question: "If, after penetration, the female changes her mind and says, 'stop,' and the male continues, is this still rape?" Assume that the facts of Zak's case make the jury's question a plausible one. At this point, the trial judge asks the defense counsel and the prosecutor to meet in chambers, in order to argue their positions on the question asked by the jury.

What are the strongest arguments that the defense counsel can make to support the position that the answer to the jury's question is, "No"?

    I. An act of intercourse that begins consensually cannot create the same sense of outrage in a victim as an act of intercourse that begins without consent at the outset.

    II. A conviction assault or battery instead of rape would be more appropriate for a defendant who continues to have forcible intercourse after a victim revokes consent.

    III. Defining intercourse as rape when a victim's consent is withdrawn in the middle of the act will create difficult line-drawing problems for juries to determine whether and how consent was revoked.

    IV. A victim sometimes says "no" to intercourse but means "yes," and therefore when a victim says "stop" in the middle of intercourse, this may mean "keep going."

A. II, III, IV

B. I, II, IV

C. I, II, III, IV

D. I, II, III

64. Kay and Jim are strangers who meet at a birthday party that happens to be held at Jim's house in St. Paul, Minnesota. Kay is from out of town, and she finds herself stranded at 2:00 a.m. when she leaves the party and heads for another friend's apartment where she plans to stay, only to discover that this friend is not home. Kay returns to Jim's apartment as a last resort, and Jim agrees to let her sleep on the couch in the living room. Jim has three roommates who are sleeping in their own rooms, and after saying good night to Kay, Jim goes off to sleep in his room while Kay settles down on the couch. Two hours later, Jim gets up to check on Kay, and he wakes her up when he walks into the living room. He walks over to where she is lying on the couch and kisses her. She kisses back. He then gets on top of her and grinds his hips, simulating intercourse. Both of them are dressed at this point. Kay testifies later that she stopped kissing Jim, told him several times to get off, and tried to push him away. She also testifies that he pulled her pants down to her knees, and she couldn't get up because he was kneeling on her pants. Jim later testifies that he thought Kay was trying to pull down his pants so he pulled hers down. He thought she made no attempt to leave before or after he lay down on top of her. He thought she only muttered, "no," once, and he did not think that she was pushing him away, only grinding her hips along with his. Both Kay and Jim testify that Jim penetrated Kay within a minute or two of getting on top of her. After the act of sexual intercourse took place, Jim

got off Kay and she was unresponsive when he asked her how she felt. He apologized and went to his room. Kay stayed on the couch for two more hours, and then takes a cab to the airport to catch her early flight home to Chicago. When she arrives home in Chicago, she calls the local police, and Jim is arrested later for sexual assault. Assume that the Minnesota statute provides: "any person who subjects another person to sexual penetration and overcomes the victim by force or threat of force, express or implied, without the victim's consent" is guilty of sexual assault. State court authority holds that "consent" is defined as "positive cooperation in an act or attitude as an exercise of free will," and that a defendant may raise the defense of a reasonable, good faith mistake as to the lack of consent of the victim. At Jim's trial, his jury is instructed on these two points, and Jim's defense counsel, Siri, argues that Jim has produced enough evidence of the affirmative defense of reasonable, good faith mistake as to Kay's consent to merit acquittal. Jim is convicted and on appeal, Siri argues that Jim's conviction should be reversed because no reasonable jury could have rejected his mistake defense.

What are the strongest arguments that Jim's defense counsel will make to persuade the appellate court to reverse Jim's conviction because of the evidence of a reasonable, good faith mistake?

  I. It was reasonable for Jim to interpret Kay's pushing on him as grinding her hips, which suggested her positive cooperation in the later sex act.

  II. It was reasonable for Jim to interpret Kay's kissing him back as a signal that she would positively cooperate in the later sex act.

  III. Jim's apology is irrelevant to Kay's demonstration of positive cooperation in the sex act.

IV. Kay's behavior in staying in Jim's house for two hours after the sex act is probative of positive cooperation in the sex act.

A. I, II, III

B. I, II, IV

C. I, II, III, IV

D. I, III, IV

65. Kay and Jim are strangers who meet at a birthday party that happens to be held at Jim's house in St. Paul, Minnesota. Kay is from out of town, and she finds herself stranded at 2:00 a.m. when she leaves the party and heads for another friend's apartment where she plans to stay, only to discover that this friend is not home. Kay returns to Jim's apartment as a last resort, and Jim agrees to let her sleep on the couch in the living room. Jim has three roommates who are sleeping in their own rooms, and after saying good night to Kay, Jim goes off to sleep in his room while Kay settles down on the couch. Two hours later, Jim gets up to check on Kay, and he wakes her up when he walks into the living room. He walks over to where she is lying on the couch and kisses her. She kisses back. He then gets on top of her and grinds his hips, simulating intercourse. Both of them are dressed at this point. Kay testifies later that she stopped kissing Jim, told him several times to get off, and tried to push him away. She also testifies that he pulled her pants down to her knees, and she couldn't get up because he was kneeling on her pants. Jim later testifies that he thought Kay was trying to pull down his pants so he pulled hers down. He thought she made no attempt to leave before or after he lay down on top of her. He thought she only muttered, "no," once, and he did not

think that she was pushing him away, only grinding her hips along with his. Both Kay and Jim testify that Jim penetrated Kay within a minute or two of getting on top of her. After the act of sexual intercourse took place, Jim got off Kay and she was unresponsive when he asked her how she felt. He apologized and went to his room. Kay stayed on the couch for two more hours, and then takes a cab to the airport to catch her early flight home to Chicago. When she arrives home in Chicago, she calls the local police, and Jim is arrested later for sexual assault. Assume that the Minnesota statute provides: "any person who subjects another person to sexual penetration and overcomes the victim by force or threat of force, express or implied, without the victim's consent" is guilty of sexual assault. State court authority holds that "consent" is defined as "positive cooperation in an act or attitude as an exercise of free will," and that a defendant may raise the defense of a reasonable, good faith mistake as to the lack of consent of the victim. At Jim's trial, his jury instructed on these two points, and Jim's defense counsel, Siri, argues that Jim has produced enough evidence of the affirmative defense of reasonable, good faith mistake as to Kay's consent to merit acquittal. Jim is convicted and on appeal, Siri argues that Jim's conviction should be reversed because no reasonable jury could have rejected his mistake defense.

What are the strongest arguments that the prosecutor will make to persuade the appellate court to affirm Jim's conviction because the evidence showed that any mistake he made about Kay's consent was not reasonable and in good faith?

    I. Jim's mistake was not reasonable because he unreasonably imagined that Kay made no attempt to leave when he was actually holding her down by kneeling on her pants.

    II. Jim's mistake was not reasonable because he should have asked Kay what it meant when she said, "no," instead of assuming that "no" meant "yes."

III. Jim's mistake was not reasonable because he assumed that Kay's kissing back was a sign of interest in imminent sexual intercourse.

IV. Jim's mistake was not in good faith because he either ignored or did not hear Kay telling him several times to get off.

A. I, II, III, IV

B. I, III, IV

C. I, II, IV

D. II, III, IV

66. Arlen is prosecuted for murder and his defense counsel, Lara, raises his claim of self-defense at his trial. Which of the following elements are commonly included in the statutory definition of self-defense which Lara will use to seek Arlen's acquittal?

I. The defendant had a duty to retreat if could safely do so before resorting to deadly force.

II. The defendant believed that deadly force was necessary to avoid deadly harm to the defendant.

III. The defendant believed that he was in immediate danger of deadly harm from the victim.

IV. The defendant's belief(s) were reasonable.

A. I, II, IV

B. I, II, III

C. I, II, III, IV

D. II, III, IV

67. Robyn is prosecuted for murder and her defense counsel, Ivan, raises the insanity defense at his trial. Which of the following definitions of the insanity defense is commonly used in the statutory definition of insanity which Ivan will use to seek Robyn's acquittal?

   I. That the defendant suffered a defect of reason from a disease of the mind so that either she did not know the nature and quality of her act or she did not know that her act was wrong.

   II. That the defendant suffered a defect of reason from a disease of the mind so that even though she knew the difference between right and wrong, she had lost the power to choose between the right and the wrong so that her free will was destroyed by the defect of reason.

   III. That the defendant's act was the product of mental disease or mental defect.

   IV. That the defendant, as a result of mental disease or defect, lacked the substantial capacity either to appreciate the wrongfulness of her conduct or to conform her conduct to the requirements of the law.

A. I, III, IV

B. I, II, III

C. I, II, IV

D. I, IV

68. Edgar is prosecuted for murder and his defense counsel, Manuel, raises the duress defense at his trial. Which of the following elements of duress are commonly included in the statutory definition of duress which Manuel will use to seek Edgar's acquittal?

   I. The defendant is faced with an unlawful threat of harm to self or to another.

   II. The threat causes the defendant to believe that the only way to avoid death or serious bodily harm to self or to another is to commit a crime.

   III. The defendant believes that the harm is imminent.

   IV. The defendant's belief(s) are reasonable.

A. I, III, IV

B. I, II, III, IV

C. I, II, III

D. I, II, IV

68. Sal is prosecuted for homicide and his defense counsel, Elise, raises the defense of voluntary intoxication at his trial. Which of the following elements of doctrine are commonly used to govern the intoxication defense which Elise will use to defend Sal?

I. Voluntary intoxication may serve to negate the mental states for premeditation and deliberation for intentional murder.

II. Voluntary intoxication may serve to support the defendant's beliefs in the necessity for self-defense.

III. Voluntary intoxication may serve to support the defendant's defense of insanity.

IV. Voluntary intoxication may serve to negate the reckless mental state for involuntary manslaughter.

A. I, IV

B. I, III

C. II, III

D. I, II

70. Jack is prosecuted for homicide when he uses deadly force to kill Pablo because Jack believes Pablo is a trespasser who is entering Jack's house illegally. Jack's defense counsel, Amy, raises Jack's claim of defense of property at his trial. Which of the following elements of doctrine are commonly used to govern this defense which Amy will raise in order to seek Jack's acquittal?

I. If the victim trespasser is reasonably believed to be entering for the purpose of committing a felony involving the unlawful use of force against a person in the dwelling, then the defendant may use deadly force.

II. In order to protect a dwelling against a trespasser, a defendant may use a mechanical device such as a spring gun that uses deadly force.

III. If the defendant is going to use deadly force against a trespasser who enters a dwelling, the defendant must retreat initially to a position of safety within the dwelling if possible.

IV. If the victim is reasonably believed to be entering for the purpose of committing any felony in the dwelling, then the defendant may use deadly force.

A. I, II

B. I, IV

C. III, IV

D. II, IV

71. Alan is a law enforcement officer who is charged with homicide in the shooting death of a fleeing suspect. Joanne is Alan's defense counsel, and she raises the law enforcement defense at his trial. Which of the following arguments, if they could be proved on the facts, would exonerate Alan for his use of deadly force?

I. Deadly force was used to prevent the escape of a fleeing suspect who poses a threat of serious physical harm to the officer or to others.

II. Deadly force was used to prevent the escape of a fleeing suspect who threatened the officer with a weapon.

III. Deadly force was used to prevent the escape of a fleeing suspect when there was probable cause to believe that the suspect had committed burglary.

IV. Deadly force was used to prevent the escape of a fleeing suspect when there was probable cause to believe that the suspect had committed a crime involving the infliction of serious physical harm.

A. I, II

B. II, IV

C. I, II, IV

D. I, III, IV

72. Mara is charged with a homicide crime because she uses deadly force to kill Larry when she sees Larry attacking Jill using deadly force. Jill is a stranger to Mara, and Mara saves Jill's life. Mara's defense counsel, Sid, argues that Mara may rely on the defense of others defense at her trial. Which of the following elements of doctrine are commonly used to govern the defense of others which Sid will use to seek Mara's acquittal?

I. If Mara reasonably believes that Larry is unlawfully attacking Jill with deadly force, Mara may use deadly force to defend Jill even though Larry is actually a police officer who is lawfully using deadly force to arrest Jill, as long as Mara is not aware of Larry's identity.

II. Even if Mara reasonably believes that Larry is unlawfully attacking Jill with deadly force, Mara may not used deadly force to defend Jill because Jill is a stranger and not a relative of Mara's.

III. Mara may use deadly force to defend Jill only if Mara believes that such force is necessary to save Jill from immediate harm.

IV. If Mara reasonably believes that Larry is unlawfully attacking Jill with deadly force, Mara may not use deadly force to defend Jill if Larry is actually a police officer who is lawfully using deadly force to arrest Jill, even though Mara was not aware of Larry's identity.

A. I, III, IV

B. I, II, III

C. I, IV

D. I, III

73. Roxanne is charged with a homicide crime in the death of Vicki, and her defense counsel, Percy, raises the necessity defense at her trial. Which of the following elements of doctrine are commonly used to govern the defense of others which Percy will use to seek Roxanne's acquittal?

I. To rely on the necessity defense, Roxanne must have acted with the purpose of avoiding a greater harm than Vicki's death.

II. To rely on the necessity defense, Roxanne must have acted with the purpose of avoiding the harm of physical harm to others.

III. To rely on the necessity defense, Roxanne must not be charged with an intentional homicide crime.

IV. To rely on the necessity defense, Roxanne must have been forced by circumstances to choose to avoid a greater harm than Vicki's death, and must not have been at fault in any way in creating the situation that necessitated her choice.

A. II

B. IV

C. I

D. III

74. Matt is charged with a homicide crime in the death of Melissa, and his defense counsel, Nora, raises the unconsciousness defense at Matt's trial. Which of the following elements of doctrine are commonly used to govern the unconsciousness defense that Nora will use to seek Matt's acquittal?

I. The unconsciousness defense may be raised by a defendant whose action is automatic because of some disturbance in consciousness that prevents the defendant from performing the action with a voluntary bodily movement.

II. The unconsciousness defense may be raised by a defendant who has an epileptic seizure.

III. The unconsciousness defense may be raised by a defendant who has somnambulism.

IV. The unconsciousness defense may be raised by a defendant who has amnesia.

A. I, II, III, IV

B. II, III, IV

C. I, III

D. I, II, III

75. Judy is charged with the crime of reckless manslaughter in the shooting death of Maxine. Judy's defense counsel, Herb, raises the defense of mistake of fact at Judy's trial, arguing that since Judy did not think the gun was loaded, she should be acquitted of reckless manslaughter. Which of the following elements of doctrine are commonly used to govern the defense of mistake of fact that Herb will use to seek Judy's acquittal?

I. When a mistake of fact defense is raised, the prosecutor must disprove the mistake of fact beyond a reasonable doubt.

II. A mistake of fact cannot negate the mental state of a strict liability crime.

III. A mistake of fact creates a good defense only when the mistake is reasonable.

IV. Mistake of fact is a defense when it negates one or more mental states of the crime with which the defendant is charged.

A. I, IV

B. I, II, IV

C. II, III, IV

D. I, III, IV

76. Betty is charged with a crime in Nebraska and wishes to raise the defense of mistaken reliance on legal authority. Which of the following arguments may be a valid defense?

    I.   Betty mistakenly believed that the criminal statute which she is charged with violating was unconstitutional.

    II.   Betty reasonably relied upon a decision of the Nebraska Supreme Court that interpreted the statute (which she is charged with violating) as authorizing her conduct, and then this decision was later overruled.

    III.   Betty relied on the advice of her privately retained lawyer, who gave her a legal opinion that the criminal statute which she is charged with violating did not cover her conduct.

    IV.   The statute which Betty is charged with violating is new, and was not published or reasonably made available to the public at the time Betty allegedly committed her crime a few days after the enactment of the statute.

A. I, II, IV

B. III, IV

C. II, IV

D. I, II

77. Bo was injured when he sideswiped another car as he drove along a rural road in Greenland, New Hampshire. Then a few seconds later, Bo drove his car into a tree. Bo caused damage to both the tree and the other car, but the driver of the other car was unhurt. Bo was rescued from his car wreck by a police officer. Bo told the officer that he felt like he passed out while he was driving and doesn't remember hitting the other vehicle or hitting the tree. He woke up and found himself inside the wreck of his own car. The police officer arranged for Bo to be taken to the hospital, where he was given an MRI test to determine whether he had any head injuries. The MRI indicated that Bo has a previously undiagnosed brain disorder in the portion of his brain that regulates consciousness. The doctor who examined Bo determined that this brain disorder could have caused Bo to lose consciousness immediately before the accident. The disorder developed between four and eight months before the accident. Bo did not know about the disorder, and without the MRI it is unlikely that it would have been discovered. Bo is charged with criminal damage to property, which is defined as "damaging tangible property of another by criminal negligence."

Assuming that New Hampshire recognizes the defense of unconsciousness, what arguments will be made by Bo's defense counsel, Marylou, to persuade the trial judge that there is sufficient evidence of unconsciousness for Bo to be acquitted?

  I. The MRI reveals that Bo has a disorder that could have caused Bo to pass out at the time of the accident.

  II. Bo did not know that he had the brain disorder.

III. Bo felt like he passed out and has no memory of hitting anything.

IV. Bo is accused of a negligence crime, not a crime that requires proof of intention or knowledge.

A. I, II

B. I, III, IV

C. I, II, III

D. I, II, III, IV

78. Biff and Otis are inmates of a Colorado prison who are charged with the crime of "possession of escape paraphernalia." At their trial, the evidence showed that Biff's friend and fellow inmate, Otis, was erroneously identified on the television show, "America's Most Wanted," as being a leader of the Aryan Brotherhood. A number of inmates in the racially tense prison facility saw the show, and Otis received death threats from two members of two different prison gangs, including members of the Aryan Brotherhood gang. These threats were communicated verbally while Otis was out in the prison yard on the day after the show was aired. Biff agreed to help Otis escape, and they collected a variety of escape paraphernalia. Biff used his position as an employee in the prison laundry to collect sheets and other useful items. Two weeks after the initial verbal threats were made to Otis by gang members, Otis received a "kite" (a note) in which an inmate told him that he was still a target of a gang execution squad among the inmates. So Biff and Otis decided that they needed to act quickly. But just as they were starting to make their escape, Biff convinced Otis that their best hope would be to get caught trying to escape, which would result in their

getting placed into disciplinary segregation without being labeled as snitches for reporting the death threats. They considered this to be a safer strategy than asking for "protective custody" in the special housing units reserved for this purpose, because they knew that those units were not free from violence. Biff and Otis were caught after strewing their escape materials around the prison yard for two hours. At their joint trial, both defendants sought a jury instruction on the duress defense, and it was denied. Both are convicted, and both defendants appeal on the grounds that the trial judge erred in denying their request for the duress instruction.

What are the strongest arguments that the prosecutor will make on appeal to persuade the court to uphold the trial judge's decision to deny the duress instruction?

   I. These defendants are not eligible for the duress instruction because the people who threatened them did not say that death would be the consequence for the failure to commit a particular crime.

   II. Biff is not eligible for the duress instruction because it was only the life of Otis that was threatened.

   III. These defendants are not eligible for the duress instruction because neither the verbal threats nor the note refer to a date or time when the threat will be carried out.

   IV. The defendants are not eligible for the duress instruction because they had the option of seeking protective custody in lieu of attempting escape.

   A. III, IV

B. I, II, III, IV

C. I, III, IV

D. II, III, IV

79. Biff and Otis are inmates of a Colorado prison who are charged with the crime of "possession of escape paraphernalia." At their trial, the evidence showed that Biff's friend and fellow inmate, Otis, was erroneously identified on the television show, "America's Most Wanted," as being a leader of the Aryan Brotherhood. A number of inmates in the racially tense prison facility saw the show, and Otis received death threats from two members of two different prison gangs, including members of the Aryan Brotherhood gang. These threats were communicated verbally while Otis was out in the prison yard on the day after the show was aired. Biff agreed to help Otis escape, and they collected a variety of escape paraphernalia. Biff used his position as an employee in the prison laundry to collect sheets and other useful items. Two weeks after the initial verbal threats were made to Otis by gang members, Otis received a "kite" (a note) in which an inmate told him that he was still a target of a gang execution squad among the inmates. So Biff and Otis decided that they needed to act quickly. But just as they were starting to make their escape, Biff convinced Otis that their best hope would be to get caught trying to escape, which would result in their getting placed into disciplinary segregation without being labeled as snitches for reporting the death threats. They considered this to be a safer strategy than asking for "protective custody" in the special housing units reserved for this purpose, because they knew that those units were not free from violence. Biff and Otis were caught after strewing their escape materials around the prison yard for two hours. At their joint trial, both defendants sought a jury instruction on the duress defense, and it was

denied. Both are convicted, and both defendants appeal on the grounds that the trial judge erred in denying their request for the duress instruction.

What are the arguments that Otis's defense counsel, Nina, will make to persuade the appellate court that Otis's conviction should be reversed because no reasonable jury should have rejected the duress defense on the facts?

 I. Otis should be acquitted based on the duress defense because he received verbal death threats and the note threatening death.

 II. Otis should be acquitted based on the duress defense because the threats were made by members of prison gangs.

 III. Otis should be acquitted based on the duress defense because the protective custody housing units were not free from violence.

 IV. Otis should be acquitted based on the duress defense because prison snitches may face violent retaliation in prison when outside protective custody.

 A. I, II

 B. I, II, III, IV

 C. I, II, III

 D. I, II, IV

80. Nan is a girlfriend of Lou's, and one night she comes home to discover that her apartment in Fairbanks, Alaska, has been trashed. Lou has the only other key to Nan's

apartment. So Nan takes a can of mace to Lou's duplex apartment, and climbs up the stairs to the second floor where Lou's front door is located. Nan knocks on the door. When Lou opens the door, Nan accuses him of trashing her apartment. Lou laughs and admits to this act. Nan tells him, "I am going to spray this mace at you if you come any closer." Lou retreats toward the dining room table, grabs a carving knife, and then advances towards Nan, holding the knife up and telling Nan that she is a coward. Nan panics and turns back to run down the stairs. Then Nan races out the front door, dropping the can of mace on the front porch. Nan decides to run over to the neighbor's driveway next to the duplex apartment, in order to hide behind a large SUV that is parked there. She believes that Lou is right behind her, and she is afraid to run away down the street in case Lou sees her and gives chase. She decides that when Lou goes back inside his apartment, then she can run off safely. Lou follows Nan down the stairs and out on to the porch, and he picks up the can of mace. As Lou stands on the porch he looks up and down the street, trying to locate Nan. In the meantime, Nan happens to notice that a heavy metal tire jack is lying on the ground next to a flat tire on the SUV. Nan picks up the tire jack and makes a noise in doing so; this noise provokes Lou to bends down to look under the SUV. Lou catches sight of Nan's feet on the other side of the vehicle, and so he tiptoes around to the rear of the SUV to attempt to surprise Nan. Then Lou pops out suddenly, startling Nan by yelling, "Gotcha!" Lou is holding the knife and the can of mace, but he is not pointing either of them at Nan. Nan swings the tire jack hard at Lou's head, and Lou is caught off guard. The tire jack hits him hard and he falls to the ground. Then Nan runs quickly to a neighbor's house, and the neighbor calls the police and the ambulance. By the time the ambulance arrives, Lou has died from his head injury and Nan is arrested for intentional murder. Nan's defense counsel, Abner, argues at trial that Nan acted in self-defense. The trial judge instructs the jury on self-defense but the jury convicts Nan of intentional murder.

What are the arguments that Nan's defense counsel will make on appeal to support the reversal of Nan's conviction on the grounds that no reasonable jury would have rejected the self-defense argument?

    I. Nan regained the right of self-defense when she ran down the stairs away from Lou and dropped the can of mace on the porch.

    II. When Lou yelled, "Gotcha!" at Nan, he posed an immediate threat of death or serious bodily harm to Nan.

    III. Nan reasonably believed that it was necessary to swing the tire jack at Lou's head in order to avert the danger of death or serious bodily harm posed by Lou.

    IV. Lou had the duty to retreat when Nan threatened to spray mace at him.

A. I, II, III

B. II, III, IV

C. I, II, III, IV

D. II, III

81. Nan is a girlfriend of Lou's, and one night she comes home to discover that her apartment in Fairbanks, Alaska, has been trashed. Lou has the only other key to Nan's apartment. So Nan takes a can of mace to Lou's duplex apartment, and climbs up the stairs to the second floor where Lou's front door is located. Nan knocks on the door. When Lou opens the door, Nan accuses him of trashing her apartment. Lou laughs and admits to this act. Nan

tells him, "I am going to spray this mace at you if you come any closer." Lou retreats toward the dining room table, grabs a carving knife, and then advances towards Nan, holding the knife up and telling Nan that she is a coward. Nan panics and turns back to run down the stairs. Then Nan races out the front door, dropping the can of mace on the front porch. Nan decides to run over to the neighbor's driveway next to the duplex apartment, in order to hide behind a large SUV that is parked there. She believes that Lou is right behind her, and she is afraid to run away down the street in case Lou sees her and gives chase. She decides that when Lou goes back inside his apartment, then she can run off safely. Lou follows Nan down the stairs and out on to the porch, and he picks up the can of mace. As Lou stands on the porch he looks up and down the street, trying to locate Nan. In the meantime, Nan happens to notice that a heavy metal tire jack is lying on the ground next to a flat tire on the SUV. Nan picks up the tire jack and makes a noise in doing so; this noise provokes Lou to bends down to look under the SUV. Lou catches sight of Nan's feet on the other side of the vehicle, and so he tiptoes around to the rear of the SUV to attempt to surprise Nan. Then Lou pops out suddenly, startling Nan by yelling, "Gotcha!" Lou is holding the knife and the can of mace, but he is not pointing either of them at Nan. Nan swings the tire jack hard at Lou's head, and Lou is caught off guard. The tire jack hits him hard and he falls to the ground. Then Nan runs quickly to a neighbor's house, and the neighbor calls the police and the ambulance. By the time the ambulance arrives, Lou has died from his head injury and Nan is arrested for intentional murder. Nan's defense counsel, Abner, argues at trial that Nan acted in self-defense. The trial judge instructs the jury on self-defense but the jury convicts Nan of intentional murder.

What are the strongest arguments that the prosecutor will make to persuade the court to affirm Nan's conviction because the jury correctly rejected her self-defense argument?

I. Lou was not pointing either the knife or the can of mace at Nan, and so he did not pose an immediate threat of death or serious bodily harm to her.

II. Lou regained the right of self-defense when he popped out at Nan and startled her by yelling, "Gotcha!"

III. Nan had the duty to retreat from Lou's apartment.

IV. Nan lost the right of self-defense when she hid behind the SUV and armed herself with the tire jack.

A. II

B. I, II

C. I

D. III, IV

82. Joanne marries an unmarried man named Dean in Arkansas, and then Joanne is prosecuted for bigamy when it is discovered that Joanne is still legally married to Claudius. The bigamy statute is silent as to the mental state that the prosecutor must prove concerning the defendant's awareness of the legal status of his or her prior marriage. Joanne is convicted of bigamy and appeals her conviction on the grounds of mistake of fact concerning the legal validity of her previous marriage to Claudius.

Which of the following mistake defenses raised by Joanne might be rejected by an appellate court?

I. Joanne reasonably thought that she had obtained a lawful divorce from her first husband.

II. Joanne reasonably thought her first husband was dead.

III. Joanne reasonably thought that her first marriage was illegal because she was too young to be married lawfully at the time of that marriage.

IV. Joanne thought that she had obtained a lawful divorce from her first husband in West Virginia, but she was negligent in her failure to discover that the divorce would not be recognized in Arkansas.

A. I, II, IV

B. I, II, III

C. II, III, IV

D. I, II, III, IV

83. Jon spends the evening with friends drinking at Jimmy's Bar in San Francisco, and after five hours he has consumed 6 beers and 4 shots of bourbon. He is angry at his former girlfriend, Lili, and so he decides to go to her house and tell her how he feels. He knocks violently on the front door and Lili opens the door and lets him in. Jon starts screaming at Lili and tries to grab her and take a swing at her. Lili runs through the house to the back bedroom, and slams her bedroom door. Jon follows her, takes a step back from the bedroom door and then charges toward it, hitting it hard with his shoulder so that the door breaks and opens. Jon enters the bedroom,

and then he picks up a knife that is lying on the bureau and attempts to strike Lili with it, but his aim is bad and his swing is wide. Lili gives Jon a sharp kick so that he drops the knife. Then Lili quickly escapes out the bedroom window to the back yard. Lili catches the attention of a passing police officer, who then arrests Jon. Jon is charged with the crime of "aggravated assault" which is defined as "attempting to cause bodily injury to another with a dangerous weapon." The criminal code defines dangerous weapon as, "gun, firearm, sharpened instrument, knife, other similar weapon." The crime of simple assault is also codified but it does not have a statutory definition. At Jon's trial on the aggravated assault crime, his defense counsel, Cherie, asks for a jury instruction on intoxication. According to Illinois law, such an instruction is available only for "specific intent" crimes. The trial judge denies the requested instruction. Jon is convicted, and on appeal, Cherie argues that the trial judge erred in denying the requested intoxication instruction.

What arguments will Jon's defense counsel make to persuade the appellate court that Jon's crime qualifies as one of specific intent?

 I. The crime of aggravated assault requires Jon's awareness that the knife was a dangerous weapon.

 II. The crime of aggravated assault requires the mental state of the intent to achieve a result of the act of causing bodily injury.

 III. The crime of aggravated assault is an attempt crime.

 IV. The lesser crime of simple assault exists, and the mental state for that lesser crime is criminal negligence.

A. II, III, IV

B. I, II, III, IV

C. I, III, IV

D. II, IV

84. Jon spends the evening with friends drinking at Jimmy's Bar in San Francisco, and after five hours he has consumed 6 beers and 4 shots of bourbon. He is angry at his former girlfriend, Lili, and so he decides to go to her house and tell her how he feels. He knocks violently on the front door and Lili opens the door and lets him in. Jon starts screaming at Lili and tries to grab her and take a swing at her. Lili runs through the house to the back bedroom, and slams her bedroom door. Jon follows her, takes a step back from the bedroom door and then charges toward it, hitting it hard with his shoulder so that the door breaks and opens. Jon enters the bedroom, and then he picks up a knife that is lying on the bureau and attempts to strike Lili with it, but his aim is bad and his swing is wide. Lili gives Jon a sharp kick so that he drops the knife. Then Lili quickly escapes out the bedroom window to the back yard. Lili catches the attention of a passing police officer, who then arrests Jon. Jon is charged with the crime of "aggravated assault" which is defined as "attempting to cause bodily injury to another with a dangerous weapon." The criminal code defines dangerous weapon as, "gun, firearm, sharpened instrument, knife, other similar weapon." The crime of simple assault is also codified but it does not have a statutory definition. At Jon's trial on the aggravated assault crime, his defense counsel, Cherie, asks for a jury instruction on intoxication. According to Illinois law, such an instruction is available only for "specific intent" crimes. The trial judge denies the requested instruction. Jon is convicted, and on appeal, Cherie argues that the

trial judge erred in denying the requested intoxication instruction.

What arguments will the prosecutor make to persuade the appellate court that Jon's crime qualifies as one of general intent?

    I. The intent needed for Jon's act is not a complex one.

    II. The intent needed for Jon's act is recklessness.

    III. Jon's crime is typically committed in an impulsive manner and is closely associated with the consumption of alcohol.

    IV. Jon's act does not require the intention to achieve a future consequence beyond the achievement of the act of battery.

    A. I, II, III, IV

    B. I, III, IV

    C. II, III, IV

    D. I, II, IV

85. Raul, Ilhyung, Mimi, and Rosa are adrift on the high seas in an overloaded lifeboat; they abandoned a sinking ship, and now the lifeboat is leaking and the four passengers are having a very difficult time bailing the water out and trying to keep their lifeboat afloat. It is riding low in the water because only three people are supposed to occupy the boat, not four people. Stormy conditions are rocking the boat in the waves, and it appears that the boat may sink at anytime. Mimi has a ship radio with her, and she has radioed nearby ships for

assistance; one ship captain has reported that her ship is on its way to the rescue, but that it will take at least 5 hours to arrive and no other ships are known to be in closer proximity to the lifeboat's location. Raul weighs 300 pounds, whereas the other three passengers each weigh only 150 pounds or less. Raul's three companions ask him to volunteer to sacrifice himself for the good of the others; when Raul does not agree, the other three passengers manage to push him overboard during a moment when he is caught off balance. The rescue ship arrives 5 hours later, just as the lifeboat is starting to sink because the three passengers are too tired to bail out the water anymore. Ilhyung, Mimi and Rosa are rescued and charged with intentional murder. The defendants request a jury instruction on the necessity defense, and this request is granted. The jury convicts the defendants, and on appeal, the defense counsel for each defendant argues that the convictions should be reversed because no reasonable jury would have rejected the necessity defense.

What argument is the most likely to be endorsed by the appellate court in resolving the appeal of the three defendants on the issue of the necessity defense?

I. The defendants' necessity defense was valid because Raul weighed 300 pounds, which created an objective basis for his selection.

II. The defendants' reliance on the necessity defense was valid because it appeared that the only way to save the lives of one or more of the passengers was to sacrifice the life of at least one person.

III. The defendants' necessity defense was not valid because the passengers did not draw lots to determine which passenger would be sacrificed.

IV. The defendants' necessity defense was not valid because under the circumstances, there was a great risk that the remaining passengers would have died because the lifeboat was prone to sinking even after one of them was sacrificed.

A. I

B. III

C. II

D. IV

86. The Uniform Controlled Substances Act has been adopted, occasionally with some modifications, in 48 states, including Iowa. Section 1 of the Act proscribes "knowing and intentional possession" of drugs, and Section 2 of the Act defines "possession" as "the exercise of actual or constructive dominion or control over a thing by one or more persons." While it appears that the Iowa legislature relied on the Act when revising the Iowa drug laws in 1970, it happens that the legislature failed to include the words, "knowing or intentional," when it enacted the Section 1 provision in the Iowa Criminal Code. The legislature did enact Section 2 as it appears in the Act. By contrast, 40 states have enacted both Sections 1 and 2 of the Act *verbatim*. Jane was arrested for "possession" of drugs under Sections 1 and 2 when the police raided a house party and found drugs in an upstairs room. Jane was a guest in a downstairs room, but she was arrested along with everyone else at the party. At trial, Jane's lawyer asked the judge to tell the jury that Jane could be convicted only if she "knowingly or intentionally" possessed drugs. This request was rejected. Instead, the trial judge simply read the text of Sections 1 and 2 to the jury. Jane was convicted, and on

appeal, her defense counsel, Wayne, argues that her conviction should be reversed because the trial judge erred in refusing Jane's requested jury instruction concerning the definition of mens rea.

On appeal, which of the following arguments will the appellate court be likely to endorse in resolving the issue presented in Jane's appeal?

I. The mens rea of strict liability should not be inferred from the legislature's action in omitting the "knowing or intentional" mens rea.

II. The "plain meaning" rule of statutory interpretation dictates that strict liability is intended for the drug possession crime here.

III. The pattern of adoption of the words "knowing and intentional" by other states relying on the model statute is not relevant for a determination of what mental state the Iowa legislature intended to use for the drug possession crime.

IV. Section 2 requires that Jane must "exercise" either "dominion or control," and this language implies a knowing or intentional mental state.

A. I, IV

B. II, III

C. I

D. II

87. In 1995, after the Oklahoma City bombing, the Congress enacted the Anti-Terrorism and Effective Death Penalty Act (AEDPA). One of the provisions of that

statute empowers the Secretary of State to designate an organization as a "foreign terrorist organization" (FTO). The criteria for the Secretary of State's decision to designate an organization as an FTO are that the organization is a foreign one, that it engages in terrorist activity, and that its terrorist activity threatens the national security. Any organization that is under consideration for the FTO designation has no right to notice concerning this designation process and no right to submit evidence for the Secretary's consideration. Even once the FTO designation is issued, the Secretary of State is not obligated to inform the organization of this status. The Secretary's only obligation is to publish the decision concerning the FTO designation in the Federal Register; on the date of this publication, the consequences of the FTO designation take effect. These consequences are significant. Members of the FTO are forbidden entry into the United States. The Secretary of the Treasury may freeze the assets of an FTO that are located in the United States. The judicial review provided for the Secretary's FTO designation is extremely limited. The AEDPA statute also makes it a crime for anyone to provide "material support" and resources to an organization that has been designated as an FTO. The statute reads as follows: "Whoever, within the United States or subject to the jurisdiction of the United States, knowingly provides material support or resources to a foreign terrorist organization shall be imprisoned under this statute not more than 15 years." The term "material support" in this criminal statute is defined to include financial contributions. Anyone who is prosecuted under this statute is precluded from raising any question concerning the validity of the FTO designation for the organization to which he or she is alleged to have knowingly provided material support.

Assume that in October 2003, the Kurdistan Workers Party, also known as the Partiya Karkeran Kurdistan (PKK), was designated as an FTO. The PKK had engaged in a wide range of activities, including peaceful political advocacy, and humanitarian aid. However, the PKK received the FTO designation because of State Department reports describing its military activities directed against both security forces and civilians in southeast Turkey. These activities were found to qualify as terrorist violence and were found to threaten the national security of the United States. The members of a group called the Humanitarian Law Project, operating in New York City, have provided financial support for many years to the PKK, in order to support the Kurds living in Turkey and to protect them from civil rights violations. One week after the date in 2003 when the PKK was designated as an FTO, one member of the Humanitarian Law Project, Rafe, sent a financial contribution to the PKK. Rafe was prosecuted for violating the federal AEDPA crime of "knowingly providing material support to a foreign terrorist organization." Rafe tells his defense counsel, Nelly, that he did not know that the PKK had been designated as an FTO when he wrote his check. At Rafe's trial, Nelly argues that the element of knowingly should be attached to both the element of "provides material support or resources" and to the element of "to a foreign terrorist organization." The prosecutor concedes that the term "knowingly" in the statute expressly modifies the element of "provides material support or resources," but the prosecutor argues that this mental state of knowingly is not intended to modify the element of "to a foreign terrorist organization." Furthermore, the prosecutor argues that no mental state should be attached to the latter element because it is a strict liability element. The trial judge accepts the prosecutor's interpretation of the elements of the crime and instructs the jury accordingly. Rafe is convicted, and on appeal, Nelly argues that his conviction should be reversed because the trial judge erred in rejecting the defense counsel's interpretation of the statute.

What are the strongest arguments that the prosecutor will make to persuade the appellate court to affirm the conviction on the grounds that the trial judge interpreted the statute correctly?

I. This is a public welfare offense statute for which strict liability is appropriate because of the need to protect the public from the dangers posed to the national security and the public safety by FTOs and donors who provide financial support to FTOs.

II. The legislative intent to convict a donor to an FTO group who has no awareness of the FTO status of that group may be inferred from the lack of notice to the FTO organizations themselves concerning the FTO designation, as well as from the secrecy of the FTO designation proceedings and the limited judicial review available to challenge the FTO status.

III. The penalty for this crime is not sufficiently severe to justify the rejection of a strict liability interpretation.

IV. This is not a common law statute and so the presumption against the use of strict liability is not appropriate here.

A. I, II, III, IV

B. I, II, III

C. I, II, IV

D. II, III, IV

88. In 1995, after the Oklahoma City bombing, the Congress enacted the Anti-Terrorism and Effective Death Penalty Act (AEDPA). One of the provisions of that

statute empowers the Secretary of State to designate an organization as a "foreign terrorist organization" (FTO). The criteria for the Secretary of State's decision to designate an organization as an FTO are that the organization is a foreign one, that it engages in terrorist activity, and that its terrorist activity threatens the national security. Any organization that is under consideration for the FTO designation has no right to notice concerning this designation process and no right to submit evidence for the Secretary's consideration. Even once the FTO designation is issued, the Secretary of State is not obligated to inform the organization of this status. The Secretary's only obligation is to publish the decision concerning the FTO designation in the Federal Register; on the date of this publication, the consequences of the FTO designation take effect. These consequences are significant. Members of the FTO are forbidden entry into the United States. The Secretary of the Treasury may freeze the assets of an FTO that are located in the United States. The judicial review provided for the Secretary's FTO designation is extremely limited. The AEDPA statute also makes it a crime for anyone to provide "material support" and resources to an organization that has been designated as an FTO. The statute reads as follows: "Whoever, within the United States or subject to the jurisdiction of the United States, knowingly provides material support or resources to a foreign terrorist organization shall be imprisoned under this statute not more than 15 years." The term "material support" in this criminal statute is defined to include financial contributions. Anyone who is prosecuted under this statute is precluded from raising any question concerning the validity of the FTO designation for the organization to which he or she is alleged to have knowingly provided material support.

Assume that in October 2003, the Kurdistan Workers Party, also known as the Partiya Karkeran Kurdistan (PKK), was designated as an FTO. The PKK had engaged in a wide range of activities, including peaceful political advocacy, and humanitarian aid. However, the PKK received the FTO designation because of State Department reports describing its military activities directed against both security forces and civilians in southeast Turkey. These activities were found to qualify as terrorist violence and were found to threaten the national security of the United States. The members of a group called the Humanitarian Law Project, operating in New York City, have provided financial support for many years to the PKK, in order to support the Kurds living in Turkey and to protect them from civil rights violations. One week after the date that the PKK was designated as an FTO, one member of the Humanitarian Law Project, Rafe, sent a financial contribution to the PKK. Rafe was prosecuted for violating the federal AEDPA crime of "knowingly providing material support to a foreign terrorist organization." Rafe tells his defense counsel, Nelly, that he did not know that the PKK had been designated as an FTO when he wrote his check. At Rafe's trial, Nelly argues that the element of knowingly should be attached to both the element of "provides material support or resources" and to the element of "to a foreign terrorist organization." The prosecutor concedes that the term "knowingly" in the statute expressly modifies the element of "provides material support or resources," but the prosecutor argues that this mental state of knowingly is not intended to modify the element of "to a foreign terrorist organization." Furthermore, the prosecutor argues that no mental state should be attached to the latter element because it is a strict liability element. The trial judge accepts the prosecutor's interpretation of the elements of the crime and instructs the jury accordingly. Rafe is convicted, and on appeal, Nelly argues that his conviction should be reversed because the trial judge erred in rejecting the defense counsel's interpretation of the statute.

What are the strongest arguments that the defense counsel will make on appeal to persuade the appellate court to reverse the conviction on the grounds that the trial judge should have accepted the defense counsel's interpretation of the statute and instructed the jury accordingly?

I. The Model Penal Code supports the use of a knowingly mental state for the element of the FTO status in this statute, even though the statute is silent concerning that mental state.

II. A strict liability interpretation should not be used because there is a long tradition of lawful donations to political and humanitarian organizations, so that many donors to FTOs might be surprised to learn that his or her conduct was criminal.

III. A donor like the defendant does not belong to a highly regulated group of people who should be on notice that their acts may be subject to criminal liability for failure to ascertain what those regulations are and to comply with them.

IV. Where a statute is ambiguous as to mental state, the rule of lenity requires that the interpretation that is most favorable to the defendant should be used, and here that would require rejection of the strict liability mental state and use of the defendant's proposed mental state of "knowingly."

A. II, III, IV

B. I, II, III, IV

C. I, II, IV

D. I, III, IV

89. Matt Quinn appeals his conviction for violating the Archaeological Resources Protection Act (ARPA), a federal statute that makes it a crime to excavate on public land without a permit. The ARPA statute was enacted in 1906 and it provides as follows:

> (a) No person may excavate, remove, damage, or otherwise alter or deface any archaeological resource located on public lands or Indian lands unless such activity is pursuant to a permit.
>
> (d) Any person who knowingly violates any prohibition contained in subsection (a) [or other subsections] shall, upon conviction, be fined for the amount of the costs of restoring the site or imprisoned for up to three years or both.

The legislative history of ARPA shows that in enacting the statute, Congress stated that archaeological resources on public lands are "irreplaceable parts of the Nation's heritage," and that "these resources are increasingly endangered because of their commercial attractiveness." Congress also found that "existing Federal laws do not provide adequate protection to prevent the loss and destruction of these resources and sites resulting from uncontrolled excavations and pillage." The Congressional purpose of the ARPA was "to secure, for the present and future benefit of the American people, the protection of resources and sites on public lands and Indian lands." In addition, Congress encouraged federal land managers "to carry out an active public information program and to publish the appropriate prohibitions and warnings in their respective brochures, maps, visitor guides, and to post signs at entrances to public lands." However, Congress explicitly authorized land managers to conceal the nature and location of any archaeological resource unless the land manager determined that disclosure would "not create a risk of harm to such resources or to the site at which such resources are located."

Matt was arrested for vandalizing an archaeological site in the Gila National Forest in New Mexico. The site where he was apprehended has been public property since 1967 and it is known as the East Fork site, a Mimbres-Mogollon ruin that covers about two acres. However, there is no sign at the East Fork site to indicate that the Mimbres-Mogollon ruin is on public land. A forest service officer had installed a remote sensor at the road closest to the site, and when the sensor went off, the officer went to investigate and found Matt excavating the site. Matt was found with a backpack, sleeping bag, shovel, a specialized probe tool (used to determine the alignment of rock walls), and pieces of Mimbres pottery. At Matt's trial he conceded in his testimony that he knew he was digging in a prehistoric Mimbres Pueblo, that he intended to remove artifacts, and that he had not received or applied for a permit from the Forest Service to excavate the site. Matt also wanted to testify that he did not know that he was excavating on public land, but he was not allowed to do so because the trial judge granted the prosecutor's motion to preclude Matt from testifying about this point. The defense counsel opposed the prosecutor's motion and asked the judge to instruct the jury that ARPA requires the prosecutor to prove that Matt knew he was excavating on public land." But the trial judge rejected this defense argument and instructed the jurors that they should convict Matt if he knowingly excavated an archaeological resource without a permit, even if he did not know that he was on public land. After Matt is convicted at trial, he is sentenced to one year in prison and ordered to pay restitution in the amount of roughly $20,000 for repair and restoration of the site. Matt's conviction has the status of a felony under the ARPA because he caused damage over $500. Matt's defense counsel, Carrie, appeals his conviction on the grounds that ARPA should not be interpreted as a strict liability crime and that the prosecutor should have the burden of proving that Matt knew he was on public land.

What are the strongest arguments that the defense

counsel will make to persuade the appellate court to reverse the conviction on the grounds that the prosecutor should have to prove that Matt knowingly excavated on public land?

> I. The legislative history of ARPA shows that Congress wanted to insure that the public and potential excavators are notified of the boundaries of public lands through the posting of signs, which goal is consistent with the goal of punishing only those defendants who know they are on public land and fail to get permits.
>
> II. The use of strict liability for the public land element in ARPA may criminalize a wide range of innocent conduct, and ARPA should not be used to convict innocent hikers who are unaware that they are on public land and pick up a few artifacts without realizing that this is a crime.
>
> III. Strict liability should not be used for the public land element because it will not be especially burdensome to require a prosecutor to prove that defendant knows that he or she is on public lands; usually a defendant has maps, and the maps will show that the defendant knew from the map that he or she was on public land.
>
> IV. This crime is similar to the common law crime of stealing and therefore a similar mental state should be used; here the parallel mental state for the larceny mens rea of knowing that property belongs to another is the mental state of knowing that one is on public land.

  A. I, II, III, IV

  B. I, III, IV

C. I, II

D. I, II, III

90. Matt Quinn appeals his conviction for violating the Archaeological Resources Protection Act (ARPA), a federal statute that makes it a crime to excavate on public land without a permit. The ARPA statute was enacted in 1906 and it provides as follows:

> A. No person may excavate, remove, damage, or otherwise alter or deface any archaeological resource located on public lands or Indian lands unless such activity is pursuant to a permit.
>
> B. Any person who knowingly violates any prohibition contained in subsection (a) [or other subsections] shall, upon conviction, be fined for the amount of the costs of restoring the site or imprisoned for up to three years or both.

The legislative history of ARPA shows that in enacting the statute, Congress stated that archaeological resources on public lands are "irreplaceable parts of the Nation's heritage," and that "these resources are increasingly endangered because of their commercial attractiveness." Congress also found that "existing Federal laws do not provide adequate protection to prevent the loss and destruction of these resources and sites resulting from uncontrolled excavations and pillage." The Congressional purpose of the ARPA was "to secure, for the present and future benefit of the American people, the protection of resources and sites on public lands and Indian lands." In addition, Congress encouraged federal land managers "to carry out an active public information program and to publish the appropriate prohibitions and warnings in their respective brochures, maps, visitor guides, and to post signs at entrances to public lands." However, Congress explicitly authorized land managers to conceal the nature and location of any archaeological resource unless the land manager determined that disclosure would "not create a risk of harm to such resources or to the site at which such resources are located."

Matt was arrested for vandalizing an archaeological site in the Gila National Forest in New Mexico. The site where he was apprehended has been public property since 1967 and it is known as the East Fork site, a Mimbres-Mogollon ruin that covers about two acres. However, there is no sign at the East Fork site to indicate that the Mimbres-Mogollon ruin is on public land. A forest service officer had installed a remote sensor at the road closest to the site, and when the sensor went off, the officer went to investigate and found Matt excavating the site. Matt was found with a backpack, sleeping bag, shovel, a specialized probe tool (used to determine the alignment of rock walls), and pieces of Mimbres pottery. At Matt's trial he conceded in his testimony that he knew he was digging in a prehistoric Mimbres Pueblo, that he intended to remove artifacts, and that he had not received or applied for a permit from the Forest Service to excavate the site. Matt also wanted to testify that he did not know that he was excavating on public land, but he was not allowed to do so because the trial judge granted the prosecutor's motion to preclude Matt from testifying about this point. The defense counsel opposed the prosecutor's motion and asked the judge to instruct the jury that ARPA requires the prosecutor to prove that Matt knew he was excavating on public land." But the trial judge rejected this defense argument and instructed the jurors that they should convict Matt if he knowingly excavated an archaeological resource without a permit, even if he did not know that he was on public land. After Matt is convicted at trial, he is sentenced to one year in prison and ordered to pay restitution in the amount of roughly $20,000 for repair and restoration of the site.

Matt's conviction has the status of a felony under the ARPA because he caused damage over $500. Matt's defense counsel, Carrie, appeals his conviction on the grounds that ARPA should not be interpreted as a strict liability crime and that the prosecutor should have the burden of proving that Matt knew he was on public land.

What are the strongest arguments that the prosecutor will make to persuade the appellate court to affirm the conviction on the grounds that the trial judge properly refused to allow Matt to testify concerning his lack of knowledge that he was on public land, and correctly rejected the defense counsel's interpretation of the mens rea requirements for the statute?

    I. Since the ARPA was enacted in 1906, it is likely that the knowingly mental state was intended to attach only to the primary conduct element, which is "to excavate any archaeological resource," and not to the attendant circumstance element of being on public land.

    II. The ARPA statute will be difficult to enforce if the prosecutor must prove that the defendant knew he or she was excavating on public land; many public land boundaries may be unmarked and so it will be easy for a defendant to claim that he or she wandered unknowingly on to public land.

    III. The ARPA crime is a public welfare offense that is meant to deter the destruction of public resources and the public heritage of historic sites, for which strict liability is appropriate as it is for some environmental crimes.

    IV. There is widespread public awareness of the value of artifacts and the need to avoid excavating them; therefore, anyone excavating on any land that does not belong to him or her must possess a culpable mental state of awareness that he or she is stealing artifacts from the landowner, whether on public or private land.

A. I, II

B. III, IV

C. I, II, IV

D. I, III, IV

91. Sheldon is prosecuted under a statute that prohibits the crime of attempt when his actions make it appear that he is involved in an arson crime. Which of the following elements are likely to be included in this crime?

   I. The defendant must do an act that can have no other purpose than to achieve the commission of the crime of arson.

   II. The defendant must intend to perform acts that would satisfy the elements of the crime of arson, if the result intended by the defendant were accomplished.

   III. The defendant must commit the last proximate act for the crime, which means that he or she has done everything that he or she believes is necessary to complete the crime.

   IV. The defendant must have the same mental state that is required for the crime of arson.

A. I, III

B. I, II, IV

C. II, IV

D. II, III, IV

92. Lucia is prosecuted under a statute that prohibits the crime of solicitation when her actions make it appear that she is involved in a theft. Which of the following elements are likely to be included in this crime?

   I. The defendant must engage in an act of solicitation, which includes inducing, requesting, encouraging, or advising another person to commit theft.

   II. The defendant must intend to promote or facilitate the commission of theft.

   III. The defendant must intend that the result of theft will be achieved by the person whom he or she solicits to accomplish it.

   IV. The person who is solicited to commit the theft must agree to do so.

A. I, II, III

B. I, II

C. I, II, IV

D. I, III, IV

93. Seth is prosecuted under a statute that prohibits the crime of conspiracy when his actions make it appear that he is involved in a drug crime. Which of the following elements are likely to be included in this crime?

> I. The defendant must have entered into an agreement to commit the drug crime with an evil purpose, with knowledge of the criminality of his or her conduct.
>
> II. The defendant either must intend to agree to commit the drug crime or must intend to achieve the objective of the commission of the drug crime.
>
> III. The defendant or a co-conspirator must do an overt act in furtherance of the conspiracy to commit the drug crime, which overt act need not be a criminal act.
>
> IV. The defendant must enter into an agreement to commit the drug crime, which need not be explicit but may be tacit.

> A. III, IV
>
> B. I, II
>
> C. I, III, IV
>
> D. II, III, IV

94. Ann went to a bar in Mount Pleasant, Arkansas, and there she encountered Moe, a stranger to her, who was eating supper at the bar. Moe offered to sell Ann some jewelry, and so she bought a necklace from him. Moe appeared to be extremely drunk. As Ann got in her

car to leave, Moe unexpectedly got in the back seat. Ann decided to be polite to Moe, even though she thought he was imposing on her. Ann told Moe that she was on her way home, and she offered him a ride wherever he wanted to go. Moe told Ann that she could let him off at her house. When Ann reached her house, she and Moe got out of the car, and Moe asked if he could use Ann's bathroom. Ann was a little fearful of Moe because he appeared to be so drunk, but she agreed to let him use the bathroom. They entered her house, and as Ann escorted Moe to the bathroom, she noticed that Moe picked up a spoon that was lying on a table. Ann suspected that Moe might want to use the spoon to take drugs. Ann remained in her living room while Moe used the bathroom. The bathroom door was closed so Ann did not see Moe "shoot up" with heroin in the bathroom, using the spoon he had picked up, as well as materials that he had concealed in his jacket pockets. When Moe emerged from the bathroom, he walked into Ann's living room and then collapsed on the floor. Ann tried to revive him, but she was unable to rouse him. Moe appeared to be in a catatonic slumber. Ann decided to drag Moe outside in case he woke up inside her house and became troublesome. She managed to pull Moe out through the front door by his feet. Once Ann had pulled Moe out on to her front porch, she lifted him up by grabbing him under the shoulders, and she sat him down on her porch swing, where he slumped over. Ann's porch and porch swing were visible to any passerby on the street. Then Ann decided to spend the night at her boyfriend's house, and so she left Moe on the porch swing at her house, hoping that he would rouse himself eventually and leave. It was a balmy evening and Ann thought that the worst that would happen to Moe was that he would sleep through the night in the 70 degree temperature, and feel a bit stiff whenever he awoke on the porch swing. When Ann returned from her boyfriend's house in the morning, however, Moe was still slumped over on her porch swing and he was dead. He had died in the middle of the night of an overdose of heroin, combined with the effects of his consumption of a large amount of alcohol. Ann is charged with negligent homicide. The prosecutor at Ann's trial argues that the trial judge should instruct the jury on the subject of "legal duties," so that the jury may find that Ann owed a duty to Moe, that she violated this duty, and that Ann's failure to summon medical assistance for Moe was an "omission" that should be treated the same way as "conduct" under the negligent homicide statute. The trial judge instructs the jury as requested by the prosecutor, and that the prosecutor persuades the jury on all the points of argument in the prosecutor's favor, so that the jury convicts Ann of negligent homicide. On appeal, Ann's defense counsel, Jorge, argues that Ann's conviction should be reversed because Ann owed no legal duty to Moe that can create a basis for negligent homicide liability here.

What are the strongest arguments that the defense counsel will make to persuade the appellate court to reverse the conviction on the grounds that Ann had no legal duty that would give rise to negligent homicide liability for her omission to act?

I. Ann has no legal duty to Moe based on statute, contract, or status relationship.

II. Ann did not voluntarily assume the duty to care for Moe when he collapsed in her house because she moved him into the public view on her porch.

III. Ann should not be held to have assumed the duty to care for Moe because she was not aware of the nature or degree of the medical danger of death that he was in.

IV. Ann should not be held liable because at common law there is no duty to rescue strangers who are known to be in peril.

A. I, II, III, IV

B. I, III, IV

C. I, II, IV

D. II, III, IV

95. Ann went to a bar in Mount Pleasant, Arkansas, and there she encountered Moe, a stranger to her, who was eating supper at the bar. Moe offered to sell Ann some jewelry, and so she bought a necklace from him. Moe appeared to be extremely drunk. As Ann got in her car to leave, Moe unexpectedly got in the back seat. Ann decided to be polite to Moe, even though she thought he was imposing on her. Ann told Moe that she was on her way home, and she offered him a ride wherever he wanted to go. Moe told Ann that she could let him off at her house. When Ann reached her house, she and Moe got out of the car, and Moe asked if he could use Ann's bathroom. Ann was a little fearful of Moe because he appeared to be so drunk, but she agreed to let him use the bathroom. They entered her house, and as Ann escorted Moe to the bathroom, she noticed that Moe picked up a spoon that was lying on a table. Ann suspected that Moe might want to use the spoon to take drugs. Ann remained in her living room while Moe used the bathroom. The bathroom door was closed so Ann did not see Moe "shoot up" with heroin in the bathroom, using the spoon he had picked up, as well as materials that he had concealed in his jacket pockets. When Moe emerged from the bathroom, he walked into Ann's living room and then collapsed on the floor. Ann tried to revive him, but she was unable to rouse him. Moe appeared to be in a catatonic slumber. Ann decided to drag Moe outside in case he woke up inside her house and became troublesome. She managed to pull Moe out through the front door by his feet. Once Ann had pulled Moe out on

to her front porch, she lifted him up by grabbing him under the shoulders, and she sat him down on her porch swing, where he slumped over. Ann's porch and porch swing were visible to any passerby on the street. Then Ann decided to spend the night at her boyfriend's house, and so she left Moe on the porch swing at her house, hoping that he would rouse himself eventually and leave. It was a balmy evening and Ann thought that the worst that would happen to Moe was that he would sleep through the night in the 70 degree temperature, and feel a bit stiff whenever he awoke on the porch swing. When Ann returned from her boyfriend's house in the morning, however, Moe was still slumped over on her porch swing and he was dead. He had died in the middle of the night of an overdose of heroin, combined with the effects of his consumption of a large amount of alcohol. Ann is charged with negligent homicide. The prosecutor at Ann's trial argues that the trial judge should instruct the jury on the subject of "legal duties," so that the jury may find that Ann owed a duty to Moe, that she violated this duty, and that Ann's failure to summon medical assistance for Moe was an "omission" that should be treated the same way as "conduct" under the negligent homicide statute. The trial judge instructs the jury as requested by the prosecutor, and that the prosecutor persuades the jury on all the points of argument in the prosecutor's favor, so that the jury convicts Ann of negligent homicide. On appeal, Ann's defense counsel, Jorge, argues that Ann's conviction should be reversed because Ann owed no legal duty to Moe that can create a basis for negligent homicide liability here.

What are the strongest arguments that the prosecutor will make to persuade the appellate court to affirm the conviction on the grounds that Ann had a legal duty that creates a basis for a negligent homicide conviction due to her omission to act?

I. Ann voluntarily assumed the care of Moe by giving him a ride in her car and allowing him to enter her house.

II. Ann saw Moe take a spoon to the bathroom and suspected that he might use it to take drugs.

III. Ann was aware that Moe was helpless and that he had collapsed on her living room floor in a catatonic slumber from which he could not be roused; these symptoms should have alerted Ann that Moe faced a substantial risk of death unless he received emergency medical care.

IV. Ann failed to either attempt to ascertain Moe's identity or to make a 911 phone call, and she isolated the helpless Moe on the porch without sharing her knowledge of his potentially dangerous medical condition with anyone.

A. I, II, III

B. I, II, III, IV

C. I, II, IV

D. II, III, IV

96. Rose ingested crack cocaine throughout her pregnancy, and during her regular prenatal visits to the doctor, Rose reported that she could not stop using cocaine. The doctor warned her that it was bad for her baby, but then explained that he could not prescribe any drugs or treatment for Rose to help her stop using cocaine until after the baby's birth. When Rose's baby was born in Raleigh, North Carolina, he had cocaine metabolites in his system, and the hospital reported this

information to the health authorities. The prosecutor learned of Rose's case, and charged her with the crime of "endangering a child." The relevant North Carolina statute provides: ""Any person having the legal custody of any child or helpless person, who shall, without lawful excuse, refuse or neglect to provide the proper care and attention for such child or helpless person, so that the life, health or comfort of such child or helpless person is endangered or is likely to be endangered, shall be guilty of a misdemeanor, and may be sentenced to not more than six months in jail, and a fine of not more than $1,000." Assume that Rose is not entitled to a jury trial. She is convicted by a judge, and sentenced to six months in jail. You are Rose's lawyer on appeal. You do some research and discover that a viable fetus is treated as a "person" under North Carolina case law for purposes of wrongful death tort liability, and that there is a "feticide" statute that criminalizes the intentional or reckless killing of a viable fetus by a person who is not the mother (with an exception for cases of constitutionally authorized abortions).

What are the strongest arguments that may be made by Rose's defense counsel in order to persuade the appellate court to reverse Rose's conviction because her conduct is not covered by the North Carolina "child endangerment" statute?

    I. The statute is not intended to cover Rose's conduct because the cocaine caused a danger to her fetus, and a fetus is not a subject of "legal custody" in the same way as a child or helpless person.

    II. The statute is not intended to cover Rose's conduct because it is targeted at those who "refuse or neglect to provide care" for a child, not at those like Rose who attempted to provide the proper care for her fetus by making regular prenatal visits to the doctor, and by seeking help for her cocaine addiction.

III. The policy reasons for civil damage judgments against negligent tortfeasors who kill a fetus should not dictate criminal punishment for an addicted pregnant woman because of her addiction.

IV. The legislative decision to enact a feticide statute implies that the legislators assumed that the homicide statutes covering "persons" did not cover a fetus; therefore, the legislators must similarly assume that the "child endangerment" statute covers only children or persons but not a fetus.

A. I, II, IV

B. I, II, III, IV

C. I, II, III

D. I, III, IV

97. Which of the following statements accurately describes the doctrines that have been formulated in cases involving the Eighth Amendment prohibition on cruel and unusual punishment as applied to prosecutions of addicted defendants?

I. It is constitutional for a statute to make it a crime "for a person to be addicted to the use of narcotics."

II. It is unconstitutional for a statute to make it a crime "for a person to be found in a state of intoxication in any public place" and then for a chronic alcoholic to be convicted of this crime.

III. It is not unconstitutional for a statute to make it a crime "for a person to possess narcotics" and then for a narcotics addict to be convicted of this crime.

IV. It is not unconstitutional for a statute to make it a crime "for a person to commit theft" and then for a narcotics addict to be convicted of this crime for stealing to support his or her addiction.

A. II, III, IV

B. II, IV

C. III, IV

D. I, IV

98. Which of the following statements accurately describes the doctrine that have been formulated in cases involving the Eighth Amendment prohibition on cruel and unusual punishment as applied to prosecutions where the defendant may receive the death sentence?

I. It is unconstitutional for a state to make the death penalty mandatory for a certain defined type of murder.

II. It is constitutional for a state to permit the death penalty to be imposed on a defendant who is convicted of the rape of an adult woman that does not result in the victim's death.

III. It is constitutional for a state to permit the death penalty to be imposed on a defendant who was 15 at the time of the crime.

IV. It is constitutional for a state to permit the death penalty to be imposed on a defendant who exhibits reckless indifference to human life and plays a major role in aiding and abetting a felony in the course of which another co-felon commits a murder.

A. I, II, IV

B. II, III

C. III, IV

D. I, IV

99. Ed is convicted of the crime of Luring or Enticing a Child, and the statutory definition of this crime under Florida law makes it a felony for an adult who has previously been convicted of a sexual offense under the law of any jurisdiction to "intentionally lure or entice, or attempt to lure or entice, a child under the age of twelve into a structure, dwelling, or conveyance for other than a lawful purpose." The statute also states that if the conduct described in the statute occurs "without the consent of the child's parent or legal guardian," this "shall be prima facie evidence of other than a lawful purpose." Finally, the statute states that a defendant "may rebut this prima facie case by establishing that either he or she reasonably believed the action taken was necessary to prevent serious injury to the child; that it was for a lawful purpose, or that the actions were reasonable under the circumstances and there was no intent to harm the child." Ed is 30 years old, and when he was 18 he

pleaded guilty (this counts as a "conviction" under the statute) to statutory rape in a situation where he and his 16-year-old girlfriend had consensual sex and were caught in the act by her parents. Ed is now married and has children. He was charged with the crime of Luring or Enticing a Child because his neighbor was standing on the sidewalk in front of Ed's house in Miami and saw a 10-year-old girl in Ed's front yard delivering a newspaper to Ed on the morning of December 24. Ed took the paper and said to the girl, "Come on inside for a moment. I have something for you." The neighbor then spied Ed through the open front door of his house, and saw him standing in his living room, where he handed the girl a box of candy and shook her hand. The neighbor called the police and Ed was arrested. Ed's lawyer, Pearl, does some research and discovers that Black's Law Dictionary defines the words "lawful purpose" as follows: "To say of an act that it is 'lawful' implies that is authorized, sanctioned or at any rate not forbidden by law. 'Lawful' usually imports a moral substance or ethical permissibility." Pearl also discovers that Florida precedents do not provide guidance concerning the meaning of "lawful purpose." At Ed's trial, Pearl argues that the Florida statute is void for vagueness under the Due Process Clause of the Fourteenth Amendment. The trial judge rejects this argument and Ed is convicted. On appeal, Pearl argues that the appellate court should reverse Ed's conviction because the statute is void for vagueness.

What are the strongest arguments that the defense lawyer can make to persuade the appellate court that the statute is void for vagueness?

    I. The statute does not give fair notice as to the scope of the conduct it makes criminal, because no reasonable person could ascertain the meaning of "lawful purpose."

II. The various dictionary definitions of "lawful purpose" reveal that there is no consensus concerning the meaning of these terms, and since there are different potential meanings, the interpretation of the meaning of the statute cannot be predicted.

III. The statute cannot be saved from the vagueness flaw because there is no source that could be used for narrowing the meaning of the statute.

IV. The statute's vagueness creates an overbreadth problem because the uncertainty of its meaning has the effect of criminalizing a broad range of innocent conduct.

A. I, II, IV

B. I, II, III, IV

C. I, II, III

D. II, III, IV

100. Ken is a member of the Montana Highway Patrol. He was traveling along State Highway 200 toward the town of Flowing Wells when a vehicle passed him. Ken caught up to the vehicle and clocked the vehicle ahead of him at a steady 85 mph during the time that he followed it. As soon as the vehicle ahead of him reached a point where the road was wide enough to pull over safely, Ken signaled the driver to pull over and issued her a ticket for violating the Montana speeding statute. The basis for the ticket was the fact that the driver, Jill, had been operating her vehicle at a speed of 85 mph on a stretch of road where Ken concluded that it was unsafe and "unreasonable" to do so. The crime with which Jill was

charged was defined by the Montana code as follows:

> A person operating or driving a vehicle of any character on a public highway of this state shall drive the vehicle in a careful and prudent manner and at a rate of speed no greater than is reasonable and proper under the conditions existing at the point of operation, taking into account the amount and character of traffic, condition of brakes, weight of vehicle, grade and width of highway, condition of surface, and freedom of obstruction to the view ahead. The person operating or driving the vehicle shall drive the vehicle so as not to unduly or unreasonably endanger the life, limb, property, or other rights of a person entitled to the use of the street or highway

At Jill's trial Ken testified that the road where the speeding occurred was a narrow road, had no shoulders, and was broken up by an occasional frost heave (a bump in the road). He also testified that the road included curves and hills which obscured vision of the roadway ahead. However, Ken acknowledged that he never lost sight of Jill's vehicle. The roadway itself was bare and dry, there were no adverse weather conditions, and the incident occurred during daylight hours. Ken did not inspect the brakes on Jill's vehicle or make any observation regarding its weight. He did inspect the tires, and they were new. Jill's car is a new model Camaro, which is a sports car with a suspension system designed so that the vehicle can be operated at high speeds. Ken testified that he observed no other vehicles on the road going in their direction during the time he trailed Jill's car and that he observed a couple of vehicles approach them in the opposite direction during this time. Jill testified that her car had fewer than 10,000 miles on it, and that it was in perfect operating condition, that the highway conditions were perfect, and that she felt she was operating her car in a safe manner. She conceded that she drove at 85 mph, but testified that because she was aware of the officer's presence she was extra careful about the manner in which she operated the vehicle. Jill testified that she is 50 years old, drives 25,000 a year, and has never had an accident. After the trial judge heard the evidence, Jill's counsel argued that the statute should be struck down as void for vagueness under the Due Process Clause of the U.S. Constitution. The trial judge found Jill guilty and upheld the statute against the constitutional challenge.

What are the strongest arguments that the defense lawyer can make to persuade the appellate court that the statute is void for vagueness?

I. The vague phrases in the statute include: "a careful and prudent manner" and "at a rate of speed no greater than is reasonable and proper" and "so as not to unduly or unreasonably endanger" the rights of another person.

II. The statute requires a driver to calculate a reasonable speed based upon facts that would be known ordinarily only by a highway engineer or car manufacturer, specifically "the weight of vehicle [and the] grade and width of highway."

III. The term "reasonable and proper speed" is vague because reasonable police officers have no clear standard by which to determine what that speed might be for a particular stretch of highway, given the large number of statutory variables that are supposed to be used to define a "reasonable" speed.

IV. The evidence reveals that the police decision to define Jill's speed ignored some of the statutory factors (lack of traffic, good road conditions) and thus reveals the inherent arbitrary enforcement danger that is created by the vagueness as to how these factors are to be weighed to determine a "reasonable" speed.

A. I, II, III

B. I, II, III, IV

C. I, III, IV

D. I, II, IV

CRIMINAL LAW
MULTIPLE CHOICE

ANSWERS & ANALYSIS

CRIMINAL LAW ANSWERS AND ANALYSIS

1. **Issue: Elements of common law battery.**
    The correct answer is (B) because statements I, II and III describe the various actus reus and mens rea elements that were used for common law battery. These included either the intent to touch offensively or criminal negligence for mental states, and either an unlawful touching or a bodily injury for acts. Statement IV is not accurate because it describes an element of the new crime of assault that was added to the old crime of common law assault in many states in the 20th century. Assault is not the equivalent of common law battery but a different crime. The Model Penal Code abandoned the "battery" term, but borrowed and modified the elements of common law battery in its assault provision. Answers (A), (C) and (D) are incorrect because they do not list the likely elements and omit the inaccurate element.

2. **Issue: Elements of modern aggravated battery.**
    The correct answer is (D) because all four types of extra elements are likely to be used in aggravated battery statute, as set forth in statements I, II, III, and IV. The Model Penal Code provision on aggravated assault incorporates the elements described in statements II and III as common elements of aggravated battery. However, few state codes now limit their aggravated battery definitions to those two types of elements, and many use the elements described in statements I and IV. Answers (A), (B) and (C) are incorrect because they do not list all the common elements of the modern aggravated battery crime.

3. **Issue: Elements of common law assault.**
    The correct answer is (C) because at common law the only type of assault was an attempted battery,

which required the elements in statements I, II, and IV. The element in statement III is common in modern assault statutes, which usually incorporate a "frightening" version of the crime that is derived from tort law. The Model Penal Code borrowed and modified the elements of this definition of common law assault in its assault provision. Answers (A), (B) and (D) are incorrect because they do not list the likely elements and omit the inaccurate element.

4. **Issue: Elements of modern assault.**
The correct answer is (A) because all four elements are likely to be used in a modern assault statute, as set forth in statements I, II, III, and IV. Most modern assault statutes include not only the old common law definition of attempted battery, but also the new tort-based crime of a "frightening" type of assault. Statements I, II, and II set forth the elements of the tort-based type of assault, and statement IV sets forth the typical elements of the attempted battery type of assault. The Model Penal Code borrowed and modified the elements of the tort-based type of modern assault in its assault provision, and combined this crime with the attempted-battery type of assault. Answers (B), (C), and (D) are incorrect because they do not list the all the common elements of the modern crime.

5. **Issue: Common law battery, application to facts.**
The correct answer is (A) because the strongest arguments for Elly are those described in statements III and IV concerning her lack of intentional mental state. By contrast, statements I and I describe weaker arguments for Elly, which she is likely to lose on these facts. First, Elly can argue that she did not have the intent to cause bodily injury or to touch offensively (described in statement I) because she did not know that the

laser would hurt Vic's eye. This is evident because she said that she didn't know how the laser worked, and she had to ask Vic to tell her if he felt anything when she turned it on his face. In terms of culpable mental state, Elly was negligent or reckless at worst, and the intentional mental states do not cover these categories. However, the criminal negligence mental state described in statement II may fit Elly if the old common law interpretation of this concept is used. According to that interpretation, her criminal negligence may be inferred from her risk-taking behavior in pointing the laser at a vulnerable and sensitive part of Vic's body. Elly is even "presumed" to intend the "natural and probable consequences" of her actions, even if she had no such intent. By contrast, a modern MPC-style definition of criminal negligence would require that Elly should have been aware of a substantial risk of either offensive touching or bodily injury, and that her conduct should be a gross deviation from that of a reasonable person. Finally, the act elements in statement I are difficult for Elly to dispute, because Vic was offensively touched in his eye and because the heavy irritation is sufficient to satisfy a broad definition of bodily injury. The Model Penal Code defines bodily injury as any impairment of physical condition. A state appellate court has affirmed a battery conviction on similar facts in a divided opinion. Answers (B), (C), and (D) are incorrect because they do not list the two strongest arguments and omit the two weakest arguments.

6. **Issue: Common law battery, application to facts.**
The correct answer is (C) because the prosecutor will argue the policy ideas expressed in statements I, III, and IV. Statement II, however, is not accurate and will not serve as an argument for the prosecutor. First, statement I accurately describes

the original underlying policies behind the common law battery crime. Second, statement II explains how these policies should be extended to a laser battery situation in a modern case, because intangible forces like a laser light can cause harm to the person. Third, statement IV explains the policy argument that public knowledge of the dangerous character of lasers should justify liability for Elly because she should have been aware of a substantial risk of harm to Vic from her conduct, even if the laser that she purchased carried no warning. However, statement II is not accurate because a majority of states have abandoned the offensive touching definition of battery and require bodily injury instead, following the Model Penal Code's position on this point. A state appellate court has affirmed a battery conviction on similar facts in a divided opinion. Answers (A), (B) and (D) are incorrect because they do not list the best policy arguments and omit the inaccurate argument.

7. **Issue: Assault, application to facts.**
The correct answer is (B) because the appellate court will reverse the conviction and cite the reasons described in statements I and II. The appellate court will not cite the reversal reason mentioned in statement III and will not cite the reason of statement IV because it will not affirm. A modern statute is being used for this prosecution, so it will incorporate both the attempted battery crime and the frightening type of assault. Dan could be convicted if only one of these assault crimes could be proven, but each crime is missing something on the facts. First, a frightened victim is a prerequisite under most definitions of the frightening type of assault, and here Mike was almost blind and could not be frightened by the knife. Therefore, statement I is accurate. Second, the mental state of intent to injure is required for

the attempted battery crime, because the intent to "complete" the battery crime is always an element of an attempt. Dan only intended to frighten Mike, not to injure him. Therefore statement II is accurate. However, statement III is inaccurate because neither type of assault crime requires actual injury. Furthermore, statement IV is inaccurate because the conviction for attempted-battery assault may not be affirmed in the absence of Dan's intent to injure; thus, Dan's close proximity to Mike is not sufficient to justify an affirmance of the conviction, even though it may establish the act element of the attempted battery version of assault. Answers (A), (C) and (D) are incorrect because they do not list the accurate explanations and omit the inaccurate ones.

8. **Issue: Elements of common law larceny.**
The correct answer is (A) because all four elements were part of the definition of common law larceny, as set forth in statements I, II, III, and IV. Modern larceny statutes have abandoned the asportation requirement that the property must be carried away and courts have trivialized the requirement by interpreting even the slightest movement of the property to count as asportation. The Model Penal Code abandoned the term "larceny" term and broadened the elements of the larceny type of theft crime to cover the taking of property or exercising control over it with the appropriate mental state. Answers (B), (C) and (D) are incorrect because they do not list all the accurate elements.

9. **Issue: Elements of common law embezzlement.**
The correct answer is (D) because the elements described in statements II, III and IV are accurate descriptions of the elements of embezzlement; by contrast, the element in statement I is inaccurate because it is an element of larceny and not embezzlement. The Model Penal Code abandoned

the "embezzlement" term and broadened the elements of the embezzlement type of theft crime to cover the taking of property or exercising control over it with the appropriate mental state. Answers (A), (B), and (C) are incorrect because they do not list all the accurate elements and omit the inaccurate element.

10. **Issue: Common law larceny, application to facts.**
The correct answer is (B) because the appellate court will affirm the larceny conviction and rely on the reasons in statements II and III. The court will not rely on the reversal reasons given in statements I and IV because they are inaccurate. First, statement II is accurate, and Cate's status as a bailee means that she is an agent who acquires lawful possession of the bags but not lawful possession of the contents of the bags, according to one of the common law larceny fictions. Therefore, when she opened the bags and removed the money, that money was still in the lawful "possession" of the bank, and thus, she took the money from the bank's "possession" and thereby committed larceny. Breaking open a packaged good and taking the contents is "breaking bale" and qualifies for larceny. Second, statement III is accurate, and the fact that Cate received instructions for the delivery of the money puts her into the status of custodian who receives property for a limited or temporary purpose. Using this theory, she never had possession of the money bags, only custody of them, and therefore, she took unlawful "possession" of the bags and the money from the bank when she violated the instructions she was given concerning the delivery of the bags. Statement I is inaccurate because Cate's temporary custody is a reason to affirm the larceny conviction; statement IV is inaccurate because the possession of the money remained constructively with the bank and never

attached to the service company, even though the company was holding the money as a bailee. A lower federal court affirmed a larceny conviction on similar facts. Answers (A), (C) and (D) are incorrect because they do not list the inaccurate explanations and omit the inaccurate ones.

11. **Issue: Common law embezzlement, application to facts.**
The correct answer is (C) because the appellate court will reverse the conviction and rely on the reasons in statements I, III, and IV. The court will not rely on the affirmance reason in statement II. The facts described in statements I, III, and IV all point to the lack of evidence of the embezzlement element of entrustment. Ali was entrusted with the coins but not with the currency. However, according to the instructions that Ali was given, it appears that he could be a classic larceny defendant who was given custody of the currency but not "possession." He had access to the cash only for a limited and temporary purpose, which was to refill the coin hopper and check for problems. Therefore, when he took the cash, he did so unlawfully without authority in disregard of his instructions, and thereby committed larceny because he took the cash from the casino's "possession." A divided state appellate court reversed an embezzlement conviction on similar facts, leaving the option open of a prosecution for larceny. Answers (A), (B), and (D) are incorrect because they do not list the accurate statements and omit the inaccurate one.

12. **Issue: Elements of common law false pretenses.**
The correct answer is (C) because the elements described in statements I, II, and IV are accurate descriptions of the elements of the common law version of false pretenses, whereas statement III is inaccurate because at common law a false

representation could not concern a "future fact" like a promise, but only past or present facts. The Model Penal Code has abandoned the term "false pretenses" term and updated the definition to include a broad range of thefts by deception. Answers (A), (B), and (D) are incorrect because they do not list all the accurate elements and omit the inaccurate element.

13. **Issue: Theft by deception, application to facts.** The correct answer is (D) because the appellate court should affirm and rely on statement I to explain the decision. The court will not need to rely on statement II because it is irrelevant to the decision to affirm. Statements III and IV will not be cited because they will not be persuasive and the court will not reverse. First, statement I is accurate because this is a modern statute modeled on the Model Penal Code, which is evident from the name of the crime and the language of the statute. The reliance by the victim on the false representation is not an explicit element of the crime, and this allows the court to affirm a conviction in a situation where no such reliance exists. Rhoda's conduct in presenting the blue dress to the cashier with the inappropriate sales tag is an implied representation, knowingly made, of a present fact that is false (that the blue dress is on sale for the price marked on the tag). Therefore, sufficient evidence for a conviction exists here. Statement II is irrelevant to the decision to affirm because the cashier's state of mind is not important according to the elements of the statute. While it is true that the cashier's lack of certainty about the validity of the sales tag means that she was in a position to be deceived through reliance on the false representation, the statute does not require proof of reliance. Furthermore, statement III is inaccurate because common law elements should not be read into a MPC-based theft crime, absent evidence of

legislative intent to this effect. The MPC abandoned a variety of elements of the common law false pretenses crime, including this one. Finally, statement IV is inaccurate because the security guard's state of mind is not relevant, according to the elements of the modern theft by deception crime. However, one lower court reversed a conviction on similar facts in a divided opinion, because the majority was persuaded that the legislature intended to retain the common law element of reliance in the theft by deception crime, according to the legislative history and case law jurisprudence of the state. Answers (A), (B), and (C) are incorrect because they do not list the accurate reason and omit the inaccurate reasons.

14. **Issue: Transmission of stolen property, application to facts.**
The correct answer is (A) because statements I, II, and IV describe the traditional arguments that will help the prosecutor to justify an interpretation of the statutory terms that covers Sara's conduct. Statement III does not describe an argument that helps the prosecutor and should be omitted. The arguments in statements I, II, and IV are reflected in the jurisprudence interpreting the statute, and lower federal court affirmed a conviction on similar facts. Statement I accurately emphasizes the modern element of "transmits," a term that was added to the statute in 1988 in order to make it clear that the statute covers money wire transfers. Such a verb allows the prosecutor to argue that modern technological forms of electronic transmission are intended to be covered by the statute. Statement II accurately describes the prosecutor's position that "goods" should be interpreted as items of commercial value, so that the trial plan may be characterized as an item that is sold by lawyers to a client, and therefore has commercial value in the marketplace. Statement IV

echoes a traditional argument that a legislative omission of a term in a statute implies a legislative intent to omit that term, and here the omission of any limitation on the concept of "goods" helps the prosecutor to argue that the statute was meant to be expanded by courts to fit evolving forms of property. By contrast, statement III does not help the prosecutor because securities and money are examples of financial instruments with a concrete and narrow definition. The prosecutor wants the concept of "goods" to be broadly interpreted, and a comparison of the term "goods" with the narrower property terms in the statute is inconsistent with the prosecutor's goal. Answers (B), (C) and (D) are incorrect because they do not list the strong prosecution arguments and omit the one that does not help the prosecutor.

15. **Issue: Transmission of stolen property, application to facts.**

    The correct answer is (C) because statements I, II, and III describe the policy arguments that may be used to justify an affirmance of the conviction. All three arguments appear in lower court jurisprudence interpreting the statute, and in a lower court case affirming a conviction on similar facts. Statement IV is not supported by the jurisprudence. Moreover, even though there is some case law that implies that telephone information should not be covered by the statute, the emailed trial plan is distinguishable from such information because it can be transmitted in a form that readily produces a tangible document.
    Answers (A), (B), and (D) are incorrect because they do not list all the policy arguments that will be used and omit the argument for reversal that will not be used.

16. **Issue: Elements of common law receiving stolen property.**

The correct answer is (B) because only statements III and IV accurately describe two of the common law elements of the crime. Statement I describes a modern element that may be used to allow the crime to be expanded beyond the original common law element of the act of receiving. Statement II describes another modern element of the Model Penal Code that expands the crime beyond the original mens rea of knowledge that the property is stolen. One other common law element of the crime, not mentioned as an answer choice, is the requirement that the received property must be "stolen" property. Answers (A), (C), and (D) are incorrect because they do not list the accurate elements and omit the inaccurate elements.

17. **Issue: Receiving stolen property, application to facts.**

    The correct answer is (B) because statements I and IV accurately describe arguments that the appellate court will use in reversing Hanna's conviction. A lower court reversed a conviction on similar facts citing these explanations. Statements II and III will not be cited by the court because they are not persuasive policy reasons for rejecting liability in Hanna's case. First, both statements I and IV identify a policy reason points toward a statutory interpretation of "possession or control" that will exclude Hanna from liability. Statement I expresses the goal of expanding liability beyond the driver of a stolen car to include passengers who fortuitously are not driving but are effectively sharing in the responsibility for controlling the stolen car. This category of passengers does not include Hanna. Notably, Hanna played no role in the theft of the car, nor did she share responsibility for controlling what happened to it after the theft. She had no evident capacity to affect Max's use of the car, other than to go along with Max's plan to offer her a ride home. Statement IV expresses the goal of expanding liability beyond the driver to cover passengers who "have the capacity" to influence the driver, because they are directing the driver, for example, or because they have agreed to assist the driver in some way during the getaway period while the driver is operating the stolen car. Hanna played no such role, and thus does not fit this other category of passengers who should be liable. By contrast, statement II describes a policy justification that is too broad to serve as a justification for liability, because the mere status of a defendant as a passenger and not a driver should not automatically dictate a lack of liability. Some passengers may have more capacity for possession and control (because they have car keys, for example) than Hanna does, and such passengers may deserve conviction. Next, statement III is inaccurate because Hanna did "benefit" from using the truck because she accepted a ride in it; moreover, this "benefit" factor is used by lower courts as one element in a totality of circumstances that may be used to justify liability. Answers (A), (C), and (D) are incorrect because they do not list the accurate elements and omit the inaccurate elements.

18. **Issue: Elements of common law robbery.**
The correct answer is (D) because statements II and III accurately identify the two elements that distinguished common law robbery from common law larceny. Statements I and IV are not accurate because they identify elements that are common to both common law robbery and common law larceny. Another element of common law robbery that overlaps with larceny element is a trespassory taking from possession, but this is not mentioned as an answer choice. The Model Penal Code's definition of the robbery crime abandoned the requirement that property must be taken from the person or presence of the victim. Answers (A), (B),

and (C) are incorrect because they do not list the two distinct elements of robbery and omit the elements that overlap with larceny.

19. **Issue: Common law robbery, application to facts.**

    The correct answer is (C) because statement I is correct; Jen may be convicted of robbery but not the other two defendants, according to state court jurisprudence. For a robbery conviction to be upheld, the force or violence needed should be an amount of "force" that is more than the ordinary force needed to remove the property from the person. If such a requirement is not used as a matter of policy, then the crimes of theft and robbery may become indistinguishable, because then there may be only a slight difference between a taking for larceny and a taking by force for robbery. Also, the victim should be aware of the taking by force or violence, because that victim awareness is what creates the special harm of robbery. That victim awareness creates a risk of extra harm to a victim who may attempt to resist the taking, and to bystanders who may seek to assist the victim. The lack of awareness of a taking is a characteristic of larceny, which causes a harm that is defined as a taking by stealth. Jen can be convicted of robbery because there was resistance by the victim Jerome, which required Jen to use more than ordinary force to yank the briefcase away from him. Such a crime deserves the robbery definition because it is involves the harm of taking violently under circumstances where a risk of extra harm exists to the resisting victim and to bystanders. By contrast, neither Harvey nor Maude used more than ordinary force in their takings. Maude snatched a $100 bill and met no resistance. Harvey also met no resistance because he took by stealth, and therefore his conduct lacks both the resistance and the victim awareness needed for robbery. Answers (A),

(B), and (D) are incorrect because they do not list the defendant who can be convicted of robbery and omit those who cannot.

20. **Issue: Elements of common law burglary.**
The correct answer is (B) because statements I, II, and III accurately describe three of the elements of common law burglary. Statement IV does not accurately describe the mens rea for burglary, which is the intent to commit a felony in the dwelling. The Model Penal Code abandoned the breaking and nighttime elements in its definition of the burglary crime, and expands the crime to include entries into occupied structures as well as dwellings. Answers (A), (C) and (D) are incorrect because they do not list the common law elements and omit the element that was not part of the common law crime.

21. **Issue: Common law burglary, application to facts.**
The correct answer is (A) because statements I, II, and IV accurately describe the prosecutor's best arguments based on statutory interpretation and policy. By contrast, statement III is not an effective argument because it would require the court to interpret the statute too broadly. First, statement I makes a traditional argument based on the terms of the statute that favor the prosecutor. Second, statement II relies on the use of a statutory example to make an analogy to the lean-to, in order to demonstrate that despite some differences between a lean-to and a traditional "structure" like a building, the lean-to should be covered by the statute. Finally, statement IV identifies a policy reason for statutory coverage of the lean-to, which is that one of the purposes of the burglary crime exists to protect collections of people's possessions in dwellings from theft. However, statement III is not an effective argument for the prosecutor

because it focuses on the existence of an alarm system to justify protection of a structure; alarm systems are used for many types of property that are neither structures themselves nor related to structures (such as cars, boats, and fenced property). Therefore, this argument would provide little guidance concerning a limiting principle for the concept of a structure. Answers (B), (C) and (D) are incorrect because they do not list the prosecutor's strongest arguments and omit the weak argument.

22. **Issue: Common law burglary, application to facts.**
The correct answer is (A) because statements II, III, and IV accurately describe the statutory interpretation ideas that will be used by the appellate court for reversing Thuy's conviction. A lower court relied on similar reasoning to reach this result. Statement I will not be used as a reason because the language of the statute does not support this interpretation of the term "structure." First, statement II describes an interpretation of "structure" that is supported by the statutory text because all the statutory examples of structures are enclosed spaces. Next, statement III is similarly supported by the text because some of the examples have barriers to entry. Finally, statement IV is a traditional statutory interpretation argument whereby courts seek to ensure that different terms in a statute will be interpreted in a consistent way (here, by relying on statutory examples to interpret the broad term of "structure" in the statute). By contrast, statement I refers to "carrying on business," which is not a characteristic of the purposes of the other enumerated examples of structures in the statute. In fact, all the examples share the purpose of overnight accommodation, but not of business activities. Answers (B), (C) and (D) are incorrect because they do not list the reasons

that will be used and omit the reason that will not be used by the appellate court.

23. **Issue: Elements of common law murder.**
The correct answer is (D) because the murder types listed in statements II, III and IV were treated as common law murder under English common law, as all three types were treated as killings with "malice aforethought," the common law mens rea for murder. The category of deliberated and premeditated murder described in statement I was not originally a type of murder category recognized at English common law. This statutory category was invented in Pennsylvania in order to create a "first degree" murder definition that would be required for the imposition of the death penalty. The Model Penal Code abandoned the popular deliberated-and-premeditated category of murder, and rejected the concept of degrees for murder. while retaining and modifying the three common law types of murder listed in statements II, III, and IV. Answers (A), (B) and (C) are incorrect because they do not list the original types of common law murder and omit the murder crime that was not originally recognized in English law.

24. **Issue: Definitions of deliberated and premeditated murder.**
The correct answer is (B) because statements I, II, III, and IV describe definitions that each receive some support in state court jurisprudence. The Model Penal Code abandoned the deliberated-and-premeditated category of murder, in part, because of the wide range of definitions of this concept. Some states interpret this mental state in a meaningful way in their code or case law definitions, by requiring significant evidence of a defendant's actual deliberation and actual premeditation concerning the decision to kill. Statements II and III describe definitions used by

some of these states. In other states, however, the mental state is interpreted in a meaningless way, through reliance on definitions like those expressed in statements I and IV. Answers (A), (C) and (D) are incorrect because each of them omits one of the common definitions of the formula.

25. **Issue: Elements of common law voluntary manslaughter.**
The correct answer is (C) because statements I, III, and IV accurately identify three elements of common law voluntary manslaughter. Statement II is inaccurate because the element of malice aforethought is an exclusive attribute of common law murder. The Model Penal Code abandoned the "no cooling time" element of voluntary manslaughter, and modified the other common law elements of the crime, while renaming it as "extreme-emotional-disturbance" manslaughter. Answers (A), (B) and (D) are incorrect because they do not list the accurate elements and omit the inaccurate element.

26. **Issue: Elements of reckless manslaughter.**
The correct answer is (D) because statements II and III accurately describe elements that are included in modern definitions of reckless manslaughter, derived from the original common law crime of "involuntary" manslaughter. The definitions used here appear in the Model Penal Code. Statements I and IV do not accurately describe elements of reckless manslaughter, but rather, elements of voluntary manslaughter at common law. Answers (A), (B), and (C) are incorrect because they do not list the accurate elements of reckless manslaughter and omit the inaccurate element.

27. **Issue: Intentional and reckless homicides, application to facts.**
The correct answer is (A) because statements I and

III accurately describe the two recklessness crimes that fit the facts. Depraved heart murder is the common law crime which modern statutes may define as reckless murder with "extreme indifference to human life," if they emulate the Model Penal Code formula. Reckless manslaughter is a modern form of involuntary manslaughter at common law; in its MPC form, it is a reckless killing that is not murder because it lacks the element of "extreme indifference to human life." The killing here was arguably reckless, because Jock chased the victim with a pointed and loaded gun, and thereby consciously disregarded a substantial and unjustifiable risk of death that existed because of the possibility that the gun could go off accidentally during the chase. The element of extreme indifference is arguably present, and this element would elevate the crime from reckless manslaughter to reckless murder. However, the crimes listed in statements II and IV do not fit the facts. The crime listed in statement II does not fit because even though there may have been adequate provocation and heat of passion, the killing was not triggered by these influences but was caused by an accident. Likewise, the crime listed in statement IV does not fit the facts because it requires the intent to kill, and the killing here was not intentional. Answers (B), (C), and (D) are incorrect because they do not list the crimes that fit the facts and omit the crimes that do not.

28. **Issue: Intentional and reckless homicides, application to facts.**

    The correct answer is (B) because the all statements, I, II, III and IV accurately describe a crime for which conviction is possible on these facts. First, statements I and II describe two reckless homicide crimes that Jock may have committed. Jock's conduct in shooting a loaded weapon through a windshield arguably will fit either or both reckless murder and reckless manslaughter. The risk of death from Jock's conduct is substantial, and he consciously disregarded that risk. Second, statement IV describes an intentional murder formula that is sometimes interpreted as requiring only that an instant of time for deliberation and premeditation was available to the defendant before the killing took place. Even though Jock's shooting is arguably impulsive, in some jurisdictions a jury verdict of deliberated and premeditated murder could be affirmed on these facts because Jock had enough time to deliberate and premeditate. Third, statement III describes a crime, felony murder, which requires the commission of a felony, and here that felony would be burglary. Arguably, Jock broke and entered into Belle's house with the intent to commit a felony inside the house; he does not need to commit an actual crime in the house, he only needs to have the intent to do so. He was armed with a weapon, and arguably he intended to frighten Belle and the man, which intent would establish the mens rea for an assault crime. Answers (A), (C), and (D) are inaccurate because they do not list all the crimes that "may" lead to a conviction.

29. **Issue: Voluntary manslaughter, application to facts.**
The correct answer is (B) because statements II, III, and IV accurately identify arguments that the defense counsel will make; statement I is an argument that defense counsel will not make. In a traditional voluntary manslaughter statute, the elements of no cooling time, adequate provocation, and heat of passion are required, and statements II, III, and IV refer to facts that support a finding of each of these elements. However, statement I is not useful to the defense because it does not relate to the defendant's burden of providing evidence of the

elements of voluntary manslaughter. The lack of an intent to kill does not stop the prosecutor from winning a murder conviction, in the absence of evidence of the elements of voluntary manslaughter. Moreover, many state codes and state cases recognize that an extremely reckless mental state may exist either during a provoked killing that qualifies for voluntary manslaughter, or during a murder that does not qualify for a voluntary manslaughter verdict. Answers (A), (C), and (D) are not correct because they do not list the arguments the defense counsel will make and omit the argument that defense counsel will not make.

30. **Issue: Deliberated and premeditated murder, application to facts.**
The correct answer is (C) because statements I and III accurately describe two strong arguments that the defense counsel will use to try to show that the evidence is insufficient to prove deliberation and premeditation. However, statements II and IV are not strong arguments to negate the elements of deliberation and premeditation. First, in a state where appellate courts conduct a careful review of "deliberation and premeditation" evidence, it is traditional to examine the manner of killing as a factor that can demonstrate planning. Therefore, statement I describes the defense counsel's argument that a one-shot killing evidences little planning, compared to other methods of killing that are not so impulsive. Second, statement III explains how the defendant's shooting was impulsive and could not have been planned, because Jock did not know that Vic would jump into a car or where the car was parked. However, statement II about the lack of motive is a weak argument here where other motive evidence is strong, since Jock was angry about Belle's sexual infidelity. Furthermore, statement IV will not be used because the element of "extreme emotional

disturbance" is an element under the Model Penal Code definition of manslaughter that is derived from voluntary manslaughter at common law. This element is irrelevant to the deliberation and premeditation murder formula, because any emotional disturbance does not necessarily negate planning. Answers (A), (B), and (D) are inaccurate because they do not list the defense arguments that will be used and omit the arguments that will not be used.

31. **Issue: Deliberated and premeditated murder, application to facts.**
The correct answer is (A) because statements I, II and IV accurately describe three strong arguments that the prosecutor will use to explain why the facts are sufficient to show deliberation and premeditation. Statements III is not going to be used by the prosecution because it is not a relevant argument. First, statement I is a traditional argument that when a defendant comes armed to the scene of a homicide, this is evidence of planning. Second, statement II is another traditional argument that the defendant's method of killing may demonstrate planning; it is arguable that Jock's failure to shoot Vic in the house or on the street can be explained by the difficulties of hitting Vic during the chase, and that Jock shot Vic in the car as part of a plan to wait until a clear shot could be fired. Finally, statement IV is a traditional argument that evidence of motive helps to support an argument that the defendant had a reason to plan the killing. However, statement III is irrelevant to the deliberation and premeditation argument, because the heinous or wanton quality of a killing are only relevant to depraved heart murder or reckless murder, but not to deliberation and premeditation murder. Answers (B), (C), and (D) are inaccurate because they do not list the prosecution arguments that will be used and omit

the argument that will not be used.

32. **Issue: Depraved heart murder, application to facts.**

The correct answer is (B) because all four statements, I, II, III, and IV accurately describe strong arguments that will used by the prosecutor to seek affirmance of the depraved heart murder conviction. This crime is the equivalent of reckless murder under the Model Penal Code, whose elements include the mental state of MPC recklessness, plus the extra element of extreme indifference to human life. Appellate courts traditionally examine the four kinds of factors mentioned in all the statements here when reviewing a depraved heart murder conviction. First, a defendant's conduct may be compared to that of other murder defendants, as in statement I, in order to insure that a depraved-heart-murder defendant seems to have the same degree of culpability as other murder defendants. Second, the courts examine the separate elements of the recklessness concept to determine whether the defendant's level of recklessness appears to be extreme, as described in statement II. Third, the courts compare a defendant's conduct to that of defendants whose depraved heart murder convictions have been affirmed in state court jurisprudence; depraved heart murder convictions have been obtained in cases like those noted in statement III. Finally, courts examine the subjective factor of wantonness or depravity, which is the equivalent of the MPC element of extreme indifference to the value of human life. Here the prosecutor will argue that proof of Jacob's intention to kill is lacking, but that his extremely dangerous playing with a loaded shotgun, in an intoxicated state, in close proximity to another human being, demonstrates the similarities between his conduct and that of intentional killers. The prosecutor will also argue that these facts demonstrate the extreme level of risk taking by Jacob as well as his depravity and wantonness. A lower court affirmed a conviction for depraved heart murder on similar facts. Answers (A), (C) and (D) are incorrect because they do not list all the arguments that the prosecutor will make.

33. **Issue: Elements of negligent homicide.**
The correct answer is (C) because statements I, III, and IV accurately describe three of the elements of negligent homicide as defined by the Model Penal Code and most state statutes. However, statement II is inaccurate because it describes an element of reckless manslaughter, not negligent homicide. Answers (A), (B), and (D) are incorrect because they do not list the three relevant elements and omit the inappropriate element.

34. **Issue: Reckless and negligent homicides, felony murder, application to facts.**
The correct answer is (D) because statements I, II, and III accurately describe three charges that may result in conviction. However, statement IV does not describe a charge that fits the facts. First, statement III describes the most likely charge to produce a conviction because negligent homicide requires only that Carl should have been aware of a substantial and unjustifiable risk of death and that his conduct was a gross deviation from that of a reasonable person. This is the Model Penal Code formula for this crime and is widely emulated in state statutes. On these facts, Carl should have been aware of the risk of hitting the vulnerable children, because they were in the middle of the road where his wide vehicle could hit them and kill them at the speed of 35 miles per hour. The risk of death was substantial because the children could be expected either to panic and make unpredictable movements, or to fail to move away from the path of

Carl's wide vehicle because of the danger from oncoming traffic on the other side of the street. Second, statement II describes a reckless manslaughter charge that may result in conviction if a jury finds that Carl consciously disregarded a substantial risk of death to the children; such a finding seems likely, given Carl's knowledge of the danger to them from his wide van traveling at 35 miles per hour, and his knowledge that the risk of death could be lowered if only he would slow down or stop and let the children cross the street. Third, statement I describes a crime which requires the prosecutor to prove the extra element, beyond recklessness, of extreme indifference to the value of human life. Given Carl's selfish behavior of not stopping to protect children in the street, and his preference for speeding along his way for his own purposes, such an extra element may be found. However, statement IV describes a crime that has no relation to these facts, because the death did not occur during the course of a felony. While it is true that Carl was speeding before the accident, this was not true at the time of the accident. Moreover, most felony murder statutes would not make a vehicular homicide accompanied with a low level of speeding into a strict liability crime of felony murder. Answers (A), (B), and (C) do not list all the convictions that may be obtained and omit the conviction that will not be obtained.

35. **Issue: Limitations on felony murder.**
The correct answer is (D) because statements II, III, and IV accurately describe common limitations for felony murder doctrine that have evolved in many states. Statement I does not accurately describe a likely limitation on felony murder liability. The liability of co-felons for any crime, not just felony murder, will depend on accomplice liability principles. Ordinarily, co-felons who have a common plan for a crime are liable for the acts of

their co-felons, as long as these acts are foreseeable. Thus, co-felons can be liable for a felony murder caused by the act of a co-felon. Therefore, statement I does not accurately describe either the normal felony murder rule of vicarious liability for co-felons or the normal rules of accomplice liability. A few states have created special doctrines to define no-liability situations where the act of a co-felon may be treated as a purely independent act, but these special doctrines are limited to a narrow set of variables and statement I is too broad to serve as an accurate description of them. Answers (A), (B), and (C) are incorrect because they do not list the likely limitations and omit the inaccurate limitation.

36. **Issue: Deliberated and premeditated murder, application to facts.**
The correct answer is (A) because statements I, II, and IV accurately describe facts that support arguments that the defense counsel will make as to the absence of deliberation and premeditation evidence. However, statement III is not directly related to the defense counsel's task of arguing that this mental state is not present on the facts. First, in a jurisdiction that requires some actual proof of this mental state, Sol's bringing a weapon to the scene of the crime would be evidence of planning. Statement I describes an explanation for the knife that rebuts this traditional argument that an inference of motive and a plan to kill may be drawn from the presence of a weapon in the defendant's possession at the scene of a killing. Second, statement II alludes to the fact that Sol apparently had no plan for performing the killing and then fleeing the scene, as evidenced from his kind gesture of summoning the ambulance after the stabbing. Third, statement IV explains how Sol could have had no plan to kill Todd because he could not have anticipated that Todd would hit him

on the nose, especially since there is no evidence that Todd was aware of Sol's special sensitivity to his nose. However, the fact that Sol suffers from a nose obsession that reveals a potential mental, emotional, or psychological abnormality does not help the defense to show either that Sol did not plan to kill Todd or that he is incapable of planning to kill anyone. Answers (B), (C), and (D) are incorrect because they do not list the strongest arguments and omit the unrelated one.

37. **Issue: Deliberated and premeditated murder, application to facts.**

The correct answer is (A) because statements I, II, and III accurately describe facts that will help the prosecutor make good arguments that deliberation and premeditation existed on the facts; statement IV is not helpful to the prosecutor because it supports an argument that the defense counsel will make. First, in a jurisdiction that requires some actual proof of this mental state, statement I refers to a fact that provides a good argument because when Sol was being teased for 20 minutes, he had plenty of time to think about the crime ahead of time and thereby premeditate. Also he had time for actual reflection, which activity is synonymous with deliberation. Moreover, during the twenty-minute time period, Todd's teasing of Sol was provocative and created a potential motive for the later killing. Second, statement II refers to a fact that provides a good argument that Sol's conduct exhibits his planning of the crime; he did not stab Todd wildly in a fit of anger but acted in a calculated way, taking off his gloves in order to get a better grip on the knife to do more damage to Todd. Third, statement III refers to a fact that provides a good argument that the manner of killing may demonstrate planning, and that two wounds may suggest a less impulsive crime than one wound would suggest. However, statement IV does not provide an argument for the prosecutor because it refers to a fact that supports a defense argument that the good relationship between Todd and Sol suggests a lack of motive for the crime, which points to impulse rather than the type of planning that establishes premeditation and deliberation. Answers (B), (C), and (D) are incorrect because they do not list the strongest arguments and omit the inappropriate one.

38. **Issue: Voluntary manslaughter, application to facts.**

    The correct answer is (B) because statements I, II, and IV accurately describe facts that will help the defense counsel make good arguments that relate to the elements of voluntary manslaughter. However, statement IV is not helpful to the defense counsel because the common law definition of this crime does not focus on the perspective of the defendant's situation but upon the reasonable person standard for assessing a provocation that leads to a killing. First, statement I describes a fact that supports a required element of voluntary manslaughter; there must be hot blood or heat of passion, and Sol's rage supports this element. Second, statement II describes a fact that supports another required element, which is an adequate provocation to which a reasonable person would react with rage. The common law did recognize a physical assault upon a defendant as sufficient evidence of provocation to justify a jury instruction on voluntary manslaughter, and therefore Todd's hitting Sol on his nose may supply adequate provocation. Third, statement IV refers to a fact that relates to an absence of cooling time, which is another element of voluntary manslaughter. The common law required that a defendant's hot blood should not have cooled during the interval between the provocation and the killing, and also required that a reasonable person's blood would not have cooled during that interval. However, statement III refers to a special characteristic of Sol's, namely his nose obsession, which is not a factor that the common law would consider in assessing the adequacy of a provocation; the reasonable person standard did not take account of such personal attributes of individual defendants. Answers (A), (C), and (D) are incorrect because they do not list the facts that support defense arguments and omit the inappropriate one.

39. **Issue: Extreme emotional disturbance manslaughter, application to facts.**

The correct answer is (D) because statements I, II, and III accurately describe facts that will help the defense counsel make good arguments that relate to the elements of the Model Penal Code version of voluntary manslaughter, which is extreme emotional disturbance manslaughter. However, statement IV is not helpful to the defense counsel because the MPC does not retain the common law element that relates to cooling time. First, statement I refers to Sol's rage, which provides evidence of the needed element of an "extreme emotional disturbance." Second, statement II refers to Todd's striking of Sol's nose, which helps to provide the element of a "reasonable explanation or excuse" for the emotional disturbance. Third, statement III refers to a special characteristic of Sol's, namely his nose obsession, which is a factor that the MPC will allow to be considered in assessing the reasonableness of Sol's excuse for killing. The MPC uses the standard of a reasonable person "in the defendant's situation," and that situation may include personal abnormalities. However, statement IV refers to the absence of cooling time, which is irrelevant to the definition of extreme emotional disturbance manslaughter. Answers (A), (B), and (C) are incorrect because they do not list the facts that support defense arguments and omit the inappropriate one.

40. **Issue: Reckless murder, application to facts.**
The correct answer is (C) because statements II, III and IV accurately describe facts that will help the defense counsel make good arguments that relate to the elements of reckless murder. However, statement I is not helpful to the defense counsel because it refers to a fact that may be helpful to the prosecutor. First, statement II refers to a fact that shows that Donna was responsive to her neighbors' complaints and cared about controlling her dogs. This kind of care shows that she was trying to reduce the risk of harm to others, and this care is inconsistent with an attitude of "extreme indifference to human life," which is the element that distinguishes reckless murder from reckless manslaughter under the Model Penal Code. The fact referred to statement II also helps the defense counsel to argue that Donna put a lock on her gate and this shows that she was believed she was reducing the risk that the dogs would get out and hurt anyone. Second, statement III also shows that Donna was not indifferent to the lives of others, because Donna tried to train her dogs in order to reduce the risk that they would harm others. Third, statement IV refers to a fact that helps to prove a negative – Donna did not receive any warning that her dogs were potential killers, based on the past behavior of the dogs when they made their earlier escapes. Therefore the only known risk that Donna disregarded was the risk that her padlock would not stop the dogs from escaping, not the risk that the dogs would escape and cause death. However, statement I refers to a fact that is useful to the prosecutor because Donna's awareness of the likely identity of the victim helps to establish Donna's awareness of the risk that if the dogs escaped, they might retaliate against Max or Larry by killing them. This fact also helps the

prosecutor to argue that Donna callously disregarded the risk that the escaping dogs would be likely to encounter children who would be more vulnerable to lethal attack than adults. In arguing that Donna was extremely indifferent to the value of human life, the prosecutor will emphasize that Donna displayed a high level of conscious disregard of a high level of risk of death. Answers (A), (B), and (D) are incorrect because they do not list the facts that support defense arguments and omit the inappropriate fact.

41. **Issue: Reckless murder, application to facts.**
The correct answer is (B) because statements I, II, III and IV accurately describe facts that will help the prosecutor make good arguments that prove the elements of reckless murder. First, statement I refers to the fact that Donna's training of the dogs was found to be deficient by people who could be regarded as experts; also, Donna focused on training the dogs to attack, not on training them to be obedient or well socialized. Thus, Donna exhibited the characteristic of extreme indifference to human life, by not seeking to protect the public from her aggressive and dangerous dogs. She also disregarded a substantial risk of death because she knew that she had been rejected from the club for failure to train her dogs properly, and yet she still failed to create a secure enclosure for her badly trained and potentially aggressive dogs. Second, statement II refers to Donna's cold-hearted attitude to the death of Max; upon hearing of his death, Donna was not remorseful or saddened, but uncaring and full of blame for Max causing his own death by bothering her dogs. This attitude helps to show the "extreme indifference" element. Third, statement III refers to Donna's failure to monitor her dogs while they were in the yard during the pre-school hours, even though she knew that Max and Larry had been near her house in the past, and

even though she knew that the dogs had escaped in the past and might escape again by digging. By taking a sleeping pill, Donna chose to ignore the risk that the dogs would get out during the time of day when the children were likely to be nearby. Finally, statement IV refers to the fact that Donna's dogs belong to a dangerous breed. Like pit bulls and a few other breeds, Rottweilers are known to be dogs that can be vicious, aggressive, and dangerous to people if not properly trained. Donna's casual attitude toward the lack of security for keeping these particular dogs locked up expresses her extreme indifference to the value of human life. Answers (A), (C), and (D) are incorrect because they do not list all the facts that support defense arguments.

42. **Issue: Deliberated and premeditated murder, application to facts.**
The correct answer is (D) because statements I, II, and IV accurately describe facts that will help the prosecutor make good arguments that demonstrate the existence of deliberation and premeditation. However, statement III is not helpful to the prosecutor because it describes a fact that may be used by the defense counsel to support a theory that the killing was impulsive. First, in a jurisdiction that requires some actual proof of deliberation and premeditation, statement I refers to a fact that allows the prosecutor to argue that the threat to kill Dr. Krug reveals that Joe was planning the homicide many hours before it occurred. Traditionally, a defendant's pre-crime conduct and statements may be used to show planning. Second, statement II refers to a fact that supports the prosecutor's argument that Joe deliberately sought out Dr. Krug after Gabe's death in order to kill the doctor. Joe's action shows that he ignored the direction to go to the cafeteria, and waited for Dr. Krug with the plan in mind to

confront him and kill him. Third, statement IV refers to a fact that establishes the long time period that Joe had to formulate his plan to kill Dr. Krug, from the time that he met the doctor until the moment of the killing. Finally, statement III is not useful to the prosecutor because it refers to a fact that will be helpful to the defense counsel, which is that Joe grabbed a nearby chair that is not a typical weapon for a planned killing. Answers (A), (B), and (C) are incorrect because they do not list all the facts that support prosecution arguments and omit the fact that does not do so.

43. **Issue: Deliberated and premeditated murder, application to facts.**

The correct answer is (D) because statements I and IV accurately describe facts that will help the defense counsel to create arguments that the killing was impulsive and not based on planning that demonstrates deliberation and premeditation. Statements II and III refer to facts that will not be used by the defense counsel because the prosecutor can use them to argue that they demonstrate planning by Joe. First, statement I refers to the fact that Joe sought to kill Dr. Krug only when provoked by the apparent laughing expression of the doctor; this fact shows that Joe did not have a plan to kill Dr. Krug but simply overreacted to the apparently callous response to his demand for an explanation for the death. Second, statement IV refers to the fact that the purpose of Joe's confrontation with Dr. Krug was not a homicidal one, but rather, a normal purpose that any parent of a dead child might have, which is to discover an explanation for the failure of the doctors to save the child's life. However, statement II refers to Joe's potential motive for killing the doctor, which is his anger that is based on his belief that Dr. Krug ignored Gabe and didn't "do his job." A motive for a killing usually helps a prosecutor to establish the likelihood that a killing was planned and therefore premeditated. Also, statement III is not helpful to the defense counsel because Joe's sleep-deprived condition does not necessarily prevent Joe from being capable of carrying out a plan. The prosecutor can use this fact to suggest that Joe was mentally unbalanced because of sleep-deprivation and grief, which abnormal condition inspired and fueled his plan to kill. Sleep deprivation does not demonstrate *per se* that conduct probably was impulsive. Answers (A), (B), and (C) are incorrect because they do not list the facts that support defense arguments and omit the facts that do not do so.

44. **Issue: Extreme emotional disturbance manslaughter, application to facts.**

    The correct answer is (A) because statements I, III and IV accurately describe facts that will help the defense counsel make arguments that relate to the elements of the Model Penal Code version of voluntary manslaughter, which is extreme emotional disturbance manslaughter. However, statement II is not relevant to any of the elements of this modern crime, even though it would be relevant to the common law definition of the crime. First, statement I refers to the emotional states of anger and grief that create the extreme emotional disturbance element of Joe's mental state. Second, statement III refers to the reasonable explanation or excuse that Joe may offer as another element of the crime, which is the callous behavior of Dr. Krug in seeming to laugh at Joe. Statement IV refers to Joe's "situation" from which the reasonableness of the explanation or excuse should be judged, that of a sleep-deprived person; the modern MPC standard combines the reasonable person standard with a focus on a defendant's situational circumstances. However, statement II refers to a factual element of immediacy that is not necessary under a modern

MPC definition, because the MPC has abandoned the "no cooling time" element of the common law. Answers (B), (C), and (D) are incorrect because they do not list the facts that support defense arguments and omit the fact that is unrelated to those arguments.

45. **Issue: Voluntary manslaughter, application to facts.**

The correct answer is (C) because statements I, II, III, and IV all accurately describe facts that will help the prosecutor make good arguments about the insufficiency of evidence of the elements of voluntary manslaughter. First, statement I describes facts relating to the common law element of adequate provocation. Here the prosecutor will argue that neither Dr. Krug's brusque silence nor the doctor's laughing expression rise to the level of an adequate provocation. At common law, the list of adequate provocations was short, and it did not include "mere words." Second, statement II describes Joe's threat, and this evidence of early hostility helps the prosecutor to argue that if Joe experienced a "provoked reaction" to Dr. Krug's when Joe first met him, there was plenty of time for Joe's passion to "cool off" in the following hours before his final encounter with the doctor. Third, statement III describes the fact that plenty of "cooling time" did elapse between the arguable provocation of Dr. Krug's brusqueness and Joe's final encounter with Dr. Krug. Therefore, the prosecutor will argue that either a reasonable person's hot blood would have cooled during that time, or that Joe's hot blood actually did cool during that time. Finally, statement IV describes Joe's calm and calculated behavior in seeking to contact Dr. Krug despite the efforts of hospital staff to steer him elsewhere; this fact can be used by the prosecutor to negate the argument that Joe had hot blood at this point, because he lingered in a quiet and cool manner and then confronted Dr. Krug with questions, not with immediate violence. Answers (A), (B), and (D) are incorrect because they do not list the facts that support defense arguments and omit the fact that is unrelated to those arguments.

46. **Issue: Reckless manslaughter, application to facts.**

The correct answer is (B) because statements II, III, and IV accurately describe facts that a prosecutor may use to demonstrate evidence of each of the elements of the mens rea of recklessness. However, statement I refers to a fact that will not be used by the prosecutor because it is not relevant to the elements of the crime. First, statement II describes a fact that shows that Hal consciously disregarded the risk that the alcohol might slow his reaction time and impair his skiing skills; Hal's drinking also constitutes further evidence of his disregard of the heightened risk of danger that intoxicated skiers pose to sober skiers on the slopes. Second, statement III describes a fact that demonstrates Hal's disregard of the risk of death from collision that could result from his failure to turn from side to side. This failure caused him to ski at an unsafe, out-of-control speed down the mountain, according to witnesses. Third, statement IV describes Hal's prior training, which is relevant to the definition of recklessness because the "grossness" of Hal's deviation from a law-abiding person standard is supposed to be evaluated in light of the circumstances known to Hal. Hal's knowledge of the dangers of unsafe skiing at a high speed was based on his experience as a trained racer. Thus, unlike an inexperienced skier, Hal was quite aware of the risk of death that was posed by his skiing while intoxicated at high speeds in an out-of-control fashion down the mountain. However, statement I does not provide the prosecutor with a useful source of an argument. There is no evidence either that the circumstances of the prior fatal collisions were familiar to Hal or that they were caused by skiing behavior that resembled his own skiing. Thus, the collisions are not relevant to the element of Hal's disregard of the degree of risk of death involved in his conduct. Answers (A), (C), and (D) are incorrect because they do not list the facts that support the prosecutor's arguments and omit the fact that is unrelated to those arguments.

47. **Issue: Reckless manslaughter, application to facts.**
The correct answer is (C) because statements I, II, and IV accurately describe facts that the defense counsel may use to argue that elements of reckless manslaughter were not proved by the evidence. However, statement III refers to a fact that the prosecutor will use to support the conviction, and therefore will not be used by the defense counsel. First, statement I refers to Hal's testimony that he tried to slow down, which shows that Hal was not consciously disregarding the risk of collision and death, but attempting to reduce the risk by slowing down, which effort was thwarted by the external circumstances of the bumps on the trail. Second, statement II refers to the fact that Hal's consumption of alcohol was not great enough to put him outside the legal category of a law-abiding person, which is one element of the recklessness standard used by the Model Penal Code and modern statutes based upon it. Third, statement IV refers to a fact that shows that Hal reasonably perceived the risk of collision to be low because of the absence of a crowd of skiers on the slopes. The defense counsel will argue that skiing fast is not substantially risky for a trained racer, and that the risk factor that produced the accident that was a fortuitous event, based on the existence of the bumps on the trail and the unexpected proximity of

the victim to Hal. Hal did not consciously disregard the risk of this accident until it was too late for him to slow down or stop. However, statement III will not be used by the defense counsel because it describes Hal's lack of control, which helps to demonstrate the conscious disregard of the risk of a fatal collision. Statement III does not describe a safe skiing posture. Since Hal is skiing "fast" in this unsafe posture, the prosecutor will argue that Hal is an experienced skier who must have chosen to ski this way, even though the defense counsel prefers to blame the accident on the unforeseeable bumps. Answers (A), (B), and (D) are incorrect because they do not list the facts that support the defense counsel's arguments and omit the fact that is unrelated to those arguments.

48. **Issue: Felony murder, application to facts.**
The correct answer is (D) because statements I, II, III, and IV accurately describe the facts that the defense counsel will use to argue that the court should follow the doctrine used by some jurisdictions that bar felony murder liability for a co-felon like Cat who satisfies the four criteria described in these four statements. These four criteria have been incorporated into some criminal codes or endorsed in some case law. However, most states do not recognize a case law exception to felony murder liability based on this multi-factor test, and only a few state codes incorporate this multi-factor exception. Answers (A), (B), and (C) are incorrect because they do not list all the facts that will be used to support the defense counsel's arguments.

49. **Issue: Felony murder, application to facts.**
The correct answer is (A) because statements III and IV accurately describe the results that the appellate court should reach in order to conform to the norms of felony murder jurisprudence.

Statements I and II describe inaccurate results according to those norms. First, statement III is correct because the convictions of both Bob and Dan for liability in the death of Al should be reversed. Most jurisdictions follow the rule that there is no felony murder liability when a co-felon is killed by a victim, and it was Vicky's bullet that killed Al. Second, statement IV is correct because the convictions of both Bob and Dan for liability in the death of Cat should be affirmed. According to both accomplice liability theory and causation theory for felony murder, it is foreseeable that when all co-felons are armed, an accidental shooting death may occur in the course of an attempted felony, and liability for that death attaches vicariously to all co-felons, even when it is a co-felon who is the victim instead of a non-participant. It was Bob's bullet that killed Cat during the course of a felony, and so both Bob and Dan are liable for this accidental shooting under felony murder doctrine. Answers (B), (C) and (D) are incorrect because they do not list the correct resolutions of the appeals.

50. **Issue: Felony murder, application to facts.**
The correct answer is (B) because statements II and III accurately describe the results that the appellate court should reach in order to conform to the norms of felony murder jurisprudence. Statements I and IV describe inaccurate results according to those norms. First, statement II is correct because the convictions of both Bob and Dan for liability in the death of Cat should be reversed. Most jurisdictions follow the rule that there is no felony murder liability when a co-felon is killed by a police officer, and it was Eve's bullet that killed Cat. Second, statement III is correct because the convictions of both Bob and Dan for liability in the death of Vicky should be affirmed. Although ordinarily the killing of anyone on the scene by a

police officer would not create felony murder liability, the "shield" rule allows for liability to exist if one of the felons uses the victim as a shield like Dan used Vicky. This conduct puts the victim in extreme danger, and this establishes a causal link between a felon's action in pursuance of the felony and the victim's death, even though that death is caused by a non-participant in the felony. Answers (A), (C) and (D) are incorrect because they do not list the correct resolutions of the appeals.

51. **Issue: Elements of common law rape.**
The correct answer is (C) because statements I, II, III, and IV accurately describe the traditional elements of the common law crime of rape. The Model Penal Code definition of rape retained the marital rape exemption described in statement II, although with some modifications. The MPC added prohibitions of additional types of penetration, and defined the crime to prohibit the conduct of compelling a woman to submit by force or threat of serious bodily injury to be inflicted on anyone, thereby expanding the scope of the common law element described in statement III. However, the resistance element described in statement IV was abandoned by the MPC. Answers (A), (B), and (C) are incorrect because they do not identify all the traditional elements of the common law rape crime.

52. **Issue: Elements of modern sexual assault.**
The correct answer is (D) because statements I, II, III, and IV accurately describe modern elements of the rape crime, which is often renamed "sexual assault." The common reforms in modern statutes after 1975 include an expanded definition of the penetration concept, as described in statement I; an expansion of the force element to include the conduct of putting the victim in fear, as described in statement III; and a gender neutral definition of the crime, as described in statement IV. In

addition, many state statutes now do not require the prosecutor to prove the victim's lack of consent as an element of the crime, but almost half of the states retain this element in their statutes. Therefore, statement II is accurate because it is "common" to find this element in a modern statute. Moreover, despite the legislative trend of eliminating the lack of consent element, many courts allow defendants to raise the affirmative defense of consent so that the prosecutor must rebut this defense by providing some proof of lack of consent. Answers (A), (B), and (C) are incorrect because they do not identify all the common modern elements of sexual assault.

53. **Issue: Evidence prohibitions in rape shield laws.**
The correct answer is (A) because statements II, III, and IV accurately describe likely elements of statutory prohibitions in rape shield laws that would be found in roughly half the states. Statement I does not describe a typical prohibition, however, because evidence of sexual acts with the defendant is typically exempted from the rape shield evidence prohibition. Statements II and IV accurately describe related types of evidence that are typically deemed inadmissible; usually the prohibition includes not only evidence relating to sexual intercourse but evidence relating to all forms of sexual activity or sexual expression with persons other than the defendant. Statement III describes a different type of common prohibition, which relates to the reputation the victim has concerning prior sexual behavior. Answers (B), (C), (D) are not correct because they do not identify the typical prohibitions in a rape shield statute and omit the typical exemption.

54. **Issue: Exceptions to evidence prohibitions in rape shield laws.**
The correct answer is (B) because statements I, II,

III, and IV accurately describe exceptions to rape shield prohibitions on the admission of evidence in rape or sexual assault prosecutions. Statements I and II describe exceptions that typically are set forth in rape shield statutes, and statements III and IV describe exceptions that are often established in case law and sometimes found in statutes. Answers (A), (C), and (D) are not correct because they do not identify all the exceptions to rape shield law prohibitions.

55. **Issue: Requirements for prosecutor in common law rape trial.**
The correct answer is (C) because statements II, III, and IV accurately describe three typical burdens that would be placed on the prosecutor in a rape trial at common law, even though these requirements might not be expressly required by the statute defining the crime. Statements II and IV describe self-explanatory requirements; statement III refers to the Lord Hale instruction, which required jurors to be cautioned that rape is a charge that is easy to bring and difficult to defend against, and encouraged jurors to scrutinize closely the testimony of the rape victim. These three requirements were abandoned by virtually all states in the post-1975 era of rape reform. Finally, statement I refers to a requirement that never existed at common law, although evidence of lack of chastity was admissible in the pre-reform era to show either likelihood of consent or lack of credibility or both. Answers (A), (B), and (D) are not correct because they do not identify all the exceptions to rape shield law prohibitions.

56. **Issue: Mens rea for common law rape.**
The correct answer is (B) because statement II accurately describes the common law's description of the mens rea for common law rape. Statements I, III and IV do not accurately describe the mens

rea. Statement II refers to the concept of general intent, which meant at common law that the prosecutor only had to prove that the defendant intended to have sexual intercourse with the victim, so that the act of penetration was intentional. Statement IV is not accurate because the common law did not recognize the defense of a reasonable mistaken belief in consent; this defense was not established in case law until 1975. Statement III is not accurate because this intent has never been required, either at common law or even under modern statutes. Statement I is not accurate because even though the common law used strict liability with regard to the defendant's mental state concerning the victim's lack of consent, the common law did not use strict liability for all the elements of the crime. Answers (A), (C), and (D) are not correct because they do not identify the correct mens rea rules for common law rape.

57. **Issue: Sexual assault, actus reus, application to facts.**
The correct answer is (D) because statements I, III, and IV accurately describe strong prosecution arguments and statement II describes a weak argument. Statement II is weak because usually a prosecutor is required to prove that a victim's fear is reasonable (the objective component) and also that the victim actually was afraid (the subjective component). Statements I and III are traditional fear arguments made by prosecutors in cases where a victim is confronted by the surprise appearance of a naked man or men, or where a victim is frightened because a man or men who have ignored her previous resistance. On similar facts, an appellate court upheld a conviction based on fear. Statement IV is a plausible argument about legislative intent that has been accepted by some courts that are called upon to interpret the meaning of legislative abandonment of the common

law resistance requirement. Answers (A), (B), and (C) are not correct because they do not list the strong prosecution arguments and omit the weak one.

58. **Issue: Sexual assault, actus reus, application to facts.**
The correct answer is (B) because statements I, II, and III accurately describe strong defense arguments and statement IV describes a weak argument. Statement I is a strong argument because it is a traditional defense argument to link the proof for the lack of consent element to the concept that proof of resistance should be required. Even though resistance is not an element of the statute, it is a concept that often was embodied in case law requirements concerning the "resistance" type of proof needed for proving the lack of consent element. Statement II is a strong argument because it is a traditional defense argument to emphasize the need for objective proof of fear of injury, and the likely absence of fear in the absence of explicit threats. Statement III refers to a defense argument about the interpretation of the force element that has been endorsed in some precedents. Statement IV is weak because Vicki's failure to resist the initial "horsing around" before the road trip happens so early in the encounter that it does not shed much light on her lack of consent to the sex acts. Moreover, there is much case law support for the idea that even a victim's lack of physical resistance to sex acts should not bar a conviction because physical resistance may be dangerous to the victim. Answers (A), (C), and (D) are not correct because they do not list the strong defense arguments and omit the weak one.

59. **Issue: Rape, actus reus, application to facts.**
The correct answer is (C) because statements I, III, and IV refer to facts that the prosecutor will use to

make arguments about the sufficiency of force, threat of force, and lack of consent. Statement II refers to a fact that does not help the prosecutor because Zena did not notice that the door was locked. First, statement I refers to Ty's angry story and his regret that he did not, implicitly, use physical violence to punish Gia. This helps the prosecutor to show that there was a threat of force, implicitly, against Zena, because she should expect Ty to treat her the same way if he starts to treat her like a girlfriend. Second, statement III refers to Ty's awareness that Zena seems scared, which helps the prosecutor to show that Ty knowingly created fear in Zena, which fear serves as evidence of a threat. Some precedents support conviction even when a victim's fear is unreasonable, if the defendant is aware of this unreasonable fear and takes advantage of it. Third, statement IV refers to Ty's physical control over Zena; this helps the prosecutor to demonstrate some proof of the element of force. However, statement II refers to Ty's locking of Zena into his room, and this will not help the prosecutor to show either force or threat of force (or fear, as a proxy for threat), because Zena was not aware of this event. Answers (A), (B), and (D) are not correct because they do not list all the facts that can be used to create defense arguments.

60. **Issue: Rape, actus reus, application to facts.**
The correct answer is (A) because statements I, II, III, and IV refer to facts that the defense counsel will use to make arguments about the insufficiency of force, threat of force, and lack of consent (which is synonymous with the sex act being "against the will" of the victim). First, statement I refers to Zena's passive response to Ty's request for proof that she is not scared, which is that she says nothing instead of saying that she is afraid. This response helps the defense counsel to raise doubts about Zena's lack of consent, because silence can

be equated with consent. Also, some jurisdictions allow the prosecutor to use the victim's fear to prove that an implicit threat existed, and so Zena's non-fearful reaction to Ty's request helps to rebut the prosecutor's assertion that fear existed here. Second, statement II refers to Zena's willingness to stay in Ty's company, and this initial willingness helps the defense counsel to show that Zena initially did not experience any threat before she tried to leave. Third, statement III refers to Zena's assertion that she is not scared, which again helps the defense counsel to cast doubt on her lack of consent and to rebut the assertion that any fear existed on Zena's part. Finally, statement IV refers to Zena's non-responsiveness, which helps to prove her lack of resistance to the sex act, and thus to cast doubt upon her lack of consent, and doubt upon the existence of any force or threat of force that could be illustrated by any finding of resistance. Answers (B), (C), and (D) are not correct because they do not list all the facts that can be used to create defense arguments.

61. **Issue: Rape trauma syndrome evidence.**
The correct answer is (A) because statements I, III, and IV accurately describe three types of evidence that a court is likely to find to be inadmissible, whereas statement II describes the typical evidence provided by rape trauma syndrome experts that courts hold is admissible. First, statement I describes evidence that courts commonly exclude because of the danger of prejudice to the defendant; this evidence casts the expert in the role as "truth detector" for the jury and as impermissibly vouching for the victim's story. Second, statement III describes evidence that lower courts have held to be irrelevant and prejudicial because it allows the jury to convict the defendant because he fits a stereotype (just like other defendants who predictably claim consent) and not because of

evidence of guilt. Finally, statement IV describes evidence that has been held to be inadmissible because it allows the jury to infer that no woman falsely claims rape and so the defendant should be convicted. However, statement II refers to admissible evidence that is the least controversial type of expert testimony. Some courts conclude that such testimony should be admissible solely to provide this sort of information, and most courts hold it to be admissible. Answers (B), (C), and (D) are not correct because they do not list the types of evidence that are inadmissible and omit the type that is admissible.

62. **Issue: Rape, actus reus, application to facts.**
The correct answer is (B) because statements II, III, and IV describe the prosecutor's strongest arguments; statement I does not belong on this list because it is not a strong argument, although it is a possible one for the prosecutor to make. The strong arguments in statements II and III have been endorsed in lower court precedents affirming a conviction on similar facts; the strong argument in statement IV echoes the reasoning relating to other factual scenarios in modern rape precedents. Statement I is a weak argument because it can be difficult for appellate courts and juries to discern whether the prosecution has proved lack of consent or whether the defendant has shown some evidence of consent, and so statement I is not a reasonable generalization to cover all cases of arguably revoked consent. Answers (A), (C), and (D) are not correct because they do not list all the strong prosecution arguments and omit the weak one.

63. **Issue: Rape, actus reus, application to facts.**
The correct answer is (D) because statements I, II, and III accurately describe the strongest arguments for the defense counsel. Statements I and II have been endorsed in one lower court precedent

reversing a conviction on similar facts. Statement III is a plausible modern policy argument. However, statement IV describes a weak argument that does not belong on the list because of its lack of support in modern precedent. It describes a policy argument that is inconsistent with the reasoning of many modern precedents that endorse the perspective that courts and juries should recognize that "no means no," not "no can mean yes." The latter perspective is characteristic of the appellate court sentiments of pre-1975 common law precedents. Answers (A), (B), and (C) are not correct because they do not list all the strongest defense arguments and omit the weak one.

64. **Issue: Rape, mistake defense, application to facts.**
The correct answer is (B) because statements I, II, IV accurately describe arguments that the defense counsel will make to persuade the appellate court that the jury should have acquitted because of the mistake defense. Those state courts that recognize this defense, which is not yet approved in a majority of jurisdictions, typically require that the mistake must be reasonable and in good faith. Statement III is not an argument that defense counsel will make because it is not legally supportable. Statements I and II refer to two elements of Kay's behavior before the sex act occurred that could be interpreted as signaling the positive cooperation in the act that is required by the definition of consent. Statement IV refers to Kay's behavior after the sex act that could be interpreted as showing, in retrospect, that Jim had her positive cooperation in the act because she made no protest afterwards. Both types of evidence have been used by courts as evidence of consent, and logically, both types may be the source of a reasonable belief in consent by the defendant, both during the act and afterwards. However, statement

III is not a supportable argument because Jim's apology is relevant to show his state of mind during and after the act. The apology may be interpreted by the prosecutor as showing Jim's lack of good faith belief in consent, or by the defense counsel to simply show Jim's good faith belief in consent and politeness in apologizing for no real reason to an unresponsive Kay. In either case, however, the apology is not irrelevant, but a relevant fact that may shed light on either a good faith or a bad faith belief in consent. Answers (A), (C), and (D) are not correct because they do not list all the strongest defense arguments and omit the weak one.

65. **Issue: Rape, mistake defense, application to facts.**

The correct answer is (A) because statements I, II, III, and IV describe arguments that the prosecutor may make to rebut the defense counsel's arguments that Jim made a reasonable, good faith mistake. First, statements I, and III relate to facts concerning Jim's interpretation of Kay's actions that were so ambiguous that it was unreasonable to interpret them as positive cooperation in moving toward a mutually desired sex act. Kissing is not equivalent to saying "yes" to the sex act taking place only a minute later with a total stranger, and Kay's not attempting to leave is not reasonably interpreted as Kay's desiring to stay in the position with Jim on top of her. The prosecutor can argue that it was not reasonable of Jim not to realize that he was kneeling on Kay's jeans and trapping her on the couch. Second, statement II refers to Jim's unreasonable failure to take Kay's "no" literally at face value, or at least to ask her what she meant by it, if he was uncertain as to whether this contradiction of positive cooperation should be treated as a "yes." Finally, statement IV relates to the "good faith" components of Jim's defense, and this prosecutor argument focuses on the conflict between Kay's testimony and Jim's testimony. According to Kay, she told Jim several times to get off, and unless Kay is lying, Jim's testimony reveals that he either ignored her or treated her comments as being made in jest. If he did hear her and ignored her, then his claim of consent is made in bad faith. Answers (B), (C), and (D) are not correct because they do not list all the strong prosecution arguments.

66. **Issue: Elements of self-defense.**
The correct answer is (C) because statements I, II, III and IV accurately describe four common elements of self-defense. Statements II, III, and IV describe traditional elements of self-defense. Statement I refers to the duty to retreat, which used by a minority of jurisdictions that endorse the Model Penal Code position; this doctrine qualifies as one that is commonly used, even though it is not the majority rule. The elements described in statements II, III, and IV are all common law elements; the Model Penal Code requires only an honest belief in necessity, not a reasonable belief. Answers (A), (B), and (D) are not correct because they do not list all the commonly used elements of the defense.

67. **Issue: Elements of insanity defense.**
The correct answer is (D) because statements I and IV accurately describe commonly used tests for insanity; statement I describes the *M'Naghten* test used by most states and statement IV describes the Model Penal Code test used by a large minority of states. However, statement II describes the "irresistible impulse" test used only by a few states and statement III describes the "product" test invented by the District of Columbia court in the 1950s and then abandoned there in the 1970s. Answers (A), (B), and (C) are not correct because they do not list the commonly used definitions of

the defense and omit the infrequently used definitions.

68. **Issue: Elements of duress defense.**
The correct answer is (A) because statements I, III, and IV accurately describe three common elements of the duress defense. However, statement II is an overbroad description of the defense, because the defense is not recognized if the defendant believes that the only way to avoid harm is to commit the crime of intentional murder. The duress defense is a common law defense, and the Model Penal Code revised the defense to require that the threat must be one that a person of "reasonable firmness" is unable to resist. Answers (B), (C), and (D) are not correct because they do not list the commonly used elements of the defense and omit the overbroad element.

69. **Issue: Elements of intoxication defense.**
The correct answer is (B) because statements I and III accurately describe two common elements of intoxication defense doctrine, whereas statements II and IV do not accurately reflect the substantive rules of that doctrine. Statement I is accurate because most states that use degrees of murder allow intoxication to negate the mental states for first degree murder that requires premeditation and deliberation. Statement III is accurate because even though intoxication and insanity are distinct defenses, intoxication evidence may come into play in a case where the insanity defense is asserted. For example, intoxication can be so severe as to cause a disease of the mind, and thereby serve to support the insanity defense. By contrast, statement II is not accurate because the defense of self-defense usually requires a defendant to have reasonable beliefs in elements such as the imminent threat of deadly force and the necessity of responding with deadly force. The defendant must

assess these elements according to the standard of a reasonably sober person. Statement IV is also incorrect because most states follow the Model Penal Code position, which is that even though intoxication may negate the defendant's appreciation of the risk of death for reckless homicide, it is fair to treat the intoxication as proof of recklessness. Answers (A), (C), and (D) are not correct because they do not list the commonly used doctrines and omit the incorrect ones.

70. **Issue: Elements of defense of property.**
The correct answer is (B) because statements I and IV accurately describe two doctrines that govern the use of deadly force in defense of a dwelling. However, statements II and III do not accurately describe elements of that doctrine. First, statements I and IV describe somewhat different rules commonly used by modern statutes or expressed in case law; both of these rules allow for a more limited defense of property than the original common law rule that allowed a defendant to use deadly force to prevent forcible entry, as long as the defendant provided a warning to the victim. However, statement II is not a correct statement of doctrine; in fact, it is not lawful to use mechanical devices to protect against a trespasser. Similarly, statement III is not a correct statement of law because the duty to retreat usually does not exist inside a dwelling. Answers (A), (C), and (D) are not correct because they do not list the commonly used doctrines and omit the incorrect ones.

71. **Issue: Elements of law enforcement defense.**
The correct answer is (C) because statements I, II, and IV accurately describe arguments that, if proved on the facts, would exonerate an officer using the law enforcement offense. Statement III describes an argument that has been expressly rejected by the Supreme Court in *Tennessee v.*

Garner (1985) on Fourth Amendment grounds. The *Garner* opinion endorses the propositions set forth in statements I, II, and IV. Answers (A), (B), and (D) are not correct because they do not list the commonly used doctrines and omit the incorrect ones.

72. **Issue: Elements of defense of others.**
The correct answer is (A) because statements I, III, and IV accurately describe doctrines commonly used to govern the defense of others defense. Statement II is not an accurate statement of modern law. First, statements I and IV, although stating opposite positions, are both common doctrines that are used by modern courts. Second, statement III is also a common doctrine. The defense of others defense and the self-defense defense overlap with respect to this requirement. However, statement II is not a modern doctrine, but rather a rule that appears in early common law cases but is no longer commonly found in statutes or case law. Answers (B), (C), and (D) are not correct because they do not list the commonly used doctrines and omit the incorrect one.

73. **Issue: Elements of necessity defense.**
The correct answer is (C) because statement I accurately describes an element of necessity defense doctrine, and statements II, III, and IV are not accurate descriptions of doctrine. Statement I describes a common requirement for the necessity defense, which is for the defendant to act with the purpose of avoiding a greater harm. Statement II describes a rule that expresses the type or purpose required by the necessity defense too narrowly; the necessity defense provides that a crime may be committed in order to avoid the harm of damage to property as well as to avoid physical harm to others. However, statement III describes a rule that does not apply to the necessity defense, but rather

to the duress defense. If a defendant is charged with intentional homicide, for example, the necessity defense is appropriate if a defendant was forced to choose to kill one person in order to save two lives, according to the Model Penal Code position. Moreover, statement IV describes a limit on the necessity doctrine that is rarely used. Under the MPC the necessity defense is not denied to every defendant who was involved in creating a situation that led to the commission of a crime. Instead, the defendant's culpability in bringing about a situation is measured so that different levels of culpability are treated differently. If a defendant is only negligent in bringing about a situation, he or she may rely on the necessity defense unless he or she is charged with committing a negligence crime. Answers (A), (B), and (D) are not correct because they do not list the accurate necessity defense doctrine.

74. **Issue: Elements of unconsciousness defense.**
The correct answer is (D) because statements I, II, and III accurately describe elements of doctrine commonly used to govern the unconsciousness defense. Statement IV is an inaccurate statement of this doctrine. First, statement I describes a general definition of the unconsciousness defense that is recognized in the Model Penal Code and in many jurisdictions. Second, statements II and III describe two examples of the unconsciousness defense. However, statement IV is not an accurate description of doctrine because amnesia alone is not recognized as a form of unconsciousness in the absence of some other evidence of unconsciousness, such as may exist when there is a concussion or other physical trauma, or other physical conditions such as the ones described in statements II and III. Answers (A), (B), and (C) are not correct because they do not list the accurate unconsciousness doctrines and omit the inaccurate

one.

75. **Issue: Elements of mistake of fact defense.**
The correct answer is (B) because statements I, II, and IV accurately describe doctrines that govern the mistake of fact defense. However, statement III is inaccurate because it is an overbroad statement that is derived from dicta in common law cases that is not endorsed in jurisdictions where the Model Penal Code's approach to mistake is used. Statement IV states the basic Model Penal Code position, and statement II is a logical corollary to that position, because a crime that is lacking in a mental state has no mental state that can be negated by a mistake of fact. Statement I is also a corollary of the Model Penal Code approach, because the defense of mistake of fact is actually a mens rea defense that is based on the assertion that the prosecutor cannot prove the required mental state for the crime because the mistake evidence negates that mental state. In order to rebut this mental state defense, the prosecutor must assume the same burden that is always assumed by the prosecution, which is to prove the existence of every element of the crime beyond the reasonable doubt. However, statement III is inaccurate because it is overbroad and inconsistent with the mistake rules that are advocated by the Model Penal Code. For example, if the mental state for a particular crime is knowledge or purpose, then even an unreasonable mistake may negate that mental state. If the defendant was only reckless or negligent, no conviction may occur, yet the acquittal is required in a situation where it may be a reckless or negligent mistake that negated the mental state. Answers (A), (C), and (D) are not correct because they do not list the accurate mistake of fact doctrines and omit the inaccurate one.

76. **Issue: Elements of mistake of law defense.**
The correct answer is (C) because statements II and IV accurately describe the defenses that may be accepted. However, statements I and III describe defenses that are generally rejected. First, statement II describes the Model Penal Code position that is adopted by some state criminal codes that allow reliance on a decision by the state's highest court, afterward determined to be erroneous. Statement IV describes another Model Penal Code position that is endorsed by a number of state codes, regarding the defense of lack of notice of enactment of a statute. However, statement I describes a rule that is not supported by case law, because a person is expected to bring a constitutional challenge to a statute and to comply with the statute until it is struck down as unconstitutional by a judicial decision. Statement IV likewise describes a proposition that is traditionally rejected by the Model Penal Code and by a strong consensus of state courts, because of the danger that the creation of this defense would create an undesirable incentive for people to seek out lawyers who could be paid to give them immunity from prosecution through dubious legal opinions. Answers (A), (B), and (D) are incorrect because they do not list the valid arguments and omit the invalid ones.

77. **Issue: Unconsciousness defense, application to facts.**
The correct answer is (C) because statements I, II, and III accurately describe arguments that the defense counsel will make to justify an acquittal based on the defense of unconsciousness. However, statement IV does not describe an argument that is relevant to this defense. First, statement I is an appropriate argument that points to evidence of Bo's brain disorder, and the defense of unconsciousness typically requires some kind of

scientific proof of brain malfunction. Second, statement II explains why Bo was not able to avoid the risk of driving because of his ignorance of his brain disorder; some courts deny the unconsciousness defense, for example, to epileptic defendants who drive with knowledge of their disorder, and then suffer a seizure that may cause an accident. Third, statement III is an argument that points to corroborating evidence of the disorder, and a successful defense usually requires some kind of testimony from the defendant to support a finding of unconscious behavior. Finally, however, statement IV is irrelevant because unconsciousness, unlike intoxication, is a complete defense to all crimes, and therefore the mental state required by the crime will not play a role in the trial judge's determination whether sufficient evidence of unconsciousness has been produced by the defendant. Answers (A), (B), and (D) are incorrect because they do not list the valid defense arguments and omit the inappropriate one.

78. **Issue: Duress defense, application to facts.**
The correct answer is (A) because statements III and IV accurately describe the strongest arguments that will be made the prosecution to identify reasons that the two defendants may be ineligible for the duress instruction. Statements I and II are possible arguments but are not as strong as the other two arguments. First, statement III describes the prosecution's argument that the evidence does not show a sufficiently imminent threat of death or serious bodily injury; the imminence element is part of the common law requirements for the defense and part of duress doctrine in most modern codes, though not all. Second, statement IV describes the prosecution's argument that the fear of death or serious bodily injury was not reasonable because they would be safe from the hands of dangerous inmates in protective custody; the

reasonableness requirement is a common element of duress doctrine. Moreover, the option of protective custody means that commission of the crime was not the only way to avoid death or serious injury, which is also a requirement of the defense. However, statement I is not a prosecution argument because most states do not require that the threatening person must be seeking to have the defendant commit a crime; instead, duress requires that the defendant believe that the only way to avoid death or serious injury is to commit a crime. Further, statement II is not a prosecution argument because the duress defense usually is available when fear of serious harm to others is involved, even though a few states limit the defense to fear of harm to self. Some states extend the "harm to others" concept to include threatened harm to family members of the defendant, and one lower court on similar facts extended this concept to a co-inmate such as Bo in a situation where a defendant like Otis was threatened. Answers (B), (C) and (D) are incorrect because they do not list the strongest prosecution arguments and omit the weak ones.

79. **Issue: Duress defense, application to facts.**
The correct answer is (B) because statements I, II, III and IV accurately describe arguments that the defense counsel will make to justify reversal of the conviction based on the duress defense. First, statement I describes the defense counsel's argument that relates to the evidence concerning the common duress requirement that the defendant must fear death or serious bodily harm. Second, statement II describes the argument that explains the reasonableness of the defendant's fear of harm based on the violent nature of the individuals making the death threats. Reasonableness is a common element of the duress doctrine. Third, statement III is an argument to explain why the defendant's action was the only way to avoid harm,

and why reliance on protective custody was not a way to avoid death or serious injury. Finally, statement IV is an argument explaining why the defendant could not have avoided harm by informing the prison authorities of the death threats; such a course of action would have created a risk of further violent harm for being a snitch. Answers (A), (C) and (D) are incorrect because they do not list all the defense counsel arguments.

80. **Issue: Self-defense, application to facts.**
The correct answer is (D) because statements II and III accurately describe the arguments that the defense counsel will make to justify reversal of the conviction based on self-defense. However, statements I and IV do not describe arguments that the defense counsel will make. First, statement II describes an argument relating to the traditional self-defense requirement that a defendant who uses deadly force, such as a tire jack used to hit the victim in the head, must be faced with an immediate threat of death or serious bodily harm. Second, statement III describes the argument that relates to the typical requirement that the defendant must reasonably believe in the necessity of the use of deadly force in order to save herself from death or great bodily harm. By contrast, statement I does not describe a defense counsel argument because it will be the defense counsel's position that Nan never lost the right of self-defense with regard to her own use of deadly force, and therefore Nan never needed to regain this right. When Nan threatened Lou with force by saying she would spray him with mace, this was not a threat of deadly force against Lou, only a threat of non-deadly force. When Lou responded by coming at Nan with a carving knife, Lou lost the right of self-defense as the aggressor who first resorted to the use of deadly force against an adversary using non-deadly force. Therefore, Nan's act of retreat was not

necessary in order for her to regain or retain the right of self-defense; once Lou came at her with the carving knife, she could have stood her ground and responded to Lou with deadly force in self-defense once he threatened her with the knife. Moreover, statement IV does not describe a defense counsel argument because even those states that require the duty to retreat do not require a person to retreat from his or her own dwelling. Answers (A), (B), and (C) are incorrect because they do not list the defense counsel arguments and omit the arguments that will not be made by defense counsel.

81. **Issue: Self-defense, application to facts.**
The correct answer is (C) because statement I accurately describes the argument that the prosecutor will make to justify the rejection of Nan's self-defense argument. However, statements II, III and IV do not describe strong arguments for the prosecutor. First, statement I describes the prosecutor's argument relating to the common self-defense doctrine that Nan cannot use deadly force in self-defense if the victim was not threatening her with deadly force. Here the mace does not constitute deadly force and Lou was not pointing the knife at Nan, only sneaking up on her to surprise her and saying, "Gotcha!" as a joke. The prosecutor will argue that if Lou had wanted to use deadly force against Nan, he would have attacked her with the knife when he had the advantage of surprise, instead of announcing his presence without pointing the knife at her. However, statement II is not a strong argument for the prosecutor because, assuming that Lou lost the right to use deadly force in self-defense (when he became the aggressor by threatening Nan with the carving knife in the apartment), he would only regain this right under typical self-defense doctrine by effectively withdrawal from the encounter with

Nan. By continuing to chase Nan, Lou is not withdrawing in good faith or taking steps to notify Nan that he is doing so – quite the contrary is true here. Moreover, statement III is not a strong argument for the prosecutor because a majority of states do not impose the duty to retreat on a person who is faced with the threat of deadly force. Further, statement IV is not a strong argument for the prosecutor because even "duty-to-retreat" states do not require a person to retreat if he or she cannot do so in complete safety. Arguably, with Lou on her heels, Nan could not retreat safely by simply running away down the street, because Lou would have seen her and could have chased her and harmed her with the knife. Thus, Nan did not lose the right to use self-defense simply by hiding for purposes of seeking safety rather than retreating. Answers (A), (B), and (D) are incorrect because they do not list the strong prosecution argument and omit the weak ones.

82. **Issue: Mistake of fact defense, application to facts.**

The correct answer is (D) because statements I, II, III and IV accurately describe case scenarios that might result in a court's rejection of a mistake defense in a bigamy prosecution. There is state court precedent to support a denial of the mistake defense in each of these four situations. However, these scenarios also might result in the acceptance of a mistake defense as well. Some courts have rejected the use of strict liability for bigamy prosecutions and assumed that some mental state should be read into a bigamy statute in order to permit a mistake defense of various kinds to be used by a bigamy defendant. Answers (A), (B), and (C) are incorrect because they do not list all the scenarios where a court might reject the mistake defense.

83. **Issue: Intoxication defense, application to facts.**

The correct answer is (A) because statements II, III and IV accurately describe the arguments that the defense counsel will make to explain why the crime of aggravated assault is one of specific intent. However, statement I does not describe a defense argument. First, statement II seeks to characterize the definition of a crime as one that requires the intent to achieve a result; crimes with the mental state of an "intent to" do something (and crimes with the mental states of "intentionally" and "knowingly") are treated in some precedents as specific intent crimes. Second, statement III describes a related argument, which is that the assault crime here is going to be defined as an attempted battery, and that most attempt crimes are treated as specific intent crimes for the reason that the mental state typically requires the intent to achieve the completed crime. Third, statement IV describes how the legislative decision to create a lesser and greater degree of a crime, such as simple and aggravated assault, is evidence of a legislative willingness to make the greater crime eligible for the intoxication defense, and the lesser crime not eligible for this defense, so that intoxicated defendants may be convicted of the lesser crime. Here, the lesser crime of simple assault has an undefined mental state, which means that the common law mental state of criminal negligence probably is intended for this crime; this mental state is one of general intent. Therefore, the intoxication defense is not available for this crime under most codes and precedents. However, statement I is not a defense argument because it has no supporting authority. First, the aggravated assault crime is silent as to the mental state required for the element of use of a dangerous weapon. This silence implies that the mental state for this element is either strict liability or a general intent such as recklessness or negligence, not that the mental state is one of specific intent. Answers (B), (C), and (D) are incorrect because they do not list the appropriate defense arguments and omit the argument that will not be made by defense counsel.

84. **Issue: Intoxication defense, application to facts.**

The correct answer is (B) because statements I, III and IV accurately describe the arguments that the prosecutor will make to justify the affirmance of the conviction on the grounds that the intoxication instruction was properly denied because the crime of aggravated assault is one of general intent. However, statement II is not an argument that the prosecutor will make. First, statement I describes a policy argument that explains why a crime with the mental state of "intent to" do something (such as intent to do bodily injury here) should not be treated as a specific intent mental state. The theory behind this argument is that alcohol has less effect on the ability to engage in simple behavior like assault than it does on the ability to engage in more complex behavior, such as the planning of a premeditated murder. Second, statement III describes another policy argument that explains why certain crimes, no matter what their mental states, should be exempted from the intoxication defense as matter of social policy. There is precedent to support the use the policy arguments in statements I and II to exempt the crimes of battery, assault, and arson from the intoxication defense. Third, statement IV describes a traditional argument for prosecutors that singles out a particular type of "intent to" crimes as being eligible for the intoxication defense (those requiring the intent to achieve a further result beyond the basic actus reus of the crime itself). The theory behind this argument is that alcohol may impair the ability to formulate the intent for achieving this further result, but not impair significantly the intent to do the basic actus reus of the crime. However, statement II is not a prosecution argument because the mental state for aggravated assault cannot be characterized as recklessness here. The statute here defines the crime as "attempting to cause bodily injury," which is a definition that resembles one of the Model Penal Code's modern definitions of assault. The mental state concept of attempt is not defined as recklessness under modern codes, but rather as purposely seeking to achieve a result. Answers (A), (C), and (D) are incorrect because they do not list the prosecutor's arguments and omit the argument that will not be made by the prosecutor.

85. **Issue: Necessity defense, application to facts.**
The correct answer is (D) because statement IV accurately identifies the argument that the appellate court is the most likely to endorse concerning the defendants' necessity defense. There are few precedents involving similar circumstances, but a federal lower court precedent from the nineteenth century supports the notion that selections of passengers to be sacrificed in an emergency at sea should be based on a drawing of lots. See *United States v. Holmes* (1842). The famous English precedent of *Regina v. Dudley & Stephens* (1884) holds that no necessity defense is ever justified for intentional homicide, but this position is not endorsed by modern American precedents or by the Model Penal Code. Statement I is not likely to be endorsed because even though Raul's heavy weight was a seemingly objective basis for his selection by the other passengers, this factor would require a court to determine that the value of human lives are not equal, which contradicts judicial dicta in necessity cases. The MPC's version of the necessity defense is called the "choice of evils" defense; its definition is potentially broad enough to support the argument in statement I, but

it has not been held to endorse such a result on similar facts. Statement II is not likely to be endorsed because even though it expresses one of the requirements of the necessity defense (that no other option exists for avoiding the harm except for the commission of the crime), the ability of the defendant to satisfy this requirement is not a sufficient justification for the defense. The problem of how to select the one passenger who must be sacrificed is not resolved by this requirement. Statement IV is not likely to be endorsed because the facts do appear to satisfy the requirement used by some state codes and in some precedents, which is that the threatened harm must be imminent or that the emergency action must be immediately necessary. Once the emergency has arisen, the necessity defense may arise for people who respond to the emergency by committing a crime, even though it may later appear that the effort to avoid one harm (such as the loss of life) might not have been likely to succeed. Answers (A), (B), and (C) are incorrect because they do not identify the argument that the appellate court is the most likely to endorse.

86. **Issue: Mens rea, strict liability.**
The correct answer is (A) because statements I and IV accurately identify the arguments the appellate court is likely to endorse in resolving the interpretation of the mens rea required for the drug possession crime. Statements II and III do not describe arguments that are likely to be relied upon by the appellate court. First, statement I describes a principle of strict liability law, which is that strict liability should not be inferred solely from the omission of a mental state in a statute. Instead, the common law tradition is that legislative silence as to mental state does not imply an intent to use strict liability but instead an intent to use mental states that will be read into the statute through

judicial interpretation based on the history of the statute and policy concerns. Second, statement IV describes a traditional type of statutory interpretation argument for the ascertainment of the mens rea that should be read into a silent statute. This tradition is that statutory provisions should be read *in pari materia*; thus, Sections 1 and 2 of the statute, which are related to the same matter and to each other, should be read together in a consistent way. This means that the implications of the language of Section 2 can be used to interpret the meaning of Section 1. However, statement II is not likely to be used by an appellate court because the "plain meaning" rule is a generic rule of statutory interpretation that does not take precedence over more specific traditions of interpretation, such as the traditions concerning the meaning of silence as to mental state. At common law, the default mental state that could be read into a silent statute was recklessness, at least with regard to the main element of the crime. Moreover, statement III is not likely to be used because the consensus established by 40 other states is not irrelevant to the court's interpretation decision concerning mens rea; on the contrary, courts often rely on the holdings of other jurisdictions concerning the wisdom of using particular mental states for particular crimes, when the legislative intent concerning mental state is ambiguous as it is here. Answers (B), (C), and (D) are incorrect because they do not identify the arguments that the appellate court is the most likely to use and omit the arguments that a court is not likely to endorse.

87. **Issue: Mens rea, strict liability.**
The correct answer is (C) because answers I, II and IV accurately describe the strongest arguments the prosecutor will make to justify the use of strict liability as the mental state for the element of the

FTO status of an organization. However, statement III is not a strong argument for the prosecutor to make. First, statement I is a typical argument that is used to justify strict liability, because many precedents acknowledge the validity of the use of this mental state when a crime may fit the profile of a public welfare offense (PWO). Not all such offenses are presumed to be strict liability crimes when the legislature is silent concerning the mental state attached to one or more elements of the offense; but this characterization of a crime as a PWO helps to lay the foundation for a judicial finding that a strict liability interpretation may be intended by the legislature. Second, statement II is a typical argument that seeks to infer the legislative intent that strict liability should be used, according to the text and goals of the statute. Here, the legislative preference for secrecy surrounding the FTO designation process implies a lack of concern for notice to the "wrongdoers," namely the FTOs and their donors, which accords with a legislative tolerance of strict liability for defendants like Rafe who are ignorant of the FTO status of the group to which they make a donation. Third, statement IV reflects a prosecution argument that seeks to distinguish the Supreme Court's precedent of *Morissette v. United States* (1952), which held that a legislative silence concerning mental state should be interpreted as a signal that the traditional common law mental state should be read into the statute in lieu of strict liability, whenever the crime itself derives from the common law. The FTO crime here is a novel one that has no relationship with any common law crime, and so strict liability may be an appropriate interpretation of the meaning of the legislative silence as to mental state. However, statement III is not a strong prosecution argument because the Supreme Court has rejected a strict liability interpretation of a felony crime in a case where the maximum punishment was 10 years in prison in *United States v. Staples* (1994). The *Staples* Court emphasized that the harshness of such a penalty is a significant factor in justifying the rejection of a strict liability interpretation. Answers (A), (B), and (D) are incorrect because they do not list the prosecutor's strongest arguments and omit the weak one.

88. **Issue: Mens rea, strict liability.**
The correct answer is (A) because statements II, III, and IV accurately describe the defense counsel's strongest arguments against strict liability. Statement I is not a strong argument for the defense because it is incorrect. First, statement I describes a defense argument that correctly explains the Model Penal Code approach to the mens rea interpretation question here. The MPC provides that if a statute contains an express reference to a mental state (such as knowingly) for one element of the crime, and also includes one or more elements with no mental state attached to them, then the mental state expressly mentioned in the statute may be used for every element of the statute. Second, statement II is a defense argument that relies on one of the factors emphasized in the Supreme Court's ruling in *United States v. Staples* (1994) as a reason for rejecting the use of strict liability. Here the defense will argue that like the long tradition of lawful gun ownership in *Staples*, the long tradition of lawful charitable donations is a reason to fear that strict liability will cause the criminalization of a broad range of innocent activity, which is a result that should be avoided if a plausible mental state may be read into a silent statute. Third, statement III is a defense argument that identifies one of the factors mentioned by the Supreme Court in *Morissette v. United States* (1952) as supporting strict liability (the highly regulated nature of the activity of a class of defendants), and then explains how that factor is

absent in this context. Fourth, statement IV describes a traditional defense argument based on the rule of lenity, which always counsels against strict liability and in favor of choosing another mental state. A lower federal court has endorsed the defendant's proposal for reading in a "knowingly" mental state to be attached to the FTO status element in the statute and thereby rejecting the strict liability interpretation. Answers (B), (C), and (D) are incorrect because they do not identify the strongest arguments that the defense counsel will make and omit the weak one.

89. **Issue: Mens rea, strict liability.**
The correct answer is (D) because statements I, II, and III accurately describe the strongest arguments that the defense counsel will make to justify a rejection of strict liability for the public lands element. Statement IV is not a strong argument for the defendant. First, statement I is a defense argument that seeks to connect the goals of the statute, as revealed in the legislative history, with the mental state needed for prosecution of the defendants who are the target of the ARPA statute. This argument relies on the history concerning the Congressional support for a public information program that is implicitly necessary in order to stimulate public compliance with the permit requirement. Second, statement II is a traditional defense argument that refers to a factor that may lead a court to reject strict liability, as the Supreme Court in *United States v. Staples* (1994) where a knowingly mental state was read into a gun control statute. Third, statement III is another traditional argument that is used to explain why strict liability is not necessary to the enforcement of the statute, which is sometimes true of public welfare offenses as explained in the Court's litany of the rationales for strict liability in *Morissette v. United States* (1952). However, statement IV is not a strong

defense argument because the ARPA crime does not derive from any common law crime. The *Morissette* Court held that the crime of converting government property was a common law crime derived from larceny, but the ARPA crime does not relate to theft law. Instead, ARPA's goal is to protect rare and historic artifacts from destruction in order to protect an environmental and archeological heritage, which is a modern type of crime that cannot be interpreted by reference to a similar common law crime. Answers (A), (B), and (C) are incorrect because they do not identify the strongest defense arguments and omit the weak one.

90. **Issue: Mens rea, strict liability.**
The correct answer is (D) because statements I, III, and IV accurately describe the strongest arguments that the prosecutor will make to justify the use of strict liability for the public lands element. Statement II is not a strong argument for the prosecutor. First, statement I is an argument that seeks to use the historic context of the statute to interpret the likely meaning of the legislative silence concerning the mental state for the public land element. It was the Model Penal Code in 1962 which led the movement for the approach, of requiring a mental state for every element of a crime; in 1906 this tradition was not yet widely established. The common law approach to mental state was to assume that legislatures did not intend to use a mental state for an attendance circumstance element, so the prosecution can point to that approach in order to interpret the legislative silence in ARPA. Second, statement III is a traditional argument based on many precedents that acknowledge the validity of the use of strict liability when a crime may fit the profile of a public welfare offense. This ARPA crime does not resemble the typical regulation that involves a dangerous item, such as guns, hand grenades, or various toxic

substances; but public welfare offenses are not limited to this type of regulation and potentially embrace all regulations that deal with public health, welfare, safety, or other public interests. Third, statement IV is an argument that seeks to establish the inherent blameworthiness of any person who excavates an artifact from any land that is not his or her own property. The defendant's knowledge that he was damaging the property of others may be treated as a substitute for actual proof of his knowledge that he was on public land. One lower federal court has relied on these arguments to uphold the use of strict liability for the public land element of ARPA. However, statement II is only a weak prosecution argument, as there is no evidence as to how many public lands are actually unmarked; the target defendant who is armed with special equipment and motivated by commercial gain is likely to be informed of his or her location while excavating, and so the difficulty of proving the defendant's knowledge of that location seems speculative. Answers (A), (B), and (C) are incorrect because they do not identify the strongest prosecution arguments and omit the weak one.

91. **Issue: Elements of attempt.**
The correct answer is (C) because statements II and IV accurately describe traditional elements of the crime of attempt, whereas statements I and III do not. First, statement II describes the basic mental state for the attempt crime; there is general agreement that the intent to complete the crime is needed, and that recklessness or negligence are not mental states for attempts. Second, statement IV describes the additional mental state that is needed for an attempt conviction, which is the mental state for the underlying crime. However, statement I describes the "equivocality" test for defining the actus reus for attempt, which is not likely to be

used because it is approved by some precedents and rejected by others. Statement III describes the last proximate act test for defining the actus reus of attempt, and this test is not endorsed presently by any states. Answers (A), (B), and (D) are incorrect because they do not identify the typical elements of attempt and omit the answers that do not describe such elements.

92. **Issue: Elements of solicitation.**
The correct answer is (B) because statements I and II accurately describe traditional elements of the crime of solicitation, whereas statements III and III do not. First, statement I describes the basic actus reus of the crime of solicitation, which may be committed through speech, or in writing, or through other conduct. Second, statement II describes the basic mens rea of the solicitation crime that is generally required; this mens rea is sometimes defined as an intent that the crime should be committed. However, statement III is not a required mens rea for the crime of solicitation, although it does describe the most common type of intent possessed by a convicted defendant. An act also qualifies as a solicitation when a defendant solicits one person and asks that person to solicit another person to perform the crime. Finally, statement IV is not a requirement for the crime of solicitation because this crime requires no agreement. The crime is complete once the request to commit a crime is made, with the intent that the crime be committed. Answers (A), (C), and (D) are incorrect because they do not identify the typical elements of solicitation and omit the answers that do not describe such elements.

93. **Issue: Elements of conspiracy.**
The correct answer is (A) because statements III and IV accurately describe traditional elements of the crime of conspiracy, whereas statements I and

II do not. First, statement III describes the overt act requirement that is used by most states. Second, statement IV describes the basic actus reus of conspiracy, which is the act of agreement. However, statement I describes the corrupt motive doctrine, which is not a general requirement for all conspiracy convictions and which has been rejected by some courts and accepted by others. Further, statement II describes an erroneous interpretation of the mens rea for conspiracy because, in fact, both the mental states mentioned in this answer are required for conviction – the intent to agree, and the intent to achieve the criminal objective of the conspiracy. Answers (B), (C), and (D) are incorrect because they do not identify the typical elements of conspiracy and omit the answers that do not describe such elements.

94. **Issue: Actus reus, omission to act, legal duty.**
The correct answer is (B) because statements I, III, and IV accurately describe strong arguments for the defense, whereas statement II describes a weak argument. First, statement I is an argument that eliminates three of the typical bases for judicial findings of legal duty; no statute appears to govern the legal duty issue here, no contractual relationship has been established between Ann and Moe; and since Ann and Moe are strangers and not relatives or people in a formal relationship (such as employer and employee, husband and wife, or other similar partnerships), no legal duty may be imposed on the basis of a status relationship. Second, statement III is an argument that focuses on another basis for finding a legal duty under some precedents, which is the duty that may arise when a person has voluntarily assumed the care of a helpless person and then sequesters that person so that no one else can come to his or her aid. A duty based on voluntary assumption of care has been held to arise when the defendant knows the scope

of the potential peril faced by the victim, as where a caregiver realizes that a dependent child is hungry or ill, or where a caregiver realizes that a dependent, elderly relative is anorexic and not eating. Here, Ann's defense counsel may argue that Ann believed that the cause of Moe's collapse was excessive consumption of alcohol, and therefore she did not seek medical care for him because she expected him to sleep off his state of unconsciousness. Third, statement IV refers to the traditional common law position, upon which a defense counsel will rely in a case where the prosecutor seeks to impose a duty upon a defendant to rescue a stranger in known (or unknown) peril. However, statement II is not a strong defense argument because Ann's placing of Moe upon her porch did not achieve the result of making it possible for others to rescue him; he was still effectively isolated from other rescuers in that location, because any passerby would assume that he was only sleeping, not that he might need medical care. Answers (A), (C), and (D) are incorrect because they do not identify the strong defense arguments and omit the weak one.

95. **Issue: Actus reus, omission to act, legal duty.**
The correct answer is (D) because statements II, III, and IV accurately describe strong arguments for the defense, whereas statement II describes a weak argument. First, statement II is a prosecution argument that seeks to establish Ann's awareness of the potential peril faced by Moe due to a medical crisis prompted by his heroin overdose in combination with his excessive consumption of alcohol. This awareness is an important element of liability for a duty based on the voluntary assumption of care of a helpless person. Second, statement III is another argument that seeks to establish Ann's awareness of the critical nature of Moe's medical crisis, which helps to support the

policy argument that Ann owed a duty to Moe to call for medical help instead of abandoning him. Third, statement IV illustrates how the prosecutor will emphasize that Ann knew that she was the only person who was in a position to aid the helpless Moe, and that she knew that she could have provided aid by simply making one 911 phone call or attempting to determine his identity in order to notify others who could help him receive such medical aid. However, statement I is a weak prosecution argument, because it implies that broad and unprecedented duties may be imposed on all those who offer either a car ride or the use of a bathroom to a drunken stranger. This is inconsistent with the narrow scope of duties that are approved at common law. Answers (A), (B) and (C) are incorrect because they do not identify the strong prosecution arguments and omit the weak one.

96. **Issue: Legality, statutory interpretation.**
The correct answer is (B) because statements I, II, III, and IV accurately describe arguments that the defense counsel can make to persuade the appellate court that principles of legality and statutory interpretation require that the child endangerment statute should be construed as excluding Rose from prosecution. Statements I and II rely on the text of the statute for arguments based on inferences of legislative intent. Statement III explains why a tort rule concerning the need to deter tortfeasors and compensate their victims should not be extended to the very different context of criminal punishment of pregnant and addicted mothers. Statement IV relies on the statutory interpretation principle of construing related statutes together *in pari materia*, and applying an inferred legislative intent from one statutory context to another related context. The majority of states that have confronted the issue posed in this

problem have declined to define the term child to cover the harm caused to a fetus by the drug ingestion of the mother during pregnancy. These results can be explained through the legality principle that requires legislatures (rather than courts) to define new crimes. Answers (A), (C) and (D) are incorrect because they do not identify all the strong defense arguments.

97. **Issue: Cruel and unusual punishment.**
The correct answer is (C) because statements III and IV accurately describe the Eighth Amendment doctrines that apply to prosecutions of addicted defendants. However, statements I and II do not accurately describe such doctrines. The rulings described in statements III and IV have not been endorsed by the U. S. Supreme Court but have been established in lower court decisions interpreting the precedents of *Robinson v. California* (1962) and *Powell v. Texas* (1968). Statement I is not accurate because it is unconstitutional under *Robinson* to make it a crime to be an addict. Statement II is not accurate because it is constitutional under *Powell* to prosecute an alcoholic for being drunk in public. Answers (A), (B) and (D) are incorrect because they do not identify the appropriate Eighth Amendment doctrines and omit the erroneous ones.

98. **Issue: Cruel and unusual punishment.**
The correct answer is (D) because statements I and IV accurately describe the Eighth Amendment doctrines that apply to prosecutions where the death penalty may be imposed. However, statements II and III do not accurately describe those doctrines. The ruling described in statement I was established by the U. S. Supreme Court in *Roberts v. Louisiana* (1976) and *Woodson v. North Carolina* (1976); the ruling described in statement IV was established by that Court in *Tison v. Arizona*

(1987). Statement II is not accurate because it is unconstitutional under *Coker v. Georgia* (1977) to impose the death penalty for the rape of an adult woman. Statement III is not accurate because it is unconstitutional for a state to permit the death penalty to be imposed on a defendant who was 15 at the time of the crime under *Thompson v. Oklahoma* (1988). Answers (A), (B) and (C) are incorrect because they do not identify the appropriate Eighth Amendment doctrines and omit the erroneous ones.

99. **Issue: Void for vagueness, statutory interpretation.**
The correct answer is (A) because statements I, II and IV are arguments that the defense counsel will make to justify the position that the statute is void for vagueness. A lower court held a similar statute to be void for vagueness, relying in part on these arguments. However, statement III is not a valid defense argument. First, statement I is a traditional argument based on the core concept of a vague statute – it is a statute that does not provide fair notice because its meaning cannot be ascertained by a reasonable person. Second, statement II is a typical argument that focuses on particular vague words in a statute, and then locates sources of a legal definitions for those terms that illustrate their vagueness. Third, statement IV refers to one policy concern of vagueness doctrine, which is the overbreadth that may be inherent in a vague statute. Overbreadth may lead to the arbitrary enforcement of the statute against harmless individuals engaged in innocent conduct. However, statement III is not accurate because a court often can find a source to use in narrowing the terms of a statute so as to cure any vagueness. Here such sources exist, and they include the array of dictionary definitions and the examples of lawful purposes cited in the statutory text. Answers (B),

(C) and (D) are incorrect because they do not identify the strongest defense arguments and omit the inaccurate one.

100. **Issue: Void for vagueness, statutory interpretation.**
The correct answer is (B) because statements I, II, III and IV are arguments that the defense counsel will make to justify the position that the statute is void for vagueness. A lower court held a similar statute to be void for vagueness, relying in part on these arguments. First, statement I is a traditional argument that identifies the vague text in the statute, which is the starting point for any vagueness argument by the defense. Second, statement II focuses on the manner in which the statute dictates the implementation of the vague standard of "reasonable speed," which the defense can argue is vague because it is defined according to statutory factors whose meaning cannot be ascertained by a reasonable person. Third, statement III continues this defense analysis by examining how difficult it is for a law enforcement officer to discern the appropriate weighing of the statutory factors that control the definition of reasonableness. Fourth, statement IV is a traditional argument that relates to a core Due Process concern in vagueness precedents, which is that a vague statute must be invalidated if it will lead to arbitrary enforcement of the criminal law. Answers (A), (C) and (D) are incorrect because they do not identify all the strong defense arguments